Technician Unit 19

Preparing Personal Taxation Computations (FA 2003)

For assessments in June 2004
and December 2004

Assessment Kit

In this August 2003 first edition

- For assessments under the new standards

- Thorough and reliable updating of material for Finance Act 2003 tax legislation

- Many additional Practice Activities

- New Practice Examinations

- The AAT's Specimen Exam is included to attempt as a 'mock' under 'exam conditions'

- Activities grouped, broadly, according to the chapter(s) in the Interactive Text to which they relate

FOR ASSESSMENTS IN JUNE 2004 AND DECEMBER 2004 UNDER THE FINANCE ACT 2003 LEGISLATION

First edition August 2003

ISBN 0 7517 1232 9

British Library Cataloguing-in-Publication Data
A catalogue record for this book
is available from the British Library

Published by

BPP Professional Education
Aldine House, Aldine Place
London W12 8AW

www.bpp.com

Printed in Great Britain by WM Print
Frederick Street
Walsall
West Midlands
WS2 9NE

We are grateful to the Lead Body for Accounting for
permission to reproduce extracts from the Standards
of Competence for Accounting, and to the AAT for
permission to reproduce extracts from the mapping
and Guidance Notes.

Contents

Introduction

How to use this Assessment Kit– Unit 19 Standards of competence –
Exam Based Assessment technique – Assessment strategy – Building your portfolio –
Tax rates and allowances

Introduction

How to use this Assessment Kit

Aims of this Assessment Kit

To provide the knowledge and practice to help you succeed in the assessment for Technician Unit 19 *Preparing Personal Tax Computations.*

To pass the assessment successfully you need a thorough understanding in all areas covered by the standards of competence.

To tie in with the other components of the BPP Effective Study Package to ensure you have the best possible chance of success.

Interactive Text

This covers all you need to know for the assessments for Unit 19 *Preparing Personal Tax Computations.* Numerous activities throughout the text help you practise what you have just learnt.

Assessment Kit

When you have understood and practised the material in the Interactive Text, you will have the knowledge and experience to tackle the Assessment Kit for Unit 19 *Preparing Personal Tax Computations.* This aims to get you through the exam. It contains the AAT's Specimen Exam.

Passcards

These short memorable notes are focused on key topics for the Technician Units, designed to remind you of what the Interactive Text has taught you.

Recommended approach to this Assessment Kit

(a)   To achieve competence in Unit 19, you need to be able to do **everything** specified by the standards. Study the Interactive Text carefully and do not skip any of it.

(b)   Learning is an **active** process. Do **all** the activities as you work through the Interactive Text so you can be sure you really understand what you have read.

(c)   After you have covered the material in the Interactive Text, work through this **Assessment Kit**.

(d)   Try the **Practice Activities**. These are linked into each chapter of the Interactive Text, and are designed to reinforce your learning and consolidate the practice that you have had doing the activities in the Interactive Text.

(e)   Next do the **Practice Exams**. They are designed to cover the areas you might see when you do a full or exam.

(f)   Finally, try the AAT's **Specimen Exam** under 'exam conditions'.

Remember this is a **practical** course.

(a)   Try to relate the material to your experience in the workplace or any other work experience you may have had.

(b)   Try to make as many links as you can to your study of the other units at this level.

A **helpful tip**: photocopy the pages containing the blank forms, this makes it easier to work on the assessments as you flick from page to page.

Inland Revenue forms used within this Assessment Kit

Please note that at the time this Kit was printed 2003/04 versions of the Inland Revenue forms were not available. We have therefore in most cases updated the 2002/03 versions of the forms. This necessarily involves us in making 'guesses' about how the forms will change. Although, it is unlikely that the 2003/04 versions will differ significantly from what we have included here, we do suggest that you contact the Inland Revenue for updated copies before you attempt your exam.

If you have internet access you should be able to obtain the various forms from the Inland Revenue's website. (www.inlandrevenue.gov.uk)

Lecturers' Resource Pack activities

At the back of this Kit we have included a number of chapter-linked activities without answers. We have also included one exam without answers. The answers for this section are in the BPP Lecturers' Resource Pack for this Unit.

Unit 19 Standards of competence

The structure of the Standards for Unit 19

The Unit commences with a statement of the **knowledge and understanding** which underpin competence in the Unit's elements.

The Unit of Competence is then divided into **elements of competence** describing activities which the individual should be able to perform.

Each element includes:

(a) A set of **performance criteria.** This defines what constitutes competent performance.

(b) A **range statement.** This defines the situations, contexts, methods etc in which competence should be displayed.

The elements of competence for Unit 19: *Preparing Personal Taxation Computations* are set out below. Knowledge and understanding required for the Unit as a whole are listed first, followed by the performance criteria and range statements for each element.

Unit 19: Preparing Personal Taxation Computations

What is the unit about?

This unit is about preparing tax computations and returns for individuals. It is concerned with the Income Tax and Capital Gains tax liability of employed individuals, and also of self-employed individuals excluding any calculation of their business income. There are four elements in this unit.

The first element requires you to calculate income from employment, including benefits.

In the second element you must calculate property and investment income and show that you can apply deductions and reliefs and claim loss set-offs.

The third element is concerned with preparing Income Tax computations, based on your calculations of the client's earned and unearned income.

The final element requires you to prepare Capital Gains Tax computations. As well as calculating chargeable gains and losses, you need to show that you apply reliefs and exemptions correctly.

Throughout the unit you must show that you take account of current tax law and Inland Revenue practice and make submissions within statutory timescales. You also need to show that you consult with the Inland Revenue in an open and constructive manner, give timely and constructive advice to clients and maintain client confidentiality.

Knowledge and understanding

To perform this unit effectively you will need to know and understand:

The business environment

1   The duties and responsibilities of the tax practitioner (Elements 19.1, 19.2, 19.3 & 19.4)

2   The issues of taxation liability (Elements 19.1, 19.2, 19.3 & 19.4)

3   Relevant legislation and guidance from the Inland Revenue (Elements 19.1, 19.2, 19.3 & 19.4)

Taxation principles and theory

4   Basic law and practice relating to all issues covered in the range and referred to in the performance criteria (Elements 19.1, 19.2, 19.3 & 19.4)

5   Calculation of assessable employment income including benefits (Element 19.1)

6   Expenses deductible from Employment income including pension contributions and payroll giving to charities (Element 19.1)

7   Classification and calculation of income as property income, savings or dividend income (Element 19.2)

8   Identification of the main tax exempt investments (Element 19.2)

9   Calculation and set-off of rental deficits (Element 19.2)

10   Computation of taxable income taking account of gift aid payments and personal allowances for taxpayers aged under 65 (Element 19.3)

11   Calculation of tax on general, savings and dividend income (Element 19.3)

12   Identification of non-business assets disposed of including part disposals and personal shareholdings (Element 19.4)

13   Calculation of gains and losses on disposals of non-business assets including indexation allowance (Element 19.4)

14   Set-off of capital losses, taper relief and annual exemption to arrive at taxable gains (Element 19.4)

15   Calculation of capital gains tax payable on gains on non-business assets disposed of by individuals (Element 19.4)

16   Self assessment including payment of tax and filing of returns by individuals (Elements 19.3 & 19.4)

The client

17   How the taxation liabilities of individuals are affected by their employment status (Elements 19.1, 19.2, 19.3 & 19.4)

18   An understanding of the individual's employment status (Elements 19.1, 19.2, 19.3 & 19.4)

Element 19.1 Calculate income from employment

Performance criteria

In order to perform this element successfully you need to:

A   Prepare accurate computations of emoluments, including benefits

B   List allowable expenses and deductions

C   Record relevant details of income from employment accurately and legibly in the tax return

D   Make computations and submissions in accordance with current tax law and take account of current Inland Revenue practice

E   Consult with Inland Revenue staff in an open and constructive manner

F   Give timely and constructive advice to clients on the recording of information relevant to tax returns

G   Maintain client confidentiality at all times

Range statement

Performance in this element relates to the following contexts:

Emoluments

- Received by UK-resident employees
- Relating to work performed wholly or partly in the UK

Benefits

- Lower paid employees
- Higher paid employees

Allowable expenses

- Contributions to pension schemes
- Contributions to charities under the payroll deduction scheme

Element 19.2 Calculate property and investment income

Performance criteria

In order to perform this element successfully you need to:

A   Prepare schedules of dividends and interest received on shares and securities

B   Prepare schedules of property income and determine profits and losses

C   Prepare schedules of investment income from other sources

D   Apply deductions and reliefs and claim loss set-offs

E   Record relevant details of property and investment income accurately and legibly in the tax return

F   Make computations and submissions in accordance with current tax law and take account of current Inland Revenue practice

G   Consult with Inland Revenue staff in an open and constructive manner

H   Give timely and constructive advice to clients on the recording of information relevant to tax returns

I   Maintain client confidentiality at all times

Range statement

Performance in this element relates to the following contexts:

Property income taking into account

- Holiday lets
- Wear and tear

Other sources of investment income

- Banks
- Building societies
- Government savings schemes

Element 19.3 Prepare Income Tax computations

Performance criteria

In order to perform this element successfully you need to:

A   List general income, savings income and dividend income and check for completeness

B   Calculate and deduct charges and personal allowances

C   Calculate Income Tax payable

D   Record income and payments legibly and accurately in the tax return

E   Make computations and submissions in accordance with current tax law and take account of current Inland Revenue practice

F   Consult with Inland Revenue staff in an open and constructive manner

G   Give timely and constructive advice to clients on the recording of information relevant to tax returns

H   Maintain client confidentiality at all times

Range statement

Performance in this element relates to the following contexts:

There are no additional contextual requirements in this element.

Element 19.4 Prepare Capital Gains Tax computations

Performance criteria

In order to perform this element successfully you need to:

A   Identify and value disposed-of chargeable personal assets

B   Identify shares disposed of by individuals

C   Calculate chargeable gains and allowable losses

D   Apply reliefs and exemptions correctly

E   Calculate Capital Gains Tax payable

F   Record relevant details of gains and the Capital Gains Tax payable legibly and accurately in the tax return

G   Make computations and submissions in accordance with current tax law and take account of current Inland Revenue practice

H   Consult with Inland Revenue staff in an open and constructive manner

I   Give timely and constructive advice to clients on the recording of information relevant to tax returns

J   Maintain client confidentiality at all times

Range statement

Performance in this element relates to the following contexts:

Chargeable personal assets that have been

- Sold
- Gifted
- Lost
- Destroyed

Exam Based Assessment technique

Completing exam based assessments successfully at this level is half about having the knowledge, and half about doing yourself full justice on the day. You must have the right **technique**.

The day of the exam based assessment

1   Set at least one **alarm** (or get an alarm call) for a morning exam.

2   Have **something to eat** but beware of eating too much; you may feel sleepy if your system is digesting a large meal.

3   Allow plenty of **time to get to where you are sitting the exam**; have your route worked out in advance and listen to news bulletins to check for potential travel problems.

4   **Don't forget** pens, pencils, rulers, erasers.

5   Put **new batteries** into your calculator and take a spare set (or a spare calculator).

6   **Avoid discussion** about the exam with other candidates outside the venue.

Technique in the exam based assessment

1   **Read the instructions (the 'rubric') on the front of the exam carefully**

    Check that the format hasn't changed. It is surprising how often assessors' reports remark on the number of students who do not attempt all the tasks.

2   **Read the paper twice**

    Read through the paper twice – don't forget that you are given 15 minutes' reading time. Check carefully that you have got the right end of the stick before putting pen to paper. Use your 15 minutes' reading time wisely. Reading time can only be used for **reading**. You can not make notes or use a calculator during those 15 minutes.

3   **Check the time allocation for each section of the exam**

    Time allocations are given for each section of the exam. When the time for a section is up, you should go on to the next section.

4   **Read the task carefully and plan your answer**

    Read through the task again very carefully when you come to answer it. Plan your answer to ensure that you **keep to the point**. Two minutes of planning plus eight minutes of writing is virtually certain to produce a better answer than ten minutes of writing. Planning will also help you answer the exam question efficiently, for example by identifying workings that can be used for more than one task.

5   **Produce relevant answers**

    Particularly with written answers, make sure you **answer what has been set**, and not what you would have preferred to have been set. Do not, for example, answer a question on **why** something is done with an explanation of **how** it is done.

6   **Work your way steadily through the exam**

    Don't get bogged down in one task. If you are having problems with something, the chances are that everyone else is too.

7 **Produce an answer in the correct format**

The assessor will state **in the requirements** the format which should be used, for example in a report or memorandum.

8 **Do what the assessor wants**

You should ask yourself what the assessor is expecting in an answer; many tasks will demand a combination of technical knowledge and business commonsense. Be careful if you are required to give a decision or make a recommendation; you cannot just list the criteria you will use, but you will also have to say whether those criteria have been fulfilled.

9 **Lay out your numerical computations and use workings correctly**

Make sure the layout is in a style the assessor likes.

Show all your **workings** clearly and explain what they mean. Cross reference them to your answer. This will help the assessor to follow your method (this is of particular importance where there may be several possible answers).

10 **Present a tidy paper**

You are a professional, and it should show in the **presentation of your work**. You should make sure that you write legibly, label diagrams clearly and lay out your work neatly.

11 **Stay until the end of the exam**

Use any spare time **checking and rechecking** your script. Check that you have answered all the requirements of the task and that you have clearly labelled your work. Consider also whether your answer appears reasonable in the light of the information given in the question.

12 **Don't worry if you feel you have performed badly in the exam**

It is more than likely that the other candidates will have found the exam difficult too. As soon as you get up to leave the venue, **forget** that exam and think about the next – or, if it is the last one, celebrate!

13 **Don't discuss an exam with other candidates**

This is particularly the case if you **still have other exams to sit**. Even if you have finished, you should put it out of your mind until the day of the results. Forget about exams and relax!

Assessment strategy

This Unit is assessed by **examination** only.

Exam based assessment

An exam based assessment is a means of collecting evidence that you have the **essential knowledge and understanding** which underpins competence. It is also a means of collecting evidence across the **range of contexts** for the standards, and of your ability to **transfer skills**, knowledge and understanding to different situations. Thus, although examinations contain practical tests linked to the performance criteria, they also focus on the underpinning knowledge and understanding. You should, in addition, expect each examination to contain tasks taken from across a broad range of the standards.

Format of exam

There will be a three hour exam in two sections.

Section 1:	Element 19.1 (taxation of an individual who is employed)
Section 2:	Element 19.4 (taxation of capital transactions)

Elements 19.2 and 19.3 can appear in either section.

There will be an additional 15 minutes reading time.

Further guidance

The Standard is divided into four elements. Element 19.1 is called 'Calculate income from employment', Element 19.2 is called 'Calculate property and investment income'' Element 19.3 is called 'Prepare Income Tax computations' and Element 19.4 is called ' Prepare Capital Gains Tax Computations. '

The purpose of **Element 19.1** is to calculate the earnings of an individual for inclusion in their income tax computation and/or income tax return. For earnings, the following sources of income need to be considered

(i)   cash received, such as salary, bonuses, commissions

(ii)   benefits, such as car, car fuel, accommodation, living expenses connected with accommodation, assets made available to employees for private usage and cheap taxable loans.

The rules for benefits need to be considered for all levels of income.

Deductibility of allowable expenses will involve: the operation of the 'wholly, exclusively and necessarily incurred' rule, pension contributions and payroll giving to charities.

Students should understand the significance of all the major PAYE forms, such as P11D, P60 and P45. However, detailed knowledge of the mechanics of the PAYE system will not required.

Element 19.2 deals with property and investment income. For property income, students will be required to compute the profit or loss on Schedule A income. This specifically includes rental income, but excludes lease premiums and 'rent-a-room' relief. An understanding of the basis of assessment, allowable expenditure and capital expenditure is required in reference to Schedule A income.

For investment income, students must understand the tax implications of owning a variety of investment assets, such as shares, ISAs and TESSAs. Students should also have an understanding of the tax implications where interest is taxed at source, and where it is not taxed at source. There will be considerable commonality between element 19.2 and element 19.3, as the generation of the income in element 19.2 will be used in the Income Tax computations in element 19.3.

Element 19.3 concerns the preparation of income tax computations. It will not necessarily be a requirement in the examination to complete a full Inland Revenue income tax return, but relevant extracts may be used and the student will need to demonstrate understanding on how it should be properly completed. All sources of income, earned and unearned, will come under this element, though the specifics on how they are individually calculated will come under another element within this unit. Detailed knowledge is required of all personal allowances and reliefs, including personal allowances for taxpayers aged under 65, charges on income and gift aid.

Specifically excluded from this element are eligible interest payments and maintenance payments.

Also, the dates for submission of the income tax return and payment of income tax must be considered, together with the implications of making a late filing of the return.

Element 19.4 deals with the calculation of capital gains for individuals. As disposals of business assets are examined under Unit 18, the type of disposals covered by this unit include: non-business assets, shares and securities, including rights issues and bonus issues, FA 1985 pool and matching rules, chattels, part-disposal of assets, improvement expenditure, principal private residence, including periods of deemed occupation, and exempt assets.

Students should be able to compute the gain, or loss, and then be able to apply tapering relief and the annual exemption. An understanding is also required of the impact of capital gains on the tax liability, assuming gains are the top slice of an individual's income.

Specifically excluded topics are double tax relief, trusts, granting of leases and share take-overs.

Section 1 and Section 2

It is not anticipated that candidates will be required to compute certain topics more than once during the examination. For instance, Schedule A income will only be assessed once in either Section 1 or Section 2. The same principle applies for calculating certain forms of income, although the application of such income in calculating the final income tax due will not be restricted to only one section.

Finance Act 2003

Note that at the time of printing this Text the AAT had not issued any further guidance on how any of the Finance Act 2003 provisions will be examined. You are advised to check for this guidance before you sit your examination. BPP will post any information that it receives on its internet site: www.bpp.com/aat.

Building your portfolio

What is a portfolio?

A portfolio is a collection of work that demonstrates what the owner can do. In AAT language the portfolio demonstrates **competence**.

A painter will have a collection of his paintings to exhibit in a gallery, an advertising executive will have a range of advertisements and ideas that she has produced to show to a prospective client. Both the collection of paintings and the advertisements form the portfolio of that artist or advertising executive.

Your portfolio will be unique to you just as the portfolio of the artist will be unique because no one will paint the same range of pictures in the same way. It is a very personal collection of your work and should be treated as a **confidential** record.

What evidence should a portfolio include?

No two portfolios will be the same but by following some simple guidelines you can decide which of the following suggestions will be appropriate in your case.

(a) **Your current CV**

This should be at the front. It will give your personal details as well as brief descriptions of posts you have held with the most recent one shown first.

(b) **References and testimonials**

References from previous employers may be included especially those of which you are particularly proud.

(c) **Your current job description**

You should emphasise financial **responsibilities and duties**.

(d) **Your student record sheets**

These should be supplied by AAT when you begin your studies, and your training provider should also have some if necessary.

(e) **Evidence from your current workplace**

This could take many forms including **letters, memos, reports** you have written, **copies of accounts** or **reconciliations** you have prepared, **discrepancies** you have investigated etc. Remember to obtain permission to include the evidence from your line manager because some records may be sensitive. Discuss the performance criteria that are listed in your Student Record Sheets with your training provider and employer, and think of other evidence that could be appropriate to you.

(f) **Evidence from your social activities**

For example you may be the treasurer of a club in which case examples of your cash and banking records could be appropriate.

(g) **Evidence from your studies**

Few students are able to satisfy all the requirements of competence by workplace evidence alone. They therefore rely on simulations to provide the remaining evidence to complete a unit. If you are not working or not working in a relevant post, then you may need to rely more heavily on simulations as a source of evidence.

(h)   **Additional work**

Your training provider may give you work that specifically targets one or a group of performance criteria in order to complete a unit. It could take the form of questions, presentations or demonstrations. Each training provider will approach this in a different way.

(i)   **Evidence from a previous workplace**

This evidence may be difficult to obtain and should be used with caution because it must satisfy the 'rules' of evidence, that is it must be current. Only rely on this as evidence if you have changed jobs recently.

(j)   **Prior achievements**

For example you may have already completed the health and safety unit during a previous course of study, and therefore there is no need to repeat this work. Advise your training provider who will check to ensure that it is the same unit and record it as complete if appropriate.

How should it be presented?

As you assemble the evidence remember to **make a note** of it on your Student Record Sheet in the space provided and **cross reference** it. In this way it is easy to check to see if your evidence is **appropriate**. Remember one piece of evidence may satisfy a number of performance criteria so remember to check this thoroughly and discuss it with your training provider if in doubt.

To keep all your evidence together a ring binder or lever arch file is a good means of storage.

When should evidence be assembled?

You should begin to assemble evidence **as soon as you have registered as a student**. **Don't leave it all** until the last few weeks of your studies, because you may miss vital deadlines and your resulting certificate sent by the AAT may not include all the units you have completed. Give yourself and your training provider time to examine your portfolio and report your results to AAT at regular intervals. In this way the task of assembling the portfolio will be spread out over a longer period of time and will be presented in a more professional manner.

What are the key criteria that the portfolio must fulfil?

As you assemble your evidence bear in mind that it must be:

- **Valid**. It must relate to the Standards.
- **Authentic**. It must be your own work.
- **Current**. It must refer to your current or most recent job.
- **Sufficient**. It must meet all the performance criteria by the time you have completed your portfolio.

What are the most important elements in a portfolio that covers Unit 19?

You should remember that the unit is about the preparation of personal tax computations.

For Element 19.1 *Calculate income from employment* you need to be able to calculate the taxable value of benefits in order to calculate total earnings. The main source of this evidence will be copies of any P11Ds that you have prepared or from which you have extracted information in order to calculate earnings.

For Element 19.2 *Calculate property and investment income* you need evidence of any investment and property schedules you have prepared. Bank /building society statements and any dividend vouchers from which you have extracted information are useful sources of evidence. Additionally rental statements from letting agents can provide support for any computation of Schedule A income you have made.

For element 19.3 *Income tax computations* you need evidence of tax computations that you have actually prepared yourself. If you do not prepare computations in the office you will need to use AAT examinations as a source of evidence.

To fulfil the requirements of Element 19.4 *Prepare capital gains tax computations* you will need to demonstrate that you can calculate chargeable gains / allowable losses on the disposal of chargeable assets. You will also need to demonstrate that you are aware of which assets are chargeable and which are exempt.

Finally

Remember that the portfolio is **your property** and **your responsibility**. Not only could it be presented to the external verifier before your award can be confirmed; it could be used when you are seeking **promotion** or applying for a more senior and better paid post elsewhere. How your portfolio is presented can say as much about you as the evidence inside.

For further information on portfolio building, see the BPP Text *Building Your Portfolio*. This can be ordered using the form at the back of this Text or via the Internet: www.bpp.com/aat

Tax rates and allowances

A   Income tax

1   Rates

	2002/03		2003/04	
	£	%	£	%
Starting rate	1 – 1,920	10	1 – 1,960	10
Basic rate	1,921 – 29,900	22	1,961 – 30,500	22
Higher rate	29,901 and above	40	30,501 and above	40

Savings (excl. Dividend) income is taxed at 20% if it falls in the basic rate band. Dividend income in both the starting rate and the basic rate bands is taxed at 10%. Dividend income within the higher rate band is taxed at 32.5%.

2   Allowances

	2002/03	2003/04
	£	£
Personal allowance	4,615	4,615
Blind person's allowance	1,480	1,510

3   Car fuel charge – 2003/04

Set figure £14,400

4   Authorised mileage rates (AMR) 2003/04 rates

Car mileage rates

First 10,000 miles	40p per mile
Over 10,000 miles	25p per mile

Bicycles	*Motor cycles*
20p per mile	24p per mile
Passenger payments	5p per mile

5   Personal pension contribution limits

Age	*Maximum percentage* %
Up to 35	17.5
36 – 45	20.0
46 – 50	25.0
51 – 55	30.0
56 – 60	35.0
61 or more	40.0

Subject to earnings cap of £97,200 for 2002/03 and £99,000 for 2003/04.

Stakeholder pension limit £3,600.

B Rates of interest

Official rate of interest: 5% (assumed)
Rate of interest on unpaid tax: 6.5% (assumed)
Rate of interest on overpaid tax: 2.5% (assumed)

C Capital gains tax

1 Lease percentage table

Years	Percentage	Years	Percentage	Years	Percentage
50 or more	100.000	33	90.280	16	64.116
49	99.657	32	89.354	15	61.617
48	99.289	31	88.371	14	58.971
47	98.902	30	87.330	13	56.167
46	98.490	29	86.226	12	53.191
45	98.059	28	85.053	11	50.038
44	97.595	27	83.816	10	46.695
43	97.107	26	82.496	9	43.154
42	96.593	25	81.100	8	39.399
41	96.041	24	79.622	7	35.414
40	95.457	23	78.055	6	31.195
39	94.842	22	76.399	5	26.722
38	94.189	21	74.635	4	21.983
37	93.497	20	72.770	3	16.959
36	92.761	19	70.791	2	11.629
35	91.981	18	68.697	1	5.983
34	91.156	17	66.470	0	0.000

2 Annual exemption (individuals)

	£
2002/03	7,700
2003/04	7,900

3 Tapering relief for non-business assets

Number of complete years after 5.4.98 for which asset held	% of gain chargeable
0	100
1	100
2	100
3	95
4	90
5	85
6	80

Practice
Activities

Chapter 7 Shares and securities

Chapter 8 CGT: Additional aspects

Chapter 9 Administration and completion of tax return

chapter 1

An outline of Income Tax

Activity checklist

This checklist shows which performance criteria are covered by each activity in this chapter. Full details of the performance criteria are shown on page (ix) onwards. Tick off each activity as you complete it.

Activity

1		Performance Criteria 19.3A, B and C
2		Performance Criteria 19.3A, B and C
3		Performance Criteria 19.3A, B and C
4		Performance Criteria 19.3A, B and C
5		Performance Criteria 19.3A, B and C
6		Performance Criteria 19.3A, B and C
7		Performance Criteria 19.3A, B and C

All of these activities cover Knowledge and Understanding points 2, 3, 4, 10 and 11.

1 Income tax computation

John Smith, a widower aged 44, has the following income and outgoings for the tax year 2003/04.

		£	
(i)	Salary (£9,500 tax deducted under PAYE)	45,000	
(ii)	Interest on a deposit account with the Scotia Bank	800	(net)
(iii)	Donation under the gift aid scheme made on 1 September 2003	5,132	(amount paid)
(iv)	Interest on a National Savings Bank investment account	496	
(v)	Dividends received on UK shares	900	(net)

Tasks

(a)   Prepare a schedule of income for 2003/04, clearly showing the distinction between non-savings, savings and dividend income. John Smith's personal allowance should be deducted as appropriate.

(b)   Calculate the net income tax payable for 2003/04.

(c)   Explain how you have dealt with the gift aid donation in your computation.

Guidance notes

1   The major part of this question requires you to calculate an individual's overall tax position for 2003/04. Start with non-savings income.

2   Insert the types of savings (excl. dividend) income, remembering that income is always included gross in the tax computation even if the amounts are actually received net.

3   Insert the dividend income, remembering that dividends are received net of a 10% tax credit and they must be grossed up before inclusion in the tax computation.

4   After deducting the personal allowance to find the taxable income, you need to calculate tax payable. It is best to calculate tax on non-savings, savings (excl. dividend) and dividend income separately. Remember that the basic rate band is extended by the gross amount of the gift aid donation.

5   Finally, deduct tax suffered at source and the tax credit on dividend income.

2 Mr Betteredge

Mr Betteredge, a married man, has the following income:

Salary as a butler for the year to 5 April 2004	£12,105
Tips received from guests in the year to 5 April 2004	£2,960

Interest received (cash received shown):

	£
National Westminster Bank plc	457
National Savings Bank investment account	26
Mini cash ISA account	180
Nationwide Building Society ordinary account	400
National Savings Certificates	173

Tasks

(a) Prepare a Schedule of income for 2003/04 clearly showing the distinction between non-savings, savings and dividends income. Mr Betteredge's personal allowance should be deducted as appropriate.

(a) Calculate the income tax liability of Mr Betteredge for 2003/04.

3 Selina

Selina, a single woman, received the following income in 2003/04:

Salary	£18,900
Dividends received in the year to 5 April 2004	£298

Selina lives with her twelve year old daughter, Charlotte. Charlotte has no income of her own.

In 2003/04 Selina's great aunt, Miss Mary Jane Stamper, died and left her £20,000 cash and a cottage in Brighton. Selina has asked you for advice on the following matters.

Tasks

(a) Prepare a schedule of income for 2003/04 clearly showing the distinction between non-savings, and dividend income. Selina's personal allowance should be deducted as appropriate.

(b) Calculate the income tax liability for 2003/04.

(c) Advise Selina whether, if she gives the £20,000 cash to her daughter, the income arising from it could be reduced by her daughter's personal allowance?

4 Mrs Rogers

Mrs Rogers has the following income:

Salary (PAYE deducted £3,000)	£17,776

Investment income (cash received):

	£
Building society interest received on ordinary deposit account	1,500
Interest received on an individual savings account	300
National Savings Bank:	
Investment account interest	150

Dividend income (cash received)

Dividend of £1.35 per share on 10,000 quoted ordinary shares.

Tasks

(a) Prepare a schedule of income for 2003/04, clearly showing the distinction between non-savings, savings and dividend income. Mrs Rogers' personal allowance should be deducted as appropriate.

(b) Calculate Mrs Rogers' income tax payable/repayable for the year to 5 April 2004.

5 Mrs Butcher

Mrs Butcher, a widow since 1997, is aged 62. Her income in the year ended 5 April 2004 was as follows.

	£
Pension (no tax deducted before receipt)	7,204
Rent from let cottage	5,776
Interest on Government stock (received gross)	490
Dividends received from UK companies	270
Building society interest received	4,000
Premium bond prizes	250

Tasks

(a) Prepare a schedule for 2003/04 clearly showing the distinction between non savings, savings and dividend income. Mrs Butcher's personal allowance should be deducted as appropriate.

(b) Compute the income tax payable for 2003/04.

6 Eric Wright

Eric Wright (born 31 January 1940) is a partner in a firm of architects. His taxable profits for 2003/04 are £26,060.

Eric has a bank account with the Halifax Bank. His account was credited with interest of £1,600 on 31 March 2004.

Eric made a gift aid donation of £390 to Oxfam on 1 December 2003.

Eric married Doreen on 10 May 2002. Doreen, who is 61, received a taxable state pension of £4,027 in 2003/04. She also received dividends of £1,818.

Tasks

(a) Prepare a Schedule for 2003/04 clearly showing the distinction between non-saving, savings and dividend income for Eric Wright. Eric Wright's personal allowance should be deduced as appropriate.

(b) Compute the income tax payable by Eric Wright for 2003/04.

(c) Prepare a schedule for 2003/04 clearly showing the distinction between non-savings, savings and dividend income for Doreen.

(d) Compute the income tax payable by Doreen for 2003/04.

7 Melanie Wong

Melanie is employed as a head teacher in a local primary school. In 2003/04 she had earnings of £40,000. PAYE of £8,429 was deducted from these earnings.

Melanie received dividends of £4,500 during 2003/04. She also cashed in National Savings Certificates and received £250 interest in addition to the repayment of the capital invested.

Melanie made a gift aid donation of £1,170 to the RSPCA on 1 February 2004.

Tasks

(a) Prepare a schedule for Melanie Wong clearly showing the distinction between non-savings, savings (excl) dividend and dividend income for 2003/04. Melanie Wong's personal allowance should be deducted as appropriate.

(b) Compute the tax payable by/repayable to Melanie Wong for 2003/04.

chapter 2

Calculation of employment income

Activity checklist

This checklist shows which performance criteria are covered by each activity in this chapter. Full details of the performance criteria are shown on page (ix) onwards. Tick off each activity as you complete it.

Activity

8		Performance Criteria 19.1A.
9		Performance Criteria 19.1A.
10		Performance Criteria 19.1A.
11		Performance Criteria 19.1A.
12		Performance Criteria 19.1A.
13		Performance Criteria 19.1B.
14		Performance Criteria 19.1A and 19.1B.

8 Cars and lunches

The directors of Shiloh plc have appointed Mr William Sherman as chief accountant with effect from 1 April 2003. His remuneration package has been agreed as follows.

Annual salary £50,000.

Luncheon vouchers worth £5 per day for the 50 days each year that he will spend working away from the office. During the remaining 180 days that he will be in the office, he will be able to eat free of charge in the employee canteen which is open to all staff. It is likely that the cost of his meals will be £900 per year.

The company will provide him with the use of a new company car together with all petrol for both business and private use. The car will be a Jaguar costing £25,000 and it will be purchased new on 1 April 2003. The car will emit 205g/km of CO_2.

Tasks

    (a)   Calculate the total assessable benefits.

    (b)   Mr Sherman is concerned about the tax payable on the private petrol provided to him and wonders whether he should continue to be taxed on the benefit or whether he should reimburse the cost of the private petrol to his employer. Advise him, assuming a petrol cost of 65p per litre and an average mileage of 5 miles per litre. Mr Sherman will travel 4,000 private miles during 2003/04.

Guidance notes

1   There is a small exemption in relation to meal vouchers such as luncheon vouchers.

2   The car and fuel benefits depend on the level of the cars CO_2 emissions.

3   In part (b), compare the cost of extra income tax with the cost of petrol.

9 Directors

You act for a number of directors.

The following benefits are enjoyed by the various directors.

    (a)   A director has had the use of a private house bought by the company for £120,000 in 2001. The director paid all of the house expenses plus the agreed open market annual rental of £2,000. The annual value of the house is £2,000.

    (b)   A television video system, which had been provided at the start of 1999/00 for the use of a director and which had cost the company £3,500, was taken over by the director on 6 April 2003 for a payment of £600 (its market value at that date).

    (c)   On 6 April 2003 a director had a loan of £40,000 at 4% interest. On 6 December 2003, £10,000 of this loan was repaid. This is the only loan he had taken out.

(d)   Medical insurance premiums were paid for a director and his family, under a group scheme, at a cost to the company of £800. Had the director paid for this as an individual the cost would have been £1,400.

(e)   On 6 September 2003 a director was given the use of a Mercedes car which had cost £24,000. The CO_2 emissions of the car were 255g/km. The director used the Mercedes for both business and private purposes. He was required to make good the cost of any petrol used for private mileage.

(f)   On 6 April 2003 the company lent a director a computer costing £3,900 for use at home. The director used the computer for both business and private purposes.

Task

Show how each of the above benefits would be quantified for tax purposes. Assume that the official rate of interest is 5%.

Guidance notes

1   Work through each benefit separately. Calculate its value before you move on to the next benefit. Watch out for exempt benefits.

2   Remember that any benefit that is only available for part of a year must be time apportioned. This is often the case in exam questions with car and fuel benefits. Is it relevant here?

10 Taxable and exempt benefits

During 2003/04, the following benefits were provided to employees of a company. All the employees earn more than £8,500 per year.

(a)   An interest free loan of £3,000 was made to Zoë Dexter on 6 April 2003. This was used to finance her daughter's wedding.

(b)   Throughout 2003/04 Victoria Eustace was provided with a computer and printer which she uses at home for both private and business purposes. The computer equipment cost the company £2,000.

(c)   Amanda Valentine was provided with a petrol engined car on 6 June 2003. The company had acquired the car new on 1 March 2000 at a cost of £17,250. The market value of the car on 6 June 2003 was estimated to be £13,000. The car emits 155g/km of CO_2. The company pays all the running costs of the car including fuel.

(d)   Throughout 2003/04 Catherine Crawley was provided with a petrol engined car which cost £16,000. The car emits 230g/km of CO_2. The company provided her with petrol for business and private motoring but she paid £500 to the company as a partial reimbursement of the cost of private fuel.

(e)   Emma Forbes was provided with a mobile telephone throughout 2003/04. Emma used the phone for business and private calls. Stowe Ltd paid total charges in respect of the phone during 2003/04 of £300.

Task

State the amounts, if any, that are taxable benefits. Explain why any benefits are exempt benefits.

11 Accommodation

Mr Ford, the managing director of the company you work for, is provided with the exclusive private use of a flat in London. The flat is not job related accommodation for Mr Ford. The company acquired the flat for £100,000 in 2001 and Mr Ford has used it since then. The flat was fully furnished at a cost of £5,000 and the council tax paid by the company amounted to £500. The rateable value is £900. The running costs of the flat amounting to £1,200 for 2003/04 were paid directly by Mr Ford.

One of your company's other employees, Charles Rainer, was relocated on 6 April 2003 and required to live in an unfurnished company house; the annual value of this job-related accommodation was £4,000. The company had bought the house in March 2003 for £80,000. The company paid the council tax in respect of the house of £800. Mr Rainer paid all the running costs in respect of the house himself.

Task

Show the taxable amounts for 2003/04 in respect of the accommodation provided to each of the above employees.

Assume the official rate of interest is 5%.

12 Rita

Rita, who is a fashion designer for Daring Designs Limited, was re-located from London to Manchester on 6 April 2003. Her annual salary is £48,000. She was immediately provided with a house with an annual value of £4,000 for which her employer paid an annual rent of £3,500. Rita was re-imbursed relevant re-location expenditure of £12,000. Daring Designs Limited provided ancillary services for the house in 2003/04 as follows.

	£
Electricity	700
Gas	1,200
Water	500
Council tax	1,300
Property repairs	3,500

The house has been furnished by Daring Designs Limited prior to Rita's occupation at a cost of £30,000. On 6 October 2003 Rita bought all of the furniture from Daring Designs Ltd for £20,000 when its market value was £25,000.

Daring Designs Limited had made an interest free loan to Rita in 2002 of £10,000. The loan is not being used for a 'qualifying purposes'. No part of the loan has been repaid.

Task

Calculate the total amount of Rita's taxable benefits for the year 2003/04.

13 Sally

Sally, a company's marketing director earning £90,000 a year, incurs the following expenses in 2003/04.

(i) An annual first class rail season ticket costing £2,700. She uses the ticket to travel between her home and her place of work. She used to walk to work, but then her company relocated to a new site 40 miles from her home. A standard class season ticket would cost £1,800 a year.

(ii) Her telephone bill for the telephone at her home, which is as follows (for the whole year).

	£
Line rental	100
Private calls	130
Business calls	270
	500

(iii) Her subscription of £50 to the Chartered Institute of Marketing. She needs to keep up with developments in marketing so as to put herself in a position to perform her duties.

(iv) Subscriptions to various professional journals, totalling £130. Regular reading of these journals significantly improves her skill in her job.

(v) A subscription of £230 to a London club. She uses the club's bar and restaurant to meet business contacts.

Tasks

(a) Prepare a schedule to accompany Sally's tax return, setting out the deductible expenses.

(b) Prepare a memorandum for Sally explaining the tax treatment of the various items above.

14   Bill Wilson

Bill Wilson, a 35 year old married man with no children, was employed as a works manager in a large UK resident company. He was made redundant on 1 January 2004.

During the year 2003/04 he had the following income.

	£	
Salary	29,750	(to 31 December 2003)
Job Seeker's Allowance	1,025	(from 1 January 2004)
Dividends	1,350	(from UK companies)
	1,600	(from ISA investments)
Interest	360	(from UK building societies)
	240	(from ISA)
	110	(from a National Savings Bank investment account)
	250	(from 3.5% War Loan)

All the dividends and interest receipts are stated at the actual amounts received. The other items are stated at the gross amounts.

The Job Seekers allowance is a taxable state benefit.

During his employment he was provided with a two year old 1,800 cc BMW car which had a list price of £20,000. The CO_2 emissions of the car were 192 g/km. The company paid for all of the petrol.

Following the cessation of his employment Bill was provided with

- Cash of £20,000
- Use of the car until 5 April 2004.

The company was not contractually obliged to provide this.

Bill paid £400 (gross) to a registered charity under the Gift Aid scheme on 1 December 2003.

Tasks

(a)   Calculate Bill's taxable income for the tax year 2003/04.

(b)   Calculate Bill's income tax payable (prior to PAYE deductions) for the tax year 2003/04.

(c)   Give reasons where you have left any amounts out of the calculations.

(d)   List FOUR types of expenses that Bill could deduct from his employment income.

chapter 3

Employment income: additional aspects

Activity checklist

This checklist shows which performance criteria are covered by each activity in this chapter. Full details of the performance criteria are provided on page (ix) onwards. Tick off each activity as you complete it.

Activity

15		Performance Criteria 19.1B.
16		Performance Criteria 19.1B.
17		Performance Criteria 19.1B.
18		Performance Criteria 19.1B.
19		Performance Criteria 19.1B.
20		Performance Criteria 19.1A, 19.1B, 19.1D, 19.3A, 19.3B, 19.3C.
21		Performance Criteria 19.2A, 19.3A, 19.3B, 19.3C, 19.3E.

15 Ian Warburton

Ian Warburton works as a consultant for a company supplying computer systems. Ian's monthly salary was increased by 5% to £1,365 from 1 August 2003. He contributes 3% of this salary to the company's occupational pension scheme, the company adding a further 9%.

Ian had a company car which was available to him throughout the year. The car was registered in 2002 and cost the company £11,000. The car emits CO_2 of 208g/km. The company provided all petrol for Ian although he did reimburse them £200 in respect of petrol for his summer vacation. Other costs in respect of the car, all paid by the company, were insurance £800, repairs £490 and new tyres £100.

Ian was paid a Christmas bonus of £1,000 with his December 2003 salary.

Task

Calculate Ian Warburton's earnings for 2003/04.

16 David

David Rogers, aged 36, and his wife Sue, aged 34, are personal tax clients of your firm. David, who is employed as a designer, has always paid tax at the basic rate. Sue, who stays at home looking after the couples' two children, does not have any earnings of her own. David has not previously made any pension contributions but would like to consider contributing to a stakeholder pension scheme.

Task

Draft a letter to David setting out the rules governing personal pension contributions.

17 Stakeholder pensions

Bill, who was born on 18 August 1960, became employed by ABC plc on 1 June 2003. His employer does not provide an occupational pension scheme. Bill forecasts that he will have the following net relevant earnings from 2003/04.

	£
2003/04	25,000
2004/05	80,000
2005/06	60,000
2006/07	70,000
2007/08	75,000
2008/09	66,000
2009/10	70,000
2010/11	60,000

Bill has decided to contribute to a stakeholder pension scheme. He has not previously made any pension provision and has never earned more than £20,000 per annum previously.

Tasks

(a) Calculate the maximum amount of gross pension contributions for which Bill will be entitled to tax relief in 2003/04 to 2010/11.

(b) Explain how tax relief is given for personal pension payments.

Assume the relevant rules and allowances in 2003/04 remain unchanged.

Guidance notes

1 First choose a basis year for each year. The basis year can be the year concerned or any one of the five previous tax years.

2 The relevant percentage depends on the taxpayer's age at the start of the tax year concerned.

18 Roger Thesaurus

Roger Thesaurus, a widower aged 46 on 1 June 2003, has the following income and outgoings for the tax year 2003/04.

		£	
(a)	Profits from sole trade	57,000	
(b)	Interest on a deposit account with the Scotia Bank	1,197	(net)
(c)	Copyright royalty paid	6,000	
(d)	Personal pension contributions. Roger joined a stakeholder pension scheme on 6.4.03. Roger chose 1998/99 as his basis year in 2003/04. In 1998/99 his profits were £80,000	11,700	(amount paid)
(e)	Dividends received on UK shares	900	(amount received)

Tasks

(a) Calculate the income tax payable by Mr Thesaurus for 2003/04.

(b) Explain how you have dealt with the personal pension contribution and the copyright royalty.

19 PAYE forms

An employer has certain responsibilities under the PAYE system to provide the Revenue and employees with various forms.

Tasks

(a) State what PAYE forms an employer must send to the Revenue following the tax year end. State the date(s) by which these forms must be provided.

(b)   State what PAYE forms an employer must provide to an employee following the tax year end. State the date(s) by which these forms must be provided.

(c)   State which PAYE form must be provided in respect of an employee who is leaving an employment and to whom this should be provided.

20 Frederick Fuse

You have just received the following letter from Mr Frederick Fuse. Mr Frederick Fuse is the managing director of a company called Nuts and Bolts Ltd.

Hammer, Wrench and Co   25 Town Road
Accountants   Lanchester
Credit Street
Lanchester   31 May 2004

Dear Ms Drill,

Income tax year ended 5 April 2004

The information you require to calculate my income tax liability for 2003/04, is as follows.

1   I receive a gross salary of £41,000 from my employment as Managing Director of Nuts and Bolts Limited. Income tax of £13,600 was deducted under the PAYE (Pay As You Earn) scheme, according to my form P60 for the tax year 2003/04.

2   Throughout 2003/04 I had the use of a company car with CO_2 emissions of 206g/km. The list price of the car was £14,003. The company supplied me with all petrol for business and private use.

3   The company reimbursed me with entertaining expenses of £3,000. I had incurred £2,900 of this amount on business entertaining. The company also reimbursed me with £700 in respect of home telephone expenses. £100 of this was for line rental and £600 was for calls. 50% of the calls were for business purposes.

4   From 6 December 2003, I had a company computer at home which I use for both private and business use. The computer cost £10,000.

5   The only other benefit I received from the company was private medical insurance. In 2003/04 this cost the company £965. If I had paid for the private medical insurance myself it would have cost me £1,265.

6   My dividend vouchers show that I received dividends of £3,330 in 2003/04. The tax credits attaching to these dividends were £370. In addition, I received £1,100 of interest on my bank account with the Nat west plc, £4,500 of interest on a high interest account with the Lanchester Building Society, £630 of interest on an individual Savings account and £95 of interest on a National Savings Bank investment account.

7   I paid £165 a month into my stakeholder pension scheme.

If you need further information please contact me.

Yours sincerely

Frederick Fuse

Task 1

Calculate Mr Fuse's taxable earnings including benefits for 2003/04.

Task 2

Prepare a schedule of income for 2003/04, clearly showing the difference between non-savings, savings and dividend income. Mr Fuse's personal allowance should be deducted as appropriate.

Task 3

Calculate the net income tax payable for 2003/04.

Task 4

The accountant of Nuts and Bolt Limited wants Mr Fuse to contribute towards some of the benefits he has received. he has suggested the following payments for 2004/05:

Payments towards the private use of the car	£100 per month
Payments towards the cost of private petrol	£10 per month (a contribution only, the full cost of private petrol would be approximately £1,000 for the year)

State how the above contributions will affect the benefits that Mr Fuse will be taxed on for 2004/05. You may assume the rules for taxing benefits in 2003/04 will be the same as they were in 2004/05.

21 The Benns

Benn, aged 51 on 1 January 2003, is married to Mrs Benn, aged 44. The following information relates to the year ended 5 April 2004.

(i) Mr Benn's salary was £40,720. His benefits have been agreed at £5,000.

(ii) During the year he paid a personal pension contribution of £8,700.

(iii) He also had the following income.

	£
Building society interest (net)	320
Dividends (including tax credits)	230
Interest on mini cash ISA account	195

(iv) Mrs Benn owns a business that manufactures window frames. Her agreed profits taxable in 2003/04 are £9,800.

(v) Mrs Benn paid a patent royalty of £780 (net) in 2003/04.

(vi) In May 2004 Mr Benn closed a deposit account at the National Midbar Bank which he had kept for many years. Interest credited recently was as follows.

	£
June 2003	51
December 2003	56
May 2004	20

(vii)   Mrs Benn's dividends received totalled £100 (including tax credits).

Tasks

(a)   Prepare a schedule for 2003/04 clearly showing the distinction between non savings, savings and dividend income for Mr Benn. Mr Benn's personal allowance should be deducted as appropriate.

(b)   Compute Mr Benn's income tax liability for 2003/04.

(c) and (d) Repeat the above tasks for Mrs Benn.

chapter 4

Investments and land

Activity checklist

This checklist shows which performance criteria are covered by each activity in this chapter. Full details of the performance criteria are shown on page (ix) onwards. Tick off each activity as you complete it.

Activity

22		Knowledge and understanding point 2.
23		Performance Criteria 19.2A.
24		Performance Criteria 19.2B.
25		Knowledge and Understanding point 8
26		Performance Criteria 19.2B.

22 Tax rates

You have received the following letter from a client.

            23 Charles Street
            Anytown
            AN1 4BQ

H Jones
Technicians & Co
14 Duke Street
Notown
NT4 5AZ

1 October 2003

Dear Hilary

You have always been very helpful in answering my tax queries, and I hope you will not mind my troubling you with this one. I heard recently that dividends are paid net of a 10% tax credit and that building society interest is paid net of 20% tax. However, I thought you told me that I won't need to pay any extra tax on my dividend or interest income. How can this be, since my marginal rate of tax is 22%?

Yours sincerely

Anthony Smith

Anthony Smith

Task

Prepare a reply to Mr Smith's letter.

23 Dividends

An individual holds the following shares.

Share	Holding	Dividends in 2003/04
A plc ords	4,000 bought 1.1.01	3p, 1.7.03
		10p, 1.2.04
B plc ords	2,000 bought 1.7.02	6p, 1.12.03
	10,000 bought 20.11.03	4p, 1.3.04
C plc 25p 7% prefs	24,000 bought 1.1.02	Per terms of issue; no arrears
D plc ords	25,000 bought 1.8.99	2p, 5.9.03
	12,000 sold 1.9.03	6p, 14.3.04

All shares go ex dividend two weeks before the dividend payment date. Assume that all purchases and sales are made on the basis that a dividend paid to a shareholder on the register on the ex dividend date remains with that shareholder, and is not paid over to a buyer.

Task

Prepare a schedule of dividend receipts for tax purposes, showing for each company the net dividend, the tax credit and the gross dividend.

Guidance notes

1   Dividends are normally expressed in pence per share or as a percentage of the nominal share capital.

2   You need to decide, for both the ordinary and the preference dividends, whether the amounts given are net or gross.

3   Shares go ex dividend a short while before a dividend is paid, so that the company can establish a list of shareholders entitled to a dividend and arrange to pay them. It is not practical to allow the list to change right up to the day of payment.

24 Peter

Peter starts to let out property on 1 July 2003. He has the following transactions.

(a)   On 1 July 2003, he lets a house which he has owned for several years. The tenant is required to pay annual rent of £4,000, quarterly in advance. The house is let unfurnished.

(b)   On 1 October 2003 he buys a badly dilapidated house for £37,000. During October, he spends £8,000 on making the house habitable. He lets it furnished for £600 a month from 1 November 2003, but the tenant leaves on 31 January 2004. A new tenant moves in on 1 March 2004, paying £2,100 a quarter in arrears. Water rates are £390 a year, payable by Peter. Peter also pays buildings insurance of £440 for the period from 1 October 2003 to 31 August 2004. He financed the purchase (but not the repairs) with a bank loan at 10% interest. Peter decides to claim the renewals basis. He replaces some furniture on 1 May 2004, at a cost of £350. The tenant is responsible for all repair costs and council tax.

Task

Compute Peter's Schedule A income for 2003/04.

25 Mr and Mrs Faulds

Mr and Mrs Faulds are considering investment in ISAs (individual savings accounts).

Task

Draft short notes in preparation for a meeting with them scheduled for October 2003 describing the main features of this type of investment.

26 William Wiles

William Wiles acquired three houses on 6 April 2003. Houses 1 and 2 were acquired freehold, and are let as furnished holiday accommodation. House 3 was acquired on a 25 year lease, and is let furnished. During 2003/04 the houses were let as follows.

House 1 was available for letting for 42 weeks during 2003/04, and was actually let for 14 weeks at £375 per week. During the 10 weeks that the house was not available for letting, it was occupied rent free by William's sister. Running costs for 2003/04 consisted of business rates £730, insurance £310, and advertising £545.

House 2 was available for letting for 32 weeks during 2003/04, and was actually let for eight weeks at £340 per week. The house was not available for letting for 20 weeks due to a serious flood. As a result of the flood, £6,250 was spent on repairs. The damage was not covered by insurance. The other running costs for 2003/04 consisted of business rates £590, insurance £330, and advertising £225.

House 3 was unoccupied from 6 April 2003 until 31 December 2003. On 1 January 2004 the house was let on at a rent of £8,600 pa payable annually in advance. During 2003/04 he paid interest on a loan to purchase the property of £3,200 and spent £710 on redecorating the property during June 2003.

Immediately after their purchase, William furnished the three houses at a cost of £6,500 per house. He claimed a capital allowance of 40% (ie £2,600) where relevant. With the exception of the 10 week rent-free letting of house 1, all the lettings are at a full rent.

Tasks

(a) Briefly explain why both house 1 and house 2 qualify to be treated as a trade under the furnished holiday letting rules. State the tax advantages of the houses being so treated.

(b) Calculate William's allowable Schedule A loss for 2003/04, and advise him as to the possible ways of relieving the loss.

chapters 5 and 6

Capital gains tax

Activity checklist

This checklist shows which performance criteria are covered by each activity in this chapter. Full details of the performance criteria are provided on page (ix) onwards. Tick off each activity as you complete it.

Activity		
27		Performance Criteria 19.4A, 19.4C, 19.4D, 19.4E.
28		Performance Criteria 19.4A, 19.4C, 19.4D, 19.4E.
29		Performance Criteria 19.4A, 19.4C, 19.4D, 19.4E.
30		Performance Criteria 19.4D.
31		Performance Criteria 19.4C, 19.4D, 19.4E.

27 Oregon

Oregon disposed of assets in 2003/04 as follows.

(i)   On 6 June 2003, he sold an antique table for £40,000. He had bought it on 15 December 1984 for £7,000.

(ii)   On 18 July 2003 he sold a picture for £75,000. He had bought it for £37,000 in March 1982.

(iii)   On 12 November 2003 he sold a plot of land for £120,000, before expenses of sale of £2,500. He had bought the land as an investment in May 1998 for £57,000. In 2000 he spent £4,000 on new permanent drainage, and in May 2002 he spent £3,800 defending his title to the land.

Oregon's taxable income for 2003/04 is £80,000.

Tasks

(a)   Calculate the taxable gain or loss made on the disposal of the table after tapering relief if applicable.

(b)   Calculate the taxable gain or loss made on the disposal of the picture after tapering relief if applicable.

(c)   Calculate the taxable gain or loss made on the disposal of the plot of land after tapering relief if applicable.

(d)   Compute Oregon's total taxable gains after deduction of the annual exemption for 2003/04.

(e)   Compute Oregon's capital gains tax liability for 2003/04.

Assume the following indexation factors:

April 1998	162.6
December 1984	90.9
March 1982	79.4

28 John Lewis

John Lewis, a single person aged 48, carried out the following disposals of assets during 2003/04.

(a)   On 6 June 2003 he sold 4 acres of a 16 acre field he owned for £125,000. Expenses of the sale amounted to £300. John had acquired the entire field in December 2001 on the death of his uncle when it had been valued for probate at £500,000. The value of the remaining 12 acres on 6 June 2003 was £375,000.

(b)   On 2 October 2003 he sold his 1958 motor car to a friend for £2,000. He had purchased the car in December 1998 for £300 and had spent many hours restoring it as a hobby.

(c)   On 30 January 2004 he sold for £60,000 an investment property, which had been acquired in July 2000 for £25,000.

John Lewis had unused capital losses carried forward at 5 April 2001 of £2,500 and transactions in the following two years gave rise to gains and losses as follows.

	Gains £	Losses £	Annual exemption £
2001/02	8,000	1,000	7,500
2002/03	10,700	2,000	7,700

No taper relief was available to reduce the gains in either of the above years.

Tasks

(a)   Compute John Lewis's net taxable gains for 2003/04 after the deduction of losses but before taper relief.

(b)   Compute John Lewis's taxable gains for 2003/04 after the deduction of taper relief and the annual exemption.

(c)   Compute John Lewis's capital gains tax liability for 2003/04 assuming that his income before the personal allowance is:

(i)   £6,000

(ii)   £34,480

29 Wyoming

In 2003/04, Wyoming made the following disposals.

	Gain/(loss) before taper relief
Asset	£
Motor car	(3,000)
Picture	14,500
Gilt-edged securities	45,000
Quoted shares	20,000

All assets were sold for their market values and had been owned since 1997. The quoted shareholding was a non-business asset for taper relief purposes.

Wyoming aged 35, is single. His statutory total income for 2003/04 was £20,150 (all non-savings).

Tasks

(a)   Compute Wyoming's taxable income for 2003/04.

(b)   Calculate Wyoming's income tax liability for 2003/04.

(c)   Calculate Wyoming's total taxable gains for 2003/04 after deduction of taper relief and the annual exemption.

(d)   Calculate Wyoming's capital gains tax liability for 2003/04.

30 Washington

Washington died on 5 October 2003. His gains and losses in recent years had been as follows.

Year	Gains	Losses	Annual exemption
	£	£	£
2000/01	2,000	10,000	7,200
2001/02	32,500	4,500	7,500
2002/03	9,900	2,000	7,700
2003/04	15,000	27,000	7,900

Washington had no gains or losses in earlier years.

Task

Compute the original and final taxable gains for each of the years 2000/01 to 2003/04.

31 Alison Garry

Alison Garry sold two holiday cottages in 2003/04 as follows:

Cottage 1

	£
Proceeds of sale	95,000
Legal fees	(1,321)
Estate agent's fees	(1,597)
Net proceeds paid to client	92,082

Date of sale: 10 March 2004

Purchase price (June 1983): £41,000

Cottage 2

The solicitors paid Alison £85,000. She paid their fee of £850 and the estate agent's fee of £1,500 (date of sale 19 August 2003).

The cottage had cost £30,000 in March 1982. An extension had been added in June 1983 at a cost of £10,000.

Task 1

Compute the chargeable gain arising before taper relief on the disposal of cottage 1.

Task 2

Compute the chargeable gain arising before taper relief on the disposal of cottage 2.

Task 3

Compute Alison Garry's capital gains liability for 2003/04. You may assume that Alison Garry is a higher rate taxpayer.

Assume indexation factors

March 1982 = 79.4
June 1983   = 84.8
April 1998   = 162.6

chapter 7

Shares and securities

Activity checklist

This checklist shows which performance criteria are covered by each activity in this chapter. Full details of the performance criteria are covered on page (ix) onwards. Tick off each activity as you complete it.

Activity		
32		Performance Criteria 19.4B, 19.4C and 19.4D.
33		Performance Criteria 19.4B, 19.4C and 19.4D.
34		Performance Criteria 19.4A, 19.4B, 19.4C, 19.4D and 19.4E.
35		Performance Criteria 19.4A, 19.4B, 19.4C and 19.4D.

32 Eleanor

Eleanor sold 11,000 ordinary shares in Biggs plc on 17 May 2003 for £66,000. She had bought ordinary shares in the company on the following dates.

	No of shares	Cost £
19 September 1982	2,000	1,700
17 January 1985	2,000	6,000
12 December 1985	2,000	5,500
29 June 2000	3,000	17,500
3 November 2001	2,000	12,800

Task

Calculate, after taper relief but before the annual exemption, the capital gain for 2003/04. The shares are not a business asset for taper relief purposes.

Assume the following indexation factors

September 1982	81.9	December 1985	96.0
January 1985	91.2	April 1998	162.6
April 1985	94.8		

Guidance notes

1 Disposals are matched with post April 1998 acquisitions on a LIFO basis before they are matched with the FA 1985 pool.

2 We must build up the FA 1985 pool (including all the first three acquisitions). Indexation is first given up to April 1985, and then (without rounding the indexation factors) up to each later purchase or sale. Remember that the FA 1985 pool closes on 5 April 1998 so the final indexation allowance calculation will be to that date.

3 Losses are set against gains before taper relief. They should be set against the gains that suffer the lowest rate of taper relief (ie the highest percentage of the gain remains taxable).

33 Yvonne

Yvonne had the following transactions in the shares of Scotia plc. The shares are a non business asset for taper relief purposes.

		Shares	£
18 August 1985	bought	3,000	6,000
19 September 2001	bought	2,000	5,000
13 March 2004	sold	5,000	23,000
28 March 2004	bought	1,000	4,400

(Indexation factor August 1995 – April 1998 is 0.085)

Task

Calculate Yvonne's capital gain for 2003/04 after taper relief, but before the annual exemption.

34 James Ramesty

James Ramesty, managing director of Beech Limited, has sold some shares, a car and a freehold holiday home during 2003/04. James Ramesty pays income tax at the 40% rate. The details of the disposals are as follows:

- **Sale of a holiday cottage**

  The solicitor's statement of the account was as follows: £

Proceeds of sale	160,028
Legal fees	(2,000)
Estate agent's fees	(1,000)
Net proceeds paid to client	157,028

Date of sale:	1 June 2003	Address of property:	The Coppice
Date of purchase:	1 October 1983		12 Green Lane
Purchase price:	£30,000		Torquay
			Devon SL6 1JH

- **Sale of shares in N and T plc**

  Transactions in these quoted shares have been as follows:

  Shares purchased

Date	Number of shares	Cost
		£
12 March 1989	200	400
04 May 1991	2,000	10,000
07 June 2000	3,000	15,000
12 July 2001	1,000	5,000

  There was also a bonus issue of shares on 21 June 1994. 1 bonus share was issued for every 2 shares held on that date. The shares are not a business asset for taper relief purposes.

  Shares sold

  James Ramesty sold all his shares in N and T plc for £41,010 on 10 January 2004.

- **Sale of car**

	£
Proceeds of sale	5,400
Purchase price	12,000
Date of purchase	12.6.00
Date of sale	3.3.04

James Ramesty had capital losses brought forward from 2002/03 of £1,000.

Task

(a)   Calculate any chargeable gains arising on the disposals before taper relief.
(b)   Calculate net taxable gains after deducting taper relief and the annual exemption.
(c)   Calculate any capital gains tax payable for 2003/04.

Assume indexation factors

October 1983	86.4
March 1989	112.3
May 1991	133.5
April 1998	162.6

35 Nigel, Kay and Shirley

(a)   On 1 May 1990 Nigel acquired a 30 year lease as an investment for £20,000. On 1 November 2003 he assigned the lease for £75,000.

Task

Calculate Nigel's capital gain for 2003/04, before the annual exemption.

(b)   Kay purchased 20 acres of land as an investment in February 1992 for £40,000. In March 2004 she sold part of the land for £21,600 when the value of the remainder was £72,000. Kay had made no other capital disposals in 2003/04.

Task

Calculate the capital gains chargeable on Kay, after the annual exemption for 2003/04.

(c)   Shirley had the following dealings in the shares of Wingfield plc, a UK quoted company.

	Number of shares	£
January 1997 - bought	4,000	18,000
March 2000 - rights issue 1 for 4	1,000	7,000
November 2003 - bought	3,000	24,000
January 2004 - bonus issue 1 for 2	4,000	-
March 2004 - sold	7,000	56,000

The shares were not a business asset for taper relief purposes.

Task

Calculate Shirley's capital gain for 2003/04, before the annual exemption.

Assume indexation factors

May 1990	126.2
February 1992	136.3
January 1997	154.4
April 1998	162.6

chapter 8

CGT: Additional aspects

Activity checklist

This checklist shows which performance criteria are covered by each activity in this chapter. Further details of the performance criteria are provided on page (ix) onwards. Tick off each activity as you complete it.

Activity

36		Performance Criteria 19.4A, 19.4C and 19.4D.
37		Performance Criteria 19.4A, 19.4B, 19.4C, 19.4D and 19.4E.
38		Performance Criteria 19.4A, 19.4C and 19.4D.
39		Performance Criteria 19.4A, 19.4C, 19.4D and 19.4E.
40		Performance Criteria 19.4A, 19.4C and 19.4D.
41		Performance Criteria 19.4A, 19.4C, 19.4D and 19.4E.

36 Michelle

Michelle purchased an antique vase in March 1982 for £4,000 and sold it in November 2003 for £10,000. 10% sales commission was deducted from this sale price.

Task

Calculate Michelle's gain for 2003/04 (after taper relief but before the annual exemption).

Assume Indexation factors

March 1982	79.4
April 1998	162.6

37 A cottage, shares and a chattel

John Hammond, a single man aged 40, has an annual salary of £21,000. He had the following capital transactions in the year ended 5 April 2004.

(i)   On 5 May 2003 he sold his holiday cottage in Scotland for £100,000. The legal and advertising expenses of the sale were £800.

      John had purchased the property on 31 March 1982 for £25,000 and had incurred costs of £8,000 on 1 December 1983 for the building of an extension.

      The property had never been John's main residence.

(ii)   On 14 September 2003 he sold 4,000 shares in JVD Products plc for £20,000, his previous transactions being as follows.

      1 May 1997 purchased 2,000 shares cost £1,500
      6 June 2000 purchased 500 shares cost £400
      10 March 2001 purchased 500 shares cost £800
      2 August 2003 purchased 2,800 shares cost £13,900

      The shares are not a business asset for taper relief purposes.

(iii)   On 27 October 2003 he sold an oil painting to his sister for £5,000. The market value at the date of sale was £7,000. Hammond had purchased the painting on 18 May 1997 for £10,000.

Tasks

(a)   Compute the taxable gain or loss arising on the disposal of the holiday cottage, after the deduction of taper relief if appropriate.

(b)   Compute the taxable gain or loss arising on disposal of the shares, after the deduction of taper relief, if appropriate.

(c)   Compute the taxable gain or loss arising on the disposal of the oil painting, after deducting taper relief if appropriate.

(d)   Compute the income tax and capital gains tax liabilities of John Hammond for the year 2003/04.

Assume indexation factors

March 1982	79.4
December 1983	86.9
May 1997	156.9
April 1998	162.6

Guidance notes

1   The key date to remember in any CGT question is 5 April 1998.

2   All the assets were sold after 5 April 1998. Remember that the indexation allowance can only be calculated to April 1998 and not beyond that date.

3   Remember that shares acquired after 5.4.98 are treated as disposed of on a LIFO basis.

4   Calculations for disposals to connected persons proceed in the same way as normal transactions, but remember the relevance of market value and the restriction on setting off losses.

5   When you come to work out the tax liabilities, remember that the starting and basic rate bands must be used for both income and gains.

38 Geoff Williams

Geoff Williams is a single man and had the following disposals of assets during the year 2003/04.

- On 14 April 2003 he sold a Ming vase for £10,000. This he had purchased on 8 July 1992 for £2,400 plus expenses of purchase of £100. Expenses of selling amounted to £500.

- On 19 September 2003 a 25% share of a painting was sold for £20,000. The remaining 75% had a value of £90,000. The painting had originally been purchased for £40,000 in May 1987.

- Another picture, which had cost £3,000 in August 1993, was sold for £5,500 in December 2003.

Task

Calculate the chargeable gains for the tax year 2003/04.

Indexation factors

July 1992 – April 1998	0.171
May 1987 – April 1998	0.596
August 1993 – April 1998	0.156

39 Miss Wolf

Miss Wolf carried out the following capital transactions:

(a)   On 30 June 2003 she assigned the lease of a building originally acquired as an investment for £30,750; the lease expires on 30 June 2019.

She had acquired the lease for £8,000 on 1 January 1995 (RPI 146.0) and the building had never been her principal private residence. RPI April 1998 = 162.6.

(b)   On 28 July 2003 she sold a racehorse for £25,000. The horse had been bought for £3,000 on 1 July 1999.

(c) On 5 August 2003 she sold a picture for £9,000 at auction. The auctioneer's costs were 10% of the sale price. Miss Wolf had acquired the painting for £2,200 on 10 September 1999.

Miss Wolf had allowable losses of £2,203 brought forward to 2003/04. Miss Wolf's rate of income tax for the year was 40%.

Task

Prepare a statement showing Miss Wolf's capital gains tax payable for 2003/04.

40 Mr Fox

Mr Fox bought a house on 1 August 1985 (RPI 95.5) for £50,000. He lived in the house until 31 July 1988. He then went abroad to work as a self-employed engineer until 31 July 1993.

Mr Fox went back to live in the house until 31 January 1994. He then moved in with his sister.

Mr Fox sold the house on 31 July 2003 for £180,000.

Task

Calculate the gain on sale after all reliefs.

Note. RPI April 1998 is 162.6

41 John Harley

(a) John Harley purchased a property in England on 1 August 1984 for £40,000 and lived in it until 31 May 1985 when he moved overseas to take up an offer of employment. He returned to the UK on 1 August 1989 and took employment in Scotland until 31 October 1995. During these periods he lived in rented accommodation. On 1 November 1995 he moved back into his own house until he moved out permanently on 30 June 1996. The house was then put up for sale and was finally sold on 30 November 2003 for £120,000. At all times when John was not in the house it remained empty.

Task

Calculate the chargeable gain on the sale of the house. A schedule of periods of exemption and non-exemption should be given, together with the reasons for exemption where applicable. Assume indexation August 1984 – April 1998 = 0.808.

(b) Peter Robinson made the following disposals of non-business assets during the tax year 2003/04.

1 September 2003:

A wasting asset for £37,000. This Peter had purchased on 1 September 1990 for £21,000 when it had an expected useful life of 25 years.

1 February 2004:

A crystal chandelier for £7,500. This he had purchased in January 2002 for £4,000.

Task

Calculate Peter's capital gains tax payable for the year 2003/04. Peter's taxable income (after personal allowances) for income tax purposes was £27,500.

Assume indexation factors

September 1990 to April 1998   0.258

chapter 9

Administration and completion of tax return

42 Mr Brown

Mr Brown's income tax liability for 2002/03 was £16,000. He had suffered tax by deduction at source of £4,000 and paid two payments on account of £6,000 each on the due dates. He submitted his 2002/03 return on 31 January 2004. Mr Brown made a claim to reduce his payments on account for 2003/04 on the basis that this total liability for 2003/04 would be £14,000 with tax suffered of £5,000. He made the payments on account of £4,500 on 28 February and 14 August 2004. Finally, on 13 March 2005 he submitted his return for 2003/04 which showed total tax due of £17,000 and tax deducted at source of £4,000. He therefore paid a further £4,000 on the same date.

Tasks

(a)   Outline the time limits for submission of returns and payments of tax under self assessment and detail the provisions for failure to comply.

(b)   Calculate the interest on overdue tax chargeable in respect of Mr Brown's tax payments for 2003/04. You are not required to compute the surcharges payable.

Note. Assume interest is charged at 5% per annum.

43 John Jefferies

John Jefferies is a senior manager working for a large UK resident trading company. He has an annual salary of £48,000 and has a company car, provided for the whole year.

The car is a two-year old 2,000cc petrol driven Ford with a list price of £18,000 (although the company only paid £16,000 for it under a group scheme). The CO_2 emissions of the car are 239 g/km. All the running costs, including fuel, are paid for by the company.

He pays 10% of his gross salary (not including the value of the car) to a personal pension plan. This amount represents the gross amount of premiums due.

He also pays £140 per year to the Institute of Management (which his employers insist upon), and £300 per year membership to a local sports club that his employers require him to be a member of. This, they say, will enable him to maintain good relations with possible customers.

During the year ended 5 April 2004 he also received the following income.

	£
Dividends	1,800
National Savings Bank ordinary account interest	370
Child benefit (Not taxable)	1,260
Rental income	5,400

All the above amounts represent the actual cash figure received.

Expenses relating to the rental income were as follows.

	£
Council tax	700
Water rates	350
Agents fees	600
New window frames	2,400
Boiler repairs	350

He has also spent £400 on new furniture. He claims the standard wear and tear allowance allowed by the Inland Revenue.

A Schedule A loss of £1,130 was made in the year 2002/03.

John paid £390 (net) to a national charity in November 2003.

John is a widower, his wife having died in July 2001. He is aged 62.

Tasks

(a)   Calculate the taxable income of John Jefferies for 2003/04.

(b)   Calculate the income tax payable by John Jefferies for 2003/2004

(c)   Mr Jefferies has received his annual self-assessment return and requires advice on the system and on filling in his 2003/04 return. Acting as Mr Jefferies' tax advisor write to him explaining the following.

    (i)   What forms he should have, what information he needs to put on the return and from where he will get this information.

    (ii)   How long he needs to keep details of tax information.

    (iii) What deadlines he needs to meet.

    (iv) How and by when any payment should be made.

44 Kitty Bennett

Miss Bennett owns her own business: 'Longbourn Gift Shop'. Schedule D Case I profits have been calculated as £18,716 for 2003/04. There were no capital allowances deducted from this figure as Miss Bennett does not own any assets on which capital allowances could be claimed. She does not prepare a balance sheet but Miss Bennett's profit and loss account is attached. This is annotated to show the amount of tax disallowable items included within each expense caption. You will need this information when you complete Miss Bennett's tax return.

Miss Bennett made the following payments on account of her 2003/04 tax liability

    31 January 2004   £500
    31 July 2004   £500

Miss Bennett's other income is as follows.

1   **Rented property – Pemberley Court (flat)**

    Rented from 1 January [April] 2003 to 30 September 2003 at an annual rental of £4,000. [9 mth 3,000]

    Rented from 1 October 2003 to date at an annual rental of £5,000. [3 mth 1250]

Expenses 2003/04	£
Property management fees	800
Interest on £35,000 loan to purchase the flat	2,450
Repairs to roof	400

2   **Dividend Vouchers – shares held**

    Wickham plc

    Final dividend for the year ended 31 December 2002 – Paid 31 October 2003

Tax credit	Net dividend received
£400	£3,600

Interim dividend for the year ended 31 December 2003 – Paid 31 March 2004

Tax credit	Net dividend received
£300	£2,700

3 Building society interest

Date	Gross interest £	Tax deducted at source £	Net interest £
30.06.03	2,500.00	500.00	2,000.00
31.12.03	2,100.00	420.00	1,680.00

4 Bank interest

Date	Gross interest £	Tax deducted at source £	Net interest £
30.09.03	800.00	160.00	640.00
31.03.04	1,190.00	238.00	952.00

Permanent file note

Name:	Kitty Bennett
Date of birth:	13 March 1965
Tax reference:	124/8765
National Insurance Number:	NB 61 72 21 F
Marital status:	Single: no children
Occupation:	Gift shop proprietor (Longbourn Gift Shop)
Accounting year end:	31 March. Commenced 1/4/01
Property owned:	Main residence – Longbourn House, Meryton Herts (Also business address)
	Rented property – Pemberley Court (flat). Purchased August 1991 for £40,000

Kitty Bennett
Trading as 'Longbourn Gift Shop'
Profit and loss account for the year ended 31 March 2004

	£	£
Sales		124,304
Less: cost of sales		
Opening stock	5,350	
Purchases	60,859	
	66,209	
Closing stock	(7,550)	
		(58,659)
Gross profit		65,645
Less: expenses		
Wages and PAYE	25,394	
Premises costs	9,186	
Telephone (Disallowable £31)	305	
Postage, stationery and advertising	1,650	
Paper and carrier bags	617	
Motor expenses (Disallowable £302)	1,954	
Professional fees	3,980	
Bank charges and interest	1,291	
Repairs and renewals (Disallowable £130)	1,886	
Cleaning	925	
Profit on disposal of fixed assets ⎤	(1,158)	
Depreciation ⎬ (Disallowable £2,557)	3,715	
Sundry expenses ⎦	204	
		(49,949)
Net profit for the year		15,696

Task 1

Prepare a calculation of Schedule A income for 2003/04.

Task 2

Prepare schedules of Kitty Bennett's dividend and interest income for 2003/04.

Task 3

Prepare Miss Bennett's income tax computation for 2003/04.

Task 4

State how much income tax is outstanding for 2003/04 and what payments of account must be made for 2004/05.

Task 5

Complete Miss Bennett's tax return including the supplementary property and self employment pages.

INCOME AND CAPITAL GAINS *for the year ended 5 April 2004*

Step 1

Answer Questions 1 to 9 below to check if you need supplementary Pages to give details of particular income or capital gains. Pages 6 and 7 of your Tax Return Guide will help.

(Ask the Orderline for a Guide if I haven't sent you one with your Tax Return, and you want one.)

If you answer 'Yes' ask the Orderline for the appropriate supplementary Pages and Notes.

Ring the Orderline on 0845 9000 404, or fax on 0845 9000 604 for any you need

(closed Christmas Day, Boxing Day and New Year's Day).

If you do need supplementary Pages, tick the boxes below when you've got them.

Q1
Were you an employee, or office holder, or director, or agency worker or did you receive payments or benefits from a former employer (excluding a pension) in the year ended 5 April 2004?
If you were a non-resident director of a UK company but received no remuneration, see the notes to the Employment Pages, page EN3, box 1.6.
YES ▢   EMPLOYMENT ▢

Q2
Did you have any taxable income from share options, shares or share related benefits in the year? (This does not include
- dividends, **or**
- dividend shares ceasing to be subject to an Inland Revenue approved share incentive plan within three years of acquisition they go in Question 10.)
YES ▢   SHARE SCHEMES ▢

Q3
Were you self-employed (but not in partnership)?
(You should also tick 'Yes' if you were a Name at Lloyd's.)
YES ▢   SELF-EMPLOYMENT ▢

Q4
Were you in partnership?
YES ▢   PARTNERSHIP ▢

Q5
Did you receive any rent or other income from land and property in the UK?
YES ▢   LAND & PROPERTY ▢

Q6
Did you have any taxable income from overseas pensions or benefits, or from foreign companies or savings institutions, offshore funds or trusts abroad, or from land and property abroad or gains on foreign insurance policies?
YES ▢
Have you or could you have received, or enjoyed directly or indirectly, or benefited in any way from, income of a foreign entity as a result of a transfer of assets made in this or earlier years?
YES ▢
Do you want to claim foreign tax credit relief for foreign tax paid on foreign income or gains?
YES ▢   FOREIGN ▢

Q7
Did you receive, or are you deemed to have, income from a trust, settlement or the residue of a deceased person's estate?
YES ▢   TRUSTS ETC ▢

Q8
Capital gains - read the guidance on page 7 of the Tax Return Guide.
- If you have disposed of your only or main residence do you need the Capital Gains Pages?
YES ▢
- Did you dispose of other chargeable assets worth more than £31,600 in total?
YES ▢
- Were your total chargeable gains more than £7,900 or do you want to make a claim or election for the year?
YES ▢   CAPITAL GAINS ▢

Q9
Are you claiming that you were not resident, or not ordinarily resident, or not domiciled, in the UK, or dual resident in the UK and another country, for all or part of the year?
YES ▢   NON-RESIDENCE ETC ▢

Step 2
Fill in any supplementary Pages BEFORE going to Step 3.
Please use blue or black ink to fill in your Tax Return and please do not include pence. Round down your income and gains. Round up your tax credits and tax deductions. Round to the nearest pound.
When you have filled in all the supplementary Pages you need, tick this box. ▢

Step 3
Fill in Questions 10 to 24. If you answer 'Yes', fill in the relevant boxes. If not applicable, go to the next question.

INCOME *for the year ended 5 April 2004*

Q10 **Did you receive any income from UK savings and investments?** | YES | | **If yes**, tick this box and then fill in boxes 10.1 to 10.26 as appropriate. Include only your share from any joint savings and investments. If not applicable, go to Question 11.

■ *Interest*

● Interest from UK banks, building societies and deposit takers (interest from UK Internet accounts must be included) - *if you have more than one bank or building society etc. account enter **totals** in the boxes.*

- enter any bank, building society etc. interest that **has not** had tax taken off. (Most interest is taxed by your bank or building society etc. so make sure you should be filling in box 10.1, rather than boxes 10.2 to 10.4)

Taxable amount
10.1 £

- enter details of your **taxed** bank or building society etc. interest. *The Working Sheet on page 10 of your Tax Return Guide will help you fill in boxes 10.2 to 10.4.*

Amount **after** tax deducted	Tax deducted	Gross amount **before** tax
10.2 £	**10.3** £	**10.4** £

● Interest distributions from UK authorised unit trusts and open-ended investment companies (dividend distributions go below)

Amount **after** tax deducted	Tax deducted	Gross amount **before** tax
10.5 £	**10.6** £	**10.7** £

● National Savings & Investments (other than First Option Bonds and Fixed Rate Savings Bonds and the first £70 of interest from an Ordinary Account)

Taxable amount
10.8 £

● National Savings & Investments First Option Bonds and Fixed Rate Savings Bonds

Amount **after** tax deducted	Tax deducted	Gross amount **before** tax
10.9 £	**10.10** £	**10.11** £

● Other income from UK savings and investments (except dividends)

Amount **after** tax deducted	Tax deducted	Gross amount **before** tax
10.12 £	**10.13** £	**10.14** £

■ *Dividends*

● Dividends and other qualifying distributions from UK companies

Dividend/distribution	Tax credit	Dividend/distribution **plus** credit
10.15 £	**10.16** £	**10.17** £

● Dividend distributions from UK authorised unit trusts and open-ended investment companies

Dividend/distribution	Tax credit	Dividend/distribution **plus** credit
10.18 £	**10.19** £	**10.20** £

● Scrip dividends from UK companies

Dividend	Notional tax	Dividend **plus** notional tax
10.21 £	**10.22** £	**10.23** £

● Non-qualifying distributions and loans written off

Distribution/Loan	Notional tax	Taxable amount
10.24 £	**10.25** £	**10.26** £

45

INCOME *for the year ended 5 April 2004, continued*

Q11 **Did you receive a taxable UK pension, retirement annuity or Social Security benefit?**
Read the notes on pages 13 to 15 of the Tax Return Guide.

YES ☐ | If yes, tick this box and then fill in boxes 11.1 to 11.14 as appropriate. If not applicable, go to Question 12.

■ *State pensions and benefits*

Taxable amount for 2003-04

- State Retirement Pension - *enter the **total** of your entitlements for the year* **11.1** £
- Widow's Pension or Bereavement Allowance **11.2** £
- Widowed Mother's Allowance or Widowed Parent's Allowance **11.3** £
- Industrial Death Benefit Pension **11.4** £
- Jobseeker's Allowance **11.5** £
- Carer's Allowance **11.6** £
- Statutory Sick Pay, Statutory Maternity Pay and Statutory Paternity Pay paid by the Inland Revenue **11.7** £

	Tax deducted	Gross amount **before tax**
Taxable Incapacity Benefit	**11.8** £	**11.9** £

■ *Other pensions and retirement annuities*

- Pensions (other than State pensions) and retirement annuities - *if you have more than one pension or annuity, please add together and complete boxes 11.10 to 11.12. Provide details of each one in box 11.14*

Amount after tax deducted	Tax deducted	Gross amount **before tax**
11.10 £	**11.11** £	**11.12** £

11.14

- Deduction - *see the note for box 11.13 on page 15 of your Tax Return Guide*
Amount of deduction **11.13** £

Q12 **Did you make any gains on UK life insurance policies, life annuities or capital redemption policies or receive refunds of surplus funds from additional voluntary contributions?**

YES ☐ | If yes, tick this box and then fill in boxes 12.1 to 12.12 as appropriate. If not applicable, go to Question 13.

- Gains on UK annuities and friendly societies' life insurance policies where no tax is treated as paid

Number of years	Amount of gain(s)
12.1	**12.2** £

- Gains on UK life insurance policies etc. on which tax is treated as paid - *read pages 15 to 18 of your Tax Return Guide*

Number of years	Tax treated as paid	Amount of gain(s)
12.3	**12.4** £	**12.5** £

- Gains on life insurance policies in ISAs that have been made void

Number of years	Tax deducted	Amount of gain(s)
12.6	**12.7** £	**12.8** £

- Corresponding deficiency relief
Amount **12.9** £

- Refunds of surplus funds from additional voluntary contributions

Amount received	Notional tax	Amount plus notional tax
12.10 £	**12.11** £	**12.12** £

Q13 **Did you receive any other taxable income which you have not already entered elsewhere in your Tax Return?**
Fill in any supplementary Pages before answering Question 13. (Supplementary Pages follow page 10, or are available from the Orderline.)

YES ☐ | If yes, tick this box and then fill in boxes 13.1 to 13.6 as appropriate. If not applicable, go to Question 14.

- Other taxable income – also provide details in box 23.5 - *read the notes on pages 18 to 20 of your Tax Return Guide*

Amount after tax deducted	Tax deducted	Amount before tax
13.1 £	**13.2** £	**13.3** £

- Tick box 13.1A if box 13.1 includes enhanced capital allowances for environmentally friendly expenditure **13.1A** ☐

	Losses brought forward	Earlier years' losses used in 2003-04
	13.4 £	**13.5** £

2003-04 losses carried forward **13.6** £

BS 12/2002net   Tax Return: page 4

  PROFESSIONAL EDUCATION

RELIEFS *for the year ended 5 April 2004*

Q14 ▶ **Do you want to claim relief for your pension contributions?** | YES | If yes, tick this box and then fill in boxes 14.1 to 14.11 as appropriate.
Do not include contributions deducted from your pay by your employer to their pension scheme or associated AVC scheme, because tax relief is given automatically. But do include your contributions to personal pension schemes and Free-Standing AVC schemes.
If not appliable, go to Question 15.

■ *Payments to your retirement annuity contracts - only fill in boxes 14.1 to 14.5 for policies taken out before 1 July 1988. See the notes on pages 20 and 21 of your Tax Return Guide.*

Qualifying payments made in 2003-04	**14.1** £	2003-04 payments used in an earlier year	**14.2** £	Relief claimed
2003-04 payments now to be carried back	**14.3** £	Payments brought back from 2004-05	**14.4** £	box 14.1 *minus* (boxes 14.2 and 14.3, but not 14.4) **14.5** £

■ *Payments to your personal pension (including stakeholder pension) contracts - enter the amount of the payment you made with the basic rate tax added (the **gross** payment). See the note for box 14.6 on page 22 of your Tax Return Guide.*

Gross qualifying payments made in 2003-04 **14.6** £

2003-04 gross payments carried back to 2002-03 **14.7** £

Gross qualifying payments made between 6 April 2004 and 31 January 2005 brought back to 2003-04 - *see page 22 of your Tax Return Guide* **14.8** £

Relief claimed
box 14.6 *minus* box 14.7 (but not 14.8)
14.9 £

■ *Contributions to other pension schemes and Free-Standing AVC schemes*

● Amount of contributions to employer's schemes **not deducted** at source from pay **14.10** £

● Gross amount of Free-Standing Additional Voluntary Contributions paid in 2003-04 **14.11** £

Q15 ▶ **Do you want to claim any of the following reliefs?** | YES | If yes, tick this box and then fill in boxes 15.1 to 15.12, as appropriate.
If you have made any annual payments, after basic rate tax, answer 'Yes' to Question 15 and fill in box 15.9. If you have made any gifts to charity go to Question 15A.
If not applicable, go to Question 15A

● Interest eligible for relief on qualifying loans **15.1** £

● Maintenance or alimony payments you have made under a court order, Child Support Agency assessment or legally binding order or agreement
Amount claimed up to £2,150 **15.2** £

To claim this relief, either you or your former spouse must have been 65 or over on 5 April 2000. So, if **your** date of birth, which is entered in box 22.6, is after 5 April 1935 then you must enter your former **spouse's** date of birth in box 15.2A - *see pages 23 and 24 of your Tax Return Guide*
Former spouse's date of birth **15.2A** / /

● Subscriptions for Venture Capital Trust shares (up to £100,000)
Amount on which relief is claimed **15.3** £

● Subscriptions under the Enterprise Investment Scheme (up to £150,000) - *also provide details in box 23.5, see page 24 of your Tax Return Guide*
Amount on which relief is claimed **15.4** £

● Community Investment Tax relief - invested amount relating to previous tax year(s) and on which relief is due **15.5** £
Total amount on which relief is claimed

● Community Investment Tax relief - invested amount for current tax year **15.6** £
box 15.5 + box 15.6 **15.7** £

● Post-cessation expenses, pre-incorporation losses brought forward and losses on relevant discounted securities, etc. - *see pages 24 and 25 of your Tax Return Guide*
Amount of payment **15.8** £

● Annuities and annual payments
Payments made **15.9** £

● Payments to a trade union or friendly society for death benefits
Half amount of payment **15.10** £

● Payment to your employer's compulsory widow's, widower's or orphan's benefit scheme - *available in some circumstances – **first** read the notes on page 25 of your Tax Return Guide*
Relief claimed **15.11** £

● Relief claimed on a qualifying distribution on the **redemption** of bonus shares or securities.
Relief claimed **15.12** £

ALLOWANCES *for the year ended 5 April 2004*

Q15A **Do you want to claim relief on gifts to charity?**

If you have made any Gift Aid payments answer 'Yes' to Question 15A. You should include Gift Aid payments to Community Amateur Sports Clubs here. You can elect to include in this Return Gift Aid payments made between 6 April 2004 and the date you send in this Return. See page 26 in the Tax Return Guide and the leaflet enclosed on Gift Aid.

YES | *If yes, tick this box and then read page 26 of your Tax Return Guide. Fill in boxes 15A.1 to 15A.5 as appropriate. If not applicable, go to Question 16.*

- Gift Aid and payments under charitable covenants made between 6 April 2003 and 5 April 2004 — **15A.1** £
- Enter in box 15A.2 the total of any 'one off' payments included in box 15A.1 — **15A.2** £
- Enter in box 15A.3 the amount of Gift Aid payments made after 5 April 2004 but treated as if made in the tax year 2003-04 — **15A.3** £
- Gifts of qualifying investments to charities – shares and securities — **15A.4** £
- Gifts of qualifying investments to charities – real property — **15A.5** £

Q16 **Do you want to claim blind person's allowance, married couple's allowance or the Children's Tax Credit?**

*You get your personal allowance of £4,615 automatically. **If you were born before 6 April 1938, enter your date of birth in box 22.6** - you may get a higher age-related personal allowance.*

YES | *If yes, tick this box and then read pages 26 to 31 of your Tax Return Guide. Fill in boxes 16.1 to 16.33 as appropriate. If not applicable, go to Question 17.*

■ *Blind person's allowance*

Date of registration (if first year of claim) **16.1** / /   Local authority (or other register) **16.2**

■ *Married couple's allowance -* In 2003-04 married couple's allowance can only be claimed if either you, or your husband or wife, were born **before 6 April 1935**. So you can only claim the allowance in 2003-04 if either of you had reached **65 years of age before 6 April 2000. Further guidance is given beginning on page 27 of your Tax Return Guide.**

If **both** you and your husband or wife were born after 5 April 1935 you cannot claim; **do not** complete boxes 16.3 to 16.13.

If you can claim fill in boxes 16.3 and 16.4 if you are a married man or if you are a married woman and you are claiming half or all of the married couple's allowance.

- Enter your date of birth (if born before 6 April 1935) — **16.3** / /
- Enter your spouse's date of birth (**if born before 6 April 1935 and** if older than you) — **16.4** / /

Then, if you are a married man fill in boxes 16.5 to 16.9. If you are a married woman fill in boxes 16.10 to 16.13.

- Wife's full name **16.5**   • Date of marriage (if after 5 April 2003) **16.6** / /

Half | All
- Tick box 16.7, or box 16.8, if you or your wife have allocated half, or all, of the minimum amount of the allowance to her — **16.7** **16.8**

- Enter in box 16.9 the date of birth of any previous wife with whom you lived at any time during 2002-03. *Read 'Special rules if you are a man who married in the year ended 5 April 2004' on page 28 before completing box 16.9.* — **16.9** / /

Half | All
- Tick box 16.10, or box 16.11, if you or your husband have allocated half, or all, of the minimum amount of the allowance to you — **16.10** **16.11**

- Husband's full name **16.12**   • Date of marriage (if after 5 April 2003) **16.13** / /

■ *Child Tax Credit* – even if you have already completed a separate Child's Tax Credit (CTC) claim form and received the relief in your tax code, you should still fill in boxes 16.14 to 16.26, as directed. Any reference to 'partner' in this question means the person you lived with during the year to 5 April 2004 – your husband or wife, or someone you lived with as husband or wife.

Guidance for claiming CTC is on pages 29 to 31 of your Tax Return Guide. Please read the notes before completing your claim, particularly if either you, or your partner, were liable to tax above the basic rate in the year to 5 April 2004.

- Enter in box 16.14 the date of birth of a child living with you who was born on or after 6 April 1986. *If you have a child living with you who was born on or after 6 April 2003 make sure you enter their date of birth in this box in preference to claiming for an older child.* — **16.14** / /

- Tick box 16.15 if the child was your own child or one you looked after at your own expense. If not, you cannot claim CTC – go to box 16.27, if appropriate, or Question 17. — **16.15**

- Tick box 16.16 if the child lived with you **throughout** the year to 5 April 2004. If you ticked box 16.16 and — **16.16**
  - you were a lone or single claimant, you have finished this question; go to Question 17,
  - you have a partner, go to box 16.18.

- If the child lived with you for only **part of the year** you may only be entitled to a proportion of the CTC. Enter in box 16.17 your share in £s that **you have agreed** with any other claimants that you may claim for this child. But leave boxes 16.17 to 16.25 blank if you separated from, or started living with, your partner during the year to 5 April 2004. Special rules apply to work out your entitlement; ask the Orderline for *Help Sheet IR343: Claiming Children's Tax Credit when your circumstances change* which explains how to complete box 16.26. — **16.17** £

ALLOWANCES *for the year ended 5 April 2004, continued*

■ *Children's Tax Credit, continued*

If you lived with your partner (for CTC this means your husband or wife, or someone you lived with as husband and wife) for the whole of the year to 5 April 2004, fill in boxes 16.18 to 16.25 as appropriate.

- Enter in box 16.18 your partner's surname

  16.18

- Enter in box 16.19 your partner's National Insurance number

  16.19

- Tick
  - box 16.20 if you had the higher income in the year to 5 April 2004,

    16.20

  or
  - box 16.21 if **your partner** had the higher income that year

    16.21

- Tick box 16.22 if either of you were chargeable to tax above the basic rate in the year to 5 April 2004.

  16.22

If you ticked boxes 16.20 and 16.22 your entitlement will be reduced - see page 30 of your Tax Return Guide; your partner cannot claim CTC - go to box 16.28, or Question 17 as appropriate.

If you ticked boxes 16.21 and 16.22 your partner's entitlement will be reduced; you cannot claim CTC - go to box 16.27, or Question 17, as appropriate.

If neither of you were chargeable above the basic rate and you had the lower income and
- *you don't want to claim half of the entitlement to CTC, and*
- *you didn't make an election for CTC to go to the partner with the lower income*

you have finished this part of your Return - go to boxes 16.27 or 16.28, or Question 17, as appropriate (your partner should claim CTC if they have not already done so).

Otherwise, tick one of boxes 16.23 to 16.25 .

- I had the higher income and I am claiming all of our entitlement to CTC

  16.23

- We are both making separate claims for half of our entitlement to CTC

  16.24

- We elected before 6 April 2003, or because of our special circumstances, during the year to 5 April 2004 (see page 31 of your Tax Return Guide), for the partner with the lower income to claim all of our entitlement to CTC

  16.25

- If you separated from, or starting living with, your partner in the year to 5 April 2004, enter in box 16.26 the amount of CTC you are claiming *(following the guidance in Help Sheet IR343: Claiming Children's Tax Credit when your circumstances change).*

  16.26 £

■ *Transfer of surplus allowances - see page 31 of your Tax Return Guide before you fill in boxes 16.27 to 16.33.*

- Tick box 16.27 if you want your spouse to have your unused allowances

  16.27

- Tick box 16.28 if you want to have your spouse's unused allowances

  16.28

If you want to calculate your tax, enter the amount of the surplus allowance you can have.

- Blind person's surplus allowance

  16.31 £

- Married couple's surplus allowance

  16.32

OTHER INFORMATION *for the year ended 5 April 2004*

Q17 **Are you liable to make Student Loan Repayments for 2003-04 on an Income Contingent Student Loan?**
You must read the note on page 31 of your Tax Return Guide before ticking the 'Yes' box.

YES If yes, tick this box.
If not applicable, go to Question 18.

If yes, and you are calculating your tax enter in Question 18, box 18.2A the amount you work out is repayable in 2003-04

OTHER INFORMATION *for the year ended 5 April 2004, continued*

Q18 **Do you want to calculate your tax and, if appropriate, any Student Loan Repayment?** **YES** | Use your Tax Calculation Guide then fill in boxes 18.1 to 18.8 as appropriate.

- Unpaid tax for earlier years **included in your tax code for 2003-04** — **18.1** £
- Tax due for 2003-04 included in your tax code for a later year — **18.2** £
- Student Loan Repayment due — **18.2A** £
- Total tax, Class 4 NIC and Student Loan Repayment due for 2003-04 **before** you made any payments on account *(put the amount in brackets if an overpayment)* — **18.3** £
- Tax due for earlier years — **18.4** £
- Tax overpaid for earlier years — **18.5** £
- Tick box 18.6 if you are claiming to reduce your 2004-05 payments on account. Make sure you enter the **reduced** amount of your first payment in box 18.7. Then, in the 'Additional information' box, box 23.5 on page 9, say why you are making a claim — **18.6**
- Your first payment on account for 2004-05 *(include the pence)* — **18.7** £
- Any 2004-05 tax you are reclaiming now — **18.8** £

Q19 **Do you want to claim a repayment if you have paid too much tax?** *(If you do not tick 'Yes' or the tax you have overpaid is below £10, I will use the amount you are owed to reduce your next tax bill.)* **YES** | **If yes**, tick this box and then fill in boxes 19.1 to 19.12 as appropriate. If not applicable, go to Question 20.

Should the repayment be sent:
- to your bank or building society account? *Tick box 19.1 and fill in boxes 19.3 to 19.7* **19.1**
or
- to your nominee's bank or building society account? *Tick box 19.2 and fill in boxes 19.3 to 19.12* **19.2**

We prefer to make repayment direct into a bank or building society account. (But tick box 19.8A or box 19.8B if you would like a cheque to be sent to you or your nominee.)

Name of bank or building society **19.3**
Branch sort code **19.4**
Account number **19.5**
Name of account holder **19.6**
Building society reference **19.7**

If you would like a cheque to be sent to:
- you, at the address on page 1, *tick box 19.8A* **19.8A**
or
- your nominee, *tick box 19.8B* **19.8B**

If your nominee is your agent, *tick box 19.9A* **19.9A**

Agent's reference for you (if your nominee is your agent) **19.9**

I authorise
Name of your nominee/agent **19.10**
Nominee/agent address **19.11**
Postcode
to receive on my behalf the amount due **19.12** *This authority must be signed by you. A photocopy of your signature will not do.*
Signature

OTHER INFORMATION *for the year ended 5 April 2004, continued*

Q20 **Have you already had any 2003-04 tax refunded or set off by your Inland Revenue office or the Benefits Agency (in Northern Ireland, the Social Security Agency)?**
Read the notes on page 32 of your Tax Return Guide.

YES ▢

If yes, tick this box and then enter the amount of the refund in box 20.1.

20.1 £ ▢

Q21 **Is your name or address on the front of the Tax Return *wrong*?**
If you are filling in an approved substitute Tax Return, see the notes on page 32 of the Tax Return Guide.

YES ▢

If yes, please tick this box and make any corrections on the front of the form.

Q22 **Please give other personal details in boxes 22.1 to 22.7.** *This information helps us to be more efficient and effective.*

Your daytime telephone number
22.1 ▢

Your agent's telephone number
22.2 ▢

and their name and address
22.3 ▢

Postcode

Your first two forenames
22.4 ▢

Say if you are single, married, widowed, divorced or separated
22.5 ▢

Your date of birth (If you were born before 6 April 1938, you may get a higher age-related allowance.)
22.6 ▢ / /

Your National Insurance number
(if known and not on page 1 of your Tax Return)
22.7 ▢

Q23 **Please tick boxes 23.1 to 23.4 if they apply. Provide any additional information in box 23.5 below (continue on page 10, if necessary).**

Tick box 23.1 if you do **not** want any tax you owe for 2003-04 collected through your tax code.
23.1 ▢

Please tick box 23.2 if this Tax Return contains figures that are provisional because you do not yet have final figures. Pages 32 and 33 of the Tax Return Guide explain the circumstances in which provisional figures may be used and asks for some additional information to be provided in box 23.5 below.
23.2 ▢

Tick box 23.3 if you are claiming relief now for 2004-05 trading, or certain capital, losses. Enter in box 23.5 the amount and year.
23.3 ▢

Tick box 23.4 if you are claiming to have post-cessation or other business receipts taxed as income of an earlier year. Enter in box 23.5 the amount and year.
23.4 ▢

23.5 *Additional information*

BS 12/2002net

TAX RETURN: PAGE 9

Please turn over ➤

OTHER INFORMATION *for the year ended 5 April 2004, continued*

23.5 *Additional information continued*

Q24 Declaration

I have filled in and am sending back to you the following pages:

Tick *In the second box enter the number of **complete sets** of supplementary Pages enclosed*

1 TO 10 OF THIS FORM — Number of sets

EMPLOYMENT — PARTNERSHIP — Tick / Number of sets — TRUSTS, ETC — Tick

SHARE SCHEMES — Number of sets — LAND & PROPERTY — CAPITAL GAINS

SELF-EMPLOYMENT — FOREIGN — NON-RESIDENCE, ETC

Before you send your completed Tax Return back to your Inland Revenue office, you must sign the statement below. If you give false information or conceal any part of your income or chargeable gains, you may be liable to financial penalties and/or you may be prosecuted.

24.1 The information I have given in this Tax Return is correct and complete to the best of my knowledge and belief.

Signature — Date

There are very few reasons why we accept a signature from someone who is not the person making this Return but if you are signing for someone else please read the notes on page 33 of the Tax Return Guide, and:

- enter the capacity in which you are signing (for example, as executor or receiver)

24.2

- enter the name of the person you are signing for

24.3

- please **PRINT** your name and address in box 24.4

24.4

Postcode

BS 12/2002net — TAX RETURN: PAGE 10

Income for the year ended 5 April 2004

Inland Revenue

LAND AND PROPERTY

Fill in these boxes first

Name

Tax reference

If you want help, look up the box numbers in the Notes.

Are you claiming Rent a Room relief for gross rents of £4,250 or less?
(Or £2,125 if the claim is shared?)
Read the Notes on page LN2 to find out
- **whether you can claim Rent a Room relief; and**
- **how to claim relief for gross rents over £4,250**

| Yes |

If 'Yes', tick box. If this is your only income from UK property, you have finished these Pages

Is your income from furnished holiday lettings?
If not applicable, please turn over and fill in Page L2 to give details of your property income

| Yes |

If 'Yes', tick box and fill in boxes 5.1 to 5.18 before completing Page L2

Furnished holiday lettings

- **Income from furnished holiday lettings**   **5.1** £

- ■ *Expenses* (furnished holiday lettings only)

- Rent, rates, insurance, ground rents etc.   **5.2** £

- Repairs, maintenance and renewals   **5.3** £

- Finance charges, including interest   **5.4** £

- Legal and professional costs   **5.5** £

- Costs of services provided, including wages   **5.6** £

- Other expenses   **5.7** £

total of boxes 5.2 to 5.7
5.8 £

Net profit (put figures in brackets if a loss)

box 5.1 *minus* box 5.8
5.9 £

- ■ *Tax adjustments*

- Private use   **5.10** £

- Balancing charges   **5.11** £

box 5.10 + box 5.11
5.12 £

- Capital allowances   **5.13** £

- Tick box 5.13A if box 5.13 includes enhanced capital allowances for environmentally friendly expenditure   **5.13A**

Profit for the year (copy to box 5.19). If loss, enter '0' in box 5.14 and put the loss in box 5.15

boxes 5.9 + 5.12 *minus* box 5.13
5.14 £

Loss for the year (if you have entered '0' in box 5.14)

boxes 5.9 + 5.12 *minus* box 5.13
5.15 £

- ■ *Losses*

- Loss offset against 2003-04 total income   **5.16** £

- Loss carried back   see Notes, page LN4   **5.17** £

- Loss offset against other income from property (copy to box 5.38)   see Notes, page LN4   **5.18** £

SA105

BS 12/2002net   TAX RETURN ■ LAND AND PROPERTY: PAGE L1   *Please turn over*

Other property income

■ Income

● Furnished holiday lettings profits	**5.19** £	*copy from box 5.14*
● Rents and other income from land and property	**5.20** £	Tax deducted — **5.21** £
● Chargeable premiums	**5.22** £	
● Reverse premiums	**5.22A** £	boxes 5.19 + 5.20 + 5.22 + 5.22A — **5.23** £

■ Expenses (do not include figures you have already put in boxes 5.2 to 5.7 on Page L1)

● Rent, rates, insurance, ground rents etc.	**5.24** £	
● Repairs, maintenance and renewals	**5.25** £	
● Finance charges, including interest	**5.26** £	
● Legal and professional costs	**5.27** £	
● Costs of services provided, including wages	**5.28** £	
● Other expenses	**5.29** £	total of boxes 5.24 to 5.29 — **5.30** £

Net profit (put figures in brackets if a loss) box 5.23 *minus* box 5.30 — **5.31** £

■ Tax adjustments

● Private use	**5.32** £	
● Balancing charges	**5.33** £	box 5.32 + box 5.33 — **5.34** £
● Rent a Room exempt amount	**5.35** £	
● Capital allowances	**5.36** £	
● Tick box 5.36A if box 5.36 includes a claim for 100% capital allowances for flats over shops	**5.36A**	
● Tick box 5.36B if box 5.36 includes enhanced capital allowances for environmentally friendly expenditure	**5.36B**	
● 10% wear and tear	**5.37** £	
● Furnished holiday lettings losses (from box 5.18)	**5.38** £	boxes 5.35 to box 5.38 — **5.39** £

Adjusted profit (if loss enter '0' in box 5.40 and put the loss in box 5.41) boxes 5.31 + 5.34 *minus* box 5.39 — **5.40** £

Adjusted loss (if you have entered '0' in box 5.40) boxes 5.31 + 5.34 *minus* box 5.39 — **5.41** £

● Loss brought forward from previous year	**5.42** £

Profit for the year box 5.40 *minus* box 5.42 — **5.43** £

■ Losses etc

● Loss offset against total income (read the note on page LN8)	**5.44** £
● Loss to carry forward to following year	**5.45** £
● Tick box 5.46 if these Pages include details of property let jointly	**5.46**
● Tick box 5.47 if **all** property income ceased in the year to 5 April 2004 **and** you don't expect to receive such income again, in the year to 5 April 2005	**5.47**

Now fill in any other supplementary Pages that apply to you. Otherwise, go back to page 2 of your Tax Return and finish filling it in.

BS 12/2002net   TAX RETURN ■ LAND AND PROPERTY: PAGE L2

Income for the year ended 5 April 2004

SELF-EMPLOYMENT

Inland Revenue

Fill in these boxes first

Name

Tax reference

If you want help, look up the box numbers in the Notes

Business details

Name of business
3.1

Description of business
3.2

Address of business
3.3

Postcode

Accounting period - *read the Notes, page SEN2 before filling in these boxes*

Start
3.4 / /

End
3.5 / /

- Tick box 3.6 if details in boxes 3.1 or 3.3 have changed since your last Tax Return **3.6**

- Date of commencement if after 5 April 2000 **3.7** / /

- Date of cessation if before 6 April 2004 **3.8** / /

- Tick box 3.9 if the special arrangements for certain trades apply - *read the Notes, pages SEN11 and SEN12* **3.9**

- Tick box 3.10 if you entered details for all relevant accounting periods on last year's Tax Return and boxes 3.14 to 3.73 and 3.99 to 3.115 will be blank *(read Step 3 on page SEN2)* **3.10**

- Tick box 3.11 if your accounts do not cover the period from the last accounting date (explain why in the 'Additional information' box, box 3.116) **3.11**

- Tick box 3.12 if your accounting date has changed (only if this is a permanent change and you want it to count for tax) **3.12**

- Tick box 3.13 if this is the second or further change (explain in box 3.116 on Page SE4 why you have not used the same date as last year) **3.13**

Capital allowances - summary

	Capital allowances	Balancing charges
- Cars costing more than £12,000 (A separate calculation must be made for each car.)	**3.14** £	**3.15** £
- Other business plant and machinery	**3.16** £	**3.17** £
- Agricultural or Industrial Buildings Allowance (A separate calculation must be made for each block of expenditure.)	**3.18** £	**3.19** £
- Other capital allowances claimed (Separate calculations must be made.)	**3.20** £	**3.21** £
	total of column above	total of column above
Total capital allowances/balancing charges	**3.22** £	**3.23** £

- Tick box 3.22A if box 3.22 includes enhanced capital allowances for environmentally friendly expenditure **3.22A**

Income and expenses - annual turnover below £15,000

*If your annual turnover is £15,000 or more, **ignore** boxes 3.24 to 3.26. Instead fill in Page SE2*

*If your annual turnover is below £15,000, **fill in boxes 3.24 to 3.26 instead of Page SE2**. Read the Notes, page SEN2.*

- Turnover including other business receipts and goods etc. taken for personal use (and balancing charges from box 3.23) **3.24** £

- Expenses allowable for tax (including capital allowances from box 3.22) **3.25** £

	box 3.24 *minus* box 3.25
Net profit (put figure in brackets if a loss)	**3.26** £

You must now fill in Page SE3

SA103

BS 12/2002net

TAX RETURN ■ SELF-EMPLOYMENT: PAGE SE1

Income and expenses - annual turnover £15,000 or more

You must fill in this Page if your annual turnover is £15,000 or more - read the Notes, page SEN2

If you were registered for VAT, do the figures in boxes 3.29 to 3.64, include VAT? **3.27** [ ] or exclude VAT? **3.28** [ ]

Sales/business income (turnover)
3.29 £ [ ]

	Disallowable expenses included in boxes 3.46 to 3.63	Total expenses
Cost of sales	**3.30** £	**3.46** £
Construction industry subcontractor costs	**3.31** £	**3.47** £
Other direct costs	**3.32** £	**3.48** £

Gross profit/(loss) **3.49** £   box 3.29 *minus* (boxes 3.46 + 3.47 + 3.48)

Other income/profits **3.50** £

Employee costs	**3.33** £	**3.51** £
Premises costs	**3.34** £	**3.52** £
Repairs	**3.35** £	**3.53** £
General administrative expenses	**3.36** £	**3.54** £
Motor expenses	**3.37** £	**3.55** £
Travel and subsistence	**3.38** £	**3.56** £
Advertising, promotion and entertainment	**3.39** £	**3.57** £
Legal and professional costs	**3.40** £	**3.58** £
Bad debts	**3.41** £	**3.59** £
Interest	**3.42** £	**3.60** £
Other finance charges	**3.43** £	**3.61** £
Depreciation and loss/(profit) on sale	**3.44** £	**3.62** £
Other expenses	**3.45** £	**3.63** £

Put the total of boxes 3.30 to 3.45 in box 3.66 below

Total expenses **3.64** £   total of boxes 3.51 to 3.63

Net profit/(loss) **3.65** £   boxes 3.49 + 3.50 *minus* 3.64

Tax adjustments to net profit or loss

- Disallowable expenses **3.66** £   boxes 3.30 to 3.45
- Adjustments (apart from disallowable expenses) that increase profits. Examples are goods taken for personal use and amounts brought forward from an earlier year because of a claim under ESC B11 about compulsory slaughter of farm animals **3.67** £
- Balancing charges (from box 3.23) **3.68** £

Total additions to net profit (deduct from net loss) **3.69** £   boxes 3.66 + 3.67 + 3.68

- Capital allowances (from box 3.22) **3.70** £
- Deductions from net profit (add to net loss) **3.71** £

   boxes 3.70 + 3.71 **3.72** £

Net business profit for tax purposes (put figure in brackets if a loss) **3.73** £   boxes 3.65 + 3.69 *minus* 3.72

BS 12/2002net   TAX RETURN ■ SELF-EMPLOYMENT: PAGE SE2   *Now fill in Page SE3* ➡

You **must** fill in boxes 3.74 and 3.75 and **all other boxes** that apply to you, on this Page

Adjustments to arrive at taxable profit or loss

Basis period begins **3.74** [/ /] and ends **3.75** [/ /]

Profit or loss of this account for tax purposes (box 3.26 or 3.73) **3.76** £

Adjustment to arrive at profit or loss for this basis period **3.77** £

- Overlap profit brought forward **3.78** £   • Deduct overlap relief used this year **3.79** £

- Overlap profit carried forward **3.80** £

Averaging for farmers and creators of literary or artistic works (see Notes, page SEN9, if you made a loss for 2003-04) **3.81** £

Adjustment on change of basis **3.82** £

Net profit for 2003-04 (if you made a loss, enter '0') **3.83** £

Allowable loss for 2003-04 (if you made a profit, enter '0') **3.84** £

- Loss offset against other income for 2003-04 **3.85** £

- Loss to carry back **3.86** £

- Loss to carry forward
(that is allowable loss not claimed in any other way) **3.87** £

- Losses brought forward from earlier years **3.88** £

- Losses brought forward from earlier years used this year **3.89** £

| box 3.83 *minus* box 3.89 |
Taxable profit after losses brought forward **3.90** £

- Any other business income (for example, Business Start-up Allowance received in 2003-04) **3.91** £

| box 3.90 + box 3.91 |
Total taxable profits from this business **3.92** £

- Tick box 3.93 if the figure in box 3.92 is provisional **3.93**

Class 4 National Insurance contributions

- Tick box 3.94 if exception or deferment applies **3.94**

- Adjustments to profit chargeable to Class 4 National Insurance contributions **3.95** £

Class 4 National Insurance contributions due **3.96** £

Subcontractors in the construction industry

- Deductions made by contractors on account of tax (please send your CIS25s to us) **3.97** £

Tax deducted from trading income

- Any tax deducted (excluding deductions made by contractors on account of tax) from trading income **3.98** £

BS 12/2002net   TAX RETURN ■ SELF-EMPLOYMENT: PAGE SE3   *Please turn over*

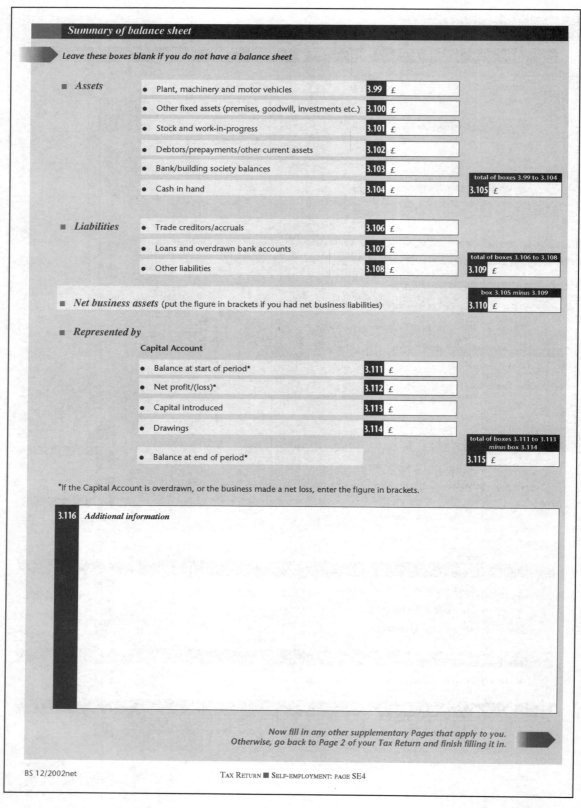

Summary of balance sheet

Leave these boxes blank if you do not have a balance sheet

Assets

- Plant, machinery and motor vehicles **3.99** £
- Other fixed assets (premises, goodwill, investments etc.) **3.100** £
- Stock and work-in-progress **3.101** £
- Debtors/prepayments/other current assets **3.102** £
- Bank/building society balances **3.103** £
- Cash in hand **3.104** £

total of boxes 3.99 to 3.104
3.105 £

Liabilities

- Trade creditors/accruals **3.106** £
- Loans and overdrawn bank accounts **3.107** £
- Other liabilities **3.108** £

total of boxes 3.106 to 3.108
3.109 £

Net business assets (put the figure in brackets if you had net business liabilities)

box 3.105 *minus* 3.109
3.110 £

Represented by

Capital Account

- Balance at start of period* **3.111** £
- Net profit/(loss)* **3.112** £
- Capital introduced **3.113** £
- Drawings **3.114** £

total of boxes 3.111 to 3.113
minus box 3.114
3.115 £

- Balance at end of period*

*If the Capital Account is overdrawn, or the business made a net loss, enter the figure in brackets.

3.116 *Additional information*

*Now fill in any other supplementary Pages that apply to you.
Otherwise, go back to Page 2 of your Tax Return and finish filling it in.*

BS 12/2002net

TAX RETURN ■ SELF-EMPLOYMENT: PAGE SE4

PROFESSIONAL EDUCATION

45 Mr Watson

You have received a copy of the following letter from John Watson.

25 Abbey Grange
Boscombe Valley

Doyle and Co
Three Gables Road
Boscombe Valley

1.5.2004

Dear Sirs,

Income tax return

Further to your recent letter I can give you the following information needed to complete my tax return for the year ended 5 April 2004.

1   Pay: £29,250, tax deducted £9,059.

2   Benefits

     Car, cost £15,850, supplied new from 1 January 2003
     The car emits 170g/km of CO_2
     My contribution for private use for the year: £600
     Petrol provided for all use

Medical insurance		£656
Travel costs reimbursed		£1,255
Entertaining costs reimbursed		£1,254
Telephone costs reimbursed	– rental	£125
	– calls	£595

     Video, cost £650 on 6 April 2003 and lent to me for private use from that date.

Please note that 40% of my telephone calls were for business purposes and that all of the travel and entertaining costs were for business purposes.

3   Dividend vouchers for my shares are enclosed.

4   Interest statements from my building society and bank accounts are enclosed.

I hope this is all you need to complete the return, but if you need any further information, please do not hesitate to contact me.

Yours faithfully

John Watson

John Watson

PERMANENT FILE NOTE

Name:	John Watson
Date of birth:	15 December 1954
Tax reference:	427/8901 (also employer's reference)
National Insurance Number:	NC 95 96 14 D
Marital status:	Married (Wife's name – Susan Mary; same tax reference, date of birth 15.01.67). The couple have no children.
Occupation:	Senior Production Manager.
	JDJ Chemicals, 12 High Street, Anytown

Additional file note: No payments on account of 2003/04 tax were made by Mr Watson.

The Red Headed League plc

Final dividend for the year ended 31 March 2003
Paid 31 October 2003

Gross dividend	Tax credit	Net dividend
£2,000	£200	£1,800

The Red Headed League plc

Interim dividend for the year ended 31 March 2004
Paid 31 March 2004

Gross dividend	Tax credit	Net dividend
£1,000	£100	£900

STRAND BUILDING SOCIETY
INTEREST STATEMENT 2003/04
HIGH INTEREST ACCOUNT
MR JOHN WATSON
ACCOUNT NUMBER 44332211A

Date	Gross interest	Tax deducted at source	Net interest
	£	£	£
30.06.03	5,960.00	1,192.00	4,768.00
31.12.03	6,110.00	1,222.00	4,888.00

BANK OF WALES INTEREST STATEMENT 2003/04 INVESTMENT ACCOUNT MR JOHN WATSON ACCOUNT NUMBER 55667788B			
Date	Gross interest	Tax deducted at source	Net interest
	£	£	£
30.09.03	550.00	110.00	440.00
31.03.04	630.00	126.00	504.00

Task 1

Prepare a calculation of taxable earnings for 2003/04.

Task 2

Prepare a schedules showing John Watson's dividend and interest income for 2003/04.

Task 3

Prepare an income tax computation for Mr Watson for 2003/04.

Task 4

Complete Mr Watson's self assessment tax return for 2003/04 including the supplementary employment pages.

Task 5

John Watson is considering changing jobs in the near future. State, for any particular activity, whether he can choose between employed and self employed status, If not, state the main considerations to be made in determining whether an individual is self employed or employed.

INCOME AND CAPITAL GAINS *for the year ended 5 April 2004*

Step 1

Answer Questions 1 to 9 below to check if you need supplementary Pages to give details of particular income or capital gains. Pages 6 and 7 of your Tax Return Guide will help.

(Ask the Orderline for a Guide if I haven't sent you one with your Tax Return, and you want one.)

If you answer 'Yes' ask the Orderline for the appropriate supplementary Pages and Notes.

Ring the Orderline on 0845 9000 404, or fax on 0845 9000 604 for any you need (closed Christmas Day, Boxing Day and New Year's Day).

If you do need supplementary Pages, tick the boxes below when you've got them.

Q1 Were you an employee, or office holder, or director, or agency worker or did you receive payments or benefits from a former employer (excluding a pension) in the year ended 5 April 2004?
If you were a non-resident director of a UK company but received no remuneration, see the notes to the Employment Pages, page EN3, box 1.6.   **YES** ☐   EMPLOYMENT ☐

Q2 Did you have any taxable income from share options, shares or share related benefits in the year? (This does not include
- dividends, **or**
- dividend shares ceasing to be subject to an Inland Revenue approved share incentive plan within three years of acquisition they go in Question 10.)   **YES** ☐   SHARE SCHEMES ☐

Q3 Were you self-employed (but not in partnership)?
(You should also tick 'Yes' if you were a Name at Lloyd's.)   **YES** ☐   SELF-EMPLOYMENT ☐

Q4 Were you in partnership?   **YES** ☐   PARTNERSHIP ☐

Q5 Did you receive any rent or other income from land and property in the UK?   **YES** ☐   LAND & PROPERTY ☐

Q6 Did you have any taxable income from overseas pensions or benefits, or from foreign companies or savings institutions, offshore funds or trusts abroad, or from land and property abroad or gains on foreign insurance policies?   **YES** ☐
Have you or could you have received, or enjoyed directly or indirectly, or benefited in any way from, income of a foreign entity as a result of a transfer of assets made in this or earlier years?   **YES** ☐
Do you want to claim foreign tax credit relief for foreign tax paid on foreign income or gains?   **YES** ☐   FOREIGN ☐

Q7 Did you receive, or are you deemed to have, income from a trust, settlement or the residue of a deceased person's estate?   **YES** ☐   TRUSTS ETC ☐

Q8 Capital gains - read the guidance on page 7 of the Tax Return Guide.
- If you have disposed of your only or main residence do you need the Capital Gains Pages?   **YES** ☐
- Did you dispose of other chargeable assets worth more than £31,600 in total?   **YES** ☐
- Were your total chargeable gains more than £7,900 or do you want to make a claim or election for the year?   **YES** ☐   CAPITAL GAINS ☐

Q9 Are you claiming that you were not resident, or not ordinarily resident, or not domiciled, in the UK, or dual resident in the UK and another country, for all or part of the year?   **YES** ☐   NON-RESIDENCE ETC ☐

Step 2

Fill in any supplementary Pages BEFORE going to Step 3.
Please use blue or black ink to fill in your Tax Return and please do not include pence. Round down your income and gains. Round up your tax credits and tax deductions. Round to the nearest pound.

When you have filled in all the supplementary Pages you need, tick this box. ☑

Step 3 Fill in Questions 10 to 24. If you answer 'Yes', fill in the relevant boxes. If not applicable, go to the next question.

TAX RETURN: PAGE 2

INCOME *for the year ended 5 April 2004*

Q10 Did you receive any income from UK savings and investments?   YES ✓   If yes, tick this box and then fill in boxes 10.1 to 10.26 as appropriate. Include only your share from any joint savings and investments. If not applicable, go to Question 11.

■ *Interest*

● Interest from UK banks, building societies and deposit takers (interest from UK Internet accounts must be included) - *if you have more than one bank or building society etc. account enter **totals** in the boxes.*

- enter any bank, building society etc. interest that **has not** had tax taken off. (Most interest is taxed by your bank or building society etc. so make sure you should be filling in box 10.1, rather than boxes 10.2 to 10.4)

Taxable amount
10.1 £

- enter details of your **taxed** bank or building society etc. interest. *The Working Sheet on page 10 of your Tax Return Guide will help you fill in boxes 10.2 to 10.4.*

Amount **after** tax deducted	Tax deducted	Gross amount **before** tax
10.2 £ 10,000	**10.3** £	**10.4** £

● Interest distributions from UK authorised unit trusts and open-ended investment companies (dividend distributions go below)

Amount **after** tax deducted	Tax deducted	Gross amount **before** tax
10.5 £	**10.6** £	**10.7** £

● National Savings & Investments (other than First Option Bonds and Fixed Rate Savings Bonds and the first £70 of interest from an Ordinary Account)

Taxable amount
10.8 £

● National Savings & Investments First Option Bonds and Fixed Rate Savings Bonds

Amount **after** tax deducted	Tax deducted	Gross amount **before** tax
10.9 £	**10.10** £	**10.11** £

● Other income from UK savings and investments (except dividends)

Amount **after** tax deducted	Tax deducted	Gross amount **before** tax
10.12 £	**10.13** £	**10.14** £

■ *Dividends*

● Dividends and other qualifying distributions from UK companies

Dividend/distribution	Tax credit	Dividend/distribution **plus** credit
10.15 £	**10.16** £	**10.17** £ 3,000

● Dividend distributions from UK authorised unit trusts and open-ended investment companies

Dividend/distribution	Tax credit	Dividend/distribution **plus** credit
10.18 £	**10.19** £	**10.20** £

● Scrip dividends from UK companies

Dividend	Notional tax	Dividend **plus** notional tax
10.21 £	**10.22** £	**10.23** £

● Non-qualifying distributions and loans written off

Distribution/Loan	Notional tax	Taxable amount
10.24 £	**10.25** £	**10.26** £

BS 12/2002net   TAX RETURN: PAGE 3   *Please turn over* ➤

INCOME *for the year ended 5 April 2004, continued*

Q11 **Did you receive a taxable UK pension, retirement annuity or Social Security benefit?**
Read the notes on pages 13 to 15 of the Tax Return Guide.

| YES | |

If yes, tick this box and then fill in boxes 11.1 to 11.14 as appropriate.
If not applicable, go to Question 12.

■ *State pensions and benefits*

Taxable amount for 2003-04

- State Retirement Pension - enter the **total** of your entitlements for the year — **11.1** £
- Widow's Pension or Bereavement Allowance — **11.2** £
- Widowed Mother's Allowance or Widowed Parent's Allowance — **11.3** £
- Industrial Death Benefit Pension — **11.4** £
- Jobseeker's Allowance — **11.5** £
- Carer's Allowance — **11.6** £
- Statutory Sick Pay, Statutory Maternity Pay and Statutory Paternity Pay paid by the Inland Revenue — **11.7** £

	Tax deducted	Gross amount **before** tax
- Taxable Incapacity Benefit	**11.8** £	**11.9** £

■ *Other pensions and retirement annuities*

	Amount after tax deducted	Tax deducted	Gross amount **before** tax
- Pensions (other than State pensions) and retirement annuities - *if you have more than one pension or annuity, please add together and complete boxes 11.10 to 11.12. Provide details of each one in box 11.14*	**11.10** £	**11.11** £	**11.12** £

11.14

	Amount of deduction
- Deduction - *see the note for box 11.13 on page 15 of your Tax Return Guide*	**11.13** £

Q12 **Did you make any gains on UK life insurance policies, life annuities or capital redemption policies or receive refunds of surplus funds from additional voluntary contributions?**

| YES | |

If yes, tick this box and then fill in boxes 12.1 to 12.12 as appropriate.
If not applicable, go to Question 13.

	Number of years		Amount of gain(s)
- Gains on UK annuities and friendly societies' life insurance policies where no tax is treated as paid	**12.1**		**12.2** £

	Number of years	Tax treated as paid	Amount of gain(s)
- Gains on UK life insurance policies etc. on which tax is treated as paid - *read pages 15 to 18 of your Tax Return Guide*	**12.3**	**12.4** £	**12.5** £

	Number of years	Tax deducted	Amount of gain(s)
- Gains on life insurance policies in ISAs that have been made void	**12.6**	**12.7** £	**12.8** £

	Amount
- Corresponding deficiency relief	**12.9** £

	Amount received	Notional tax	Amount plus notional tax
- Refunds of surplus funds from additional voluntary contributions	**12.10** £	**12.11** £	**12.12** £

Q13 **Did you receive any other taxable income which you have not already entered elsewhere in your Tax Return?**
Fill in any supplementary Pages before answering Question 13.
(Supplementary Pages follow page 10, or are available from the Orderline.)

| YES | |

If yes, tick this box and then fill in boxes 13.1 to 13.6 as appropriate.
If not applicable, go to Question 14.

	Amount **after** tax deducted	Tax deducted	Amount **before** tax
- Other taxable income – also provide details in box 23.5 - *read the notes on pages 18 to 20 of your Tax Return Guide*	**13.1** £	**13.2** £	**13.3** £

		Losses brought forward	Earlier years' losses used in 2003-04
- Tick box 13.1A if box 13.1 includes enhanced capital allowances for environmentally friendly expenditure	**13.1A**	**13.4** £	**13.5** £

2003-04 losses carried forward
13.6 £

BS 12/2002net

TAX RETURN: PAGE 4

RELIEFS *for the year ended 5 April 2004*

Q14 ▶ **Do you want to claim relief for your pension contributions?** **YES** ☐   If yes, tick this box and then fill in boxes 14.1 to 14.11 as appropriate.
If not appliable, go to Question 15.

Do not include contributions deducted from your pay by your employer to their pension scheme or associated AVC scheme, because tax relief is given automatically. But do include your contributions to personal pension schemes and Free-Standing AVC schemes.

■ *Payments to your retirement annuity contracts - only fill in boxes 14.1 to 14.5 for policies taken out before 1 July 1988.*
See the notes on pages 20 and 21 of your Tax Return Guide.

Qualifying payments made in 2003-04	**14.1** £	2003-04 payments used in an earlier year	**14.2** £	Relief claimed
2003-04 payments now to be carried back	**14.3** £	Payments brought back from 2004-05	**14.4** £	box 14.1 *minus* (boxes 14.2 and 14.3, but not 14.4) **14.5** £

■ *Payments to your personal pension (including stakeholder pension) contracts - enter the amount of the payment you made with the basic rate tax added (the **gross** payment). See the note for box 14.6 on page 22 of your Tax Return Guide.*

Gross qualifying payments made in 2003-04   **14.6** £

2003-04 gross payments carried back to 2002-03   **14.7** £

Gross qualifying payments made between 6 April 2004 and 31 January 2005 brought back to 2003-04 - *see page 22 of your Tax Return Guide*   **14.8** £   Relief claimed box 14.6 *minus* box 14.7 (but not 14.8) **14.9** £

■ *Contributions to other pension schemes and Free-Standing AVC schemes*

• Amount of contributions to employer's schemes **not deducted** at source from pay   **14.10** £

• Gross amount of Free-Standing Additional Voluntary Contributions paid in 2003-04   **14.11** £

Q15 ▶ **Do you want to claim any of the following reliefs?**   **YES** ☐   If yes, tick this box and then fill in boxes 15.1 to 15.12, as appropriate.
If you have made any annual payments, after basic rate tax, answer 'Yes' to Question 15 and fill in box 15.9. If you have made any gifts to charity go to Question 15A.   If not applicable, go to Question 15A.

• Interest eligible for relief on qualifying loans   **15.1** £

• Maintenance or alimony payments you have made under a court order, Child Support Agency assessment or legally binding order or agreement   Amount claimed up to £2,150 **15.2** £

To claim this relief, either you or your former spouse must have been 65 or over on 5 April 2000. So, if **your** date of birth, which is entered in box 22.6, is after 5 April 1935 then you must enter your former **spouse's** date of birth in box 15.2A - *see pages 23 and 24 of your Tax Return Guide*   Former spouse's date of birth **15.2A** / /

• Subscriptions for Venture Capital Trust shares (up to £100,000)   Amount on which relief is claimed **15.3** £

• Subscriptions under the Enterprise Investment Scheme (up to £150,000) - *also provide details in box 23.5, see page 24 of your Tax Return Guide*   Amount on which relief is claimed **15.4** £

• Community Investment Tax relief - invested amount relating to previous tax year(s) and on which relief is due   **15.5** £   Total amount on which relief is claimed box 15.5 + box 15.6

• Community Investment Tax relief - invested amount for current tax year   **15.6** £   **15.7** £

• Post-cessation expenses, pre-incorporation losses brought forward and losses on relevant discounted securities, etc. - *see pages 24 and 25 of your Tax Return Guide*   Amount of payment **15.8** £

• Annuities and annual payments   Payments made **15.9** £

• Payments to a trade union or friendly society for death benefits   Half amount of payment **15.10** £

• Payment to your employer's compulsory widow's, widower's or orphan's benefit scheme - *available in some circumstances – **first** read the notes on page 25 of your Tax Return Guide*   Relief claimed **15.11** £

• Relief claimed on a qualifying distribution on the **redemption** of bonus shares or securities.   Relief claimed **15.12** £

ALLOWANCES *for the year ended 5 April 2004*

Q15A **Do you want to claim relief on gifts to charity?**
If you have made any Gift Aid payments answer 'Yes' to Question 15A. You should include Gift Aid payments to Community Amateur Sports Clubs here. You can elect to include in this Return Gift Aid payments made between 6 April 2004 and the date you send in this Return. See page 26 in the Tax Return Guide and the leaflet enclosed on Gift Aid.

| **YES** ☐ |

If yes, tick this box and then read page 26 of your Tax Return Guide. Fill in boxes 15A.1 to 15A.5 as appropriate. If not applicable, go to Question 16.

- Gift Aid and payments under charitable covenants made between 6 April 2003 and 5 April 2004 — **15A.1** £
- Enter in box 15A.2 the total of any 'one off' payments included in box 15A.1 — **15A.2** £
- Enter in box 15A.3 the amount of Gift Aid payments made after 5 April 2004 but treated as if made in the tax year 2003-04 — **15A.3** £
- Gifts of qualifying investments to charities – shares and securities — **15A.4** £
- Gifts of qualifying investments to charities – real property — **15A.5** £

Q16 **Do you want to claim blind person's allowance, married couple's allowance or the Children's Tax Credit?**
You get your personal allowance of £4,615 automatically. **If you were born before 6 April 1938, enter your date of birth in box 22.6** *- you may get a higher age-related personal allowance.*

| **YES** ☐ |

If yes, tick this box and then read pages 26 to 31 of your Tax Return Guide. Fill in boxes 16.1 to 16.33 as appropriate. If not applicable, go to Question 17.

- ■ *Blind person's allowance*
  - Date of registration (if first year of claim) **16.1** / /
  - Local authority (or other register) **16.2**

■ *Married couple's allowance -* *In 2003-04 married couple's allowance can only be claimed if either you, or your husband or wife, were born* **before 6 April 1935***. So you can only claim the allowance in 2003-04 if either of you had reached* **65 years of age before 6 April 2000***. Further guidance is given beginning on page 27 of your Tax Return Guide.*

If **both** you and your husband or wife were born after 5 April 1935 you cannot claim; **do not** complete boxes 16.3 to 16.13.

If **you can claim** fill in boxes 16.3 and 16.4 if you are a married man or if you are a married woman and you are claiming half or all of the married couple's allowance.

- Enter your date of birth (if born before 6 April 1935) — **16.3** / /
- Enter your spouse's date of birth (**if** born before 6 April 1935 **and** if older than you) — **16.4** / /

Then, if you are a married man fill in boxes 16.5 to 16.9. If you are a married woman fill in boxes 16.10 to 16.13.

- Wife's full name **16.5**
- Date of marriage (if after 5 April 2003) **16.6** / /
- Tick box 16.7, or box 16.8, if you or your wife have allocated half, or all, of the minimum amount of the allowance to her — Half **16.7** All **16.8**
- Enter in box 16.9 the date of birth of any previous wife with whom you lived at any time during 2002-03. *Read 'Special rules if you are a man who married in the year ended 5 April 2004' on page 28 before completing box 16.9.* **16.9** / /
- Tick box 16.10, or box 16.11, if you or your husband have allocated half, or all, of the minimum amount of the allowance to you — Half **16.10** All **16.11**
- Husband's full name **16.12**
- Date of marriage (if after 5 April 2003) **16.13** / /

■ *Child Tax Credit -* *even if you have already completed a separate Child's Tax Credit (CTC) claim form and received the relief in your tax code, you should still fill in boxes 16.14 to 16.26, as directed. Any reference to 'partner' in this question means the person you lived with during the year to 5 April 2004 - your husband or wife, or someone you lived with as husband or wife.*

Guidance for claiming CTC is on pages 28 to 31 of your Tax Return Guide. Please read the notes before completing your claim, particularly if either you, or your partner, were liable to tax above the basic rate in the year to 5 April 2004.

- Enter in box 16.14 the date of birth of a child living with you (and who was born on or after 6 April 1986. **If you have a child living with you who was born on or after 6 April 2004 you may like to enter their date of birth in this box in preference to claiming for an older child.** **16.14** / /
- Tick box 16.15 if the child was your own child or one you looked after at your own expense. If not, you cannot claim CTC – go to box 16.27, if appropriate, or Question 17. **16.15**
- Tick box 16.16 if the child lived with you **throughout** the year to 5 April 2004. **16.16**
  If you ticked box 16.16 and
  - you were a lone or single claimant, you have finished this question; go to Question 17,
  - you have a partner, go to box 16.18.
- If the child lived with you for only **part of the year** you may only be entitled to a proportion of the CTC. Enter in box 16.17 your share in £s that **you have agreed** with any other claimants that you may claim for this child. But leave boxes 16.17 to 16.25 blank if you separated from, or started living with, your partner during the year to 5 April 2004. Special rules apply to work out your entitlement; ask the Orderline for *Help Sheet IR343: Claiming Children's Tax Credit when your circumstances change* which explains how to complete box 16.26. **16.17** £

BS 12/2002net
TAX RETURN: PAGE 6

BPP PROFESSIONAL EDUCATION

ALLOWANCES *for the year ended 5 April 2004, continued*

■ *Children's Tax Credit, continued*

If you lived with your partner (for CTC this means your husband or wife, or someone you lived with as husband and wife) for the whole of the year to 5 April 2004, fill in boxes 16.18 to 16.25 as appropriate.

- Enter in box 16.18 your partner's surname **16.18** [ ]

- Enter in box 16.19 your partner's National Insurance number **16.19** [| | | | |]

- Tick
  - box 16.20 if you had the higher income in the year to 5 April 2004, **16.20** [ ]

  or
  - box 16.21 if **your partner** had the higher income in the year **16.21** [ ]

- Tick box 16.22 if either of you were chargeable to tax above the basic rate in the year to 5 April 2004. **16.22** [ ]

*If you ticked boxes 16.20 and 16.22 your entitlement will be reduced — see page 31 of your Tax Return Guide; **your partner cannot claim CTC** - go to box 16.28, or Question 17, as appropriate.*

*If you ticked boxes 16.21 and 16.22 your partner's entitlement will be reduced; **you cannot claim CTC** - go to box 16.27, or Question 17, as appropriate.*

*If **neither** of you were chargeable above the basic rate and **you** had the lower income **and***
- *you don't want to claim half of the entitlement to CTC, and*
- *you didn't make an election for CTC to go to the partner with the lower income*

you have finished this part of your Return - go to boxes 16.27 or 16.28, or Question 17, as appropriate (your partner should claim CTC if they have not already done so).

Otherwise, tick one of boxes 16.23 to 16.25 .

- I had the higher income and I am claiming all of our entitlement to CTC **16.23** [ ]

- We are both making separate claims for half of our entitlement to CTC **16.24** [ ]

- We elected before 6 April 2003, or because of our special circumstances, during the year to 5 April 2004 (see page 31 of your Tax Return Guide), for the partner with the lower income to claim all of our entitlement to CTC **16.25** [ ]

- If you separated from, or starting living with, your partner in the year to 5 April 2004, enter in box 16.26 the amount of CTC you are claiming *(following the guidance in Help Sheet IR343: Claiming Children's Tax Credit when your circumstances change).* **16.26** £ [ ]

■ *Transfer of surplus allowances - see page 31 of your Tax Return Guide before you fill in boxes 16.27 to 16.33.*

- Tick box 16.27 if you want your spouse to have your unused allowances **16.27** [ ]

- Tick box 16.28 if you want to have your spouse's unused allowances **16.28** [ ]

If you want to calculate your tax, enter the amount of the surplus allowance you can have.

- Blind person's surplus allowance **16.31** £ [ ]

- Married couple's surplus allowance **16.32** [ ]

OTHER INFORMATION *for the year ended 5 April 2004*

Q17 ▶ **Are you liable to make Student Loan Repayments for 2003-04 on an Income Contingent Student Loan?**
You must read the note on page 31 of your Tax Return Guide before ticking the 'Yes' box.

YES [ ] If yes, tick this box.
If not applicable, go to Question 18.

If yes, and you are calculating your tax enter in Question 18, box 18.2A the amount you work out is repayable in 2003-04

OTHER INFORMATION *for the year ended 5 April 2004, continued*

Q18 Do you want to calculate your tax and, if appropriate, any Student Loan Repayment?

YES

Use your Tax Calculation Guide then fill in boxes 18.1 to 18.8 as appropriate.

- Unpaid tax for earlier years **included in your tax code for 2003-04**

  18.1 £

- Tax due for 2003-04 included in your tax code for a later year

  18.2 £

- Student Loan Repayment due

  18.2A £

- Total tax, Class 4 NIC and Student Loan Repayment due for 2003-04 **before** you made any payments on account *(put the amount in brackets if an overpayment)*

  18.3 £

- Tax due for earlier years

  18.4 £

- Tax overpaid for earlier years

  18.5 £

- Tick box 18.6 if you are claiming to reduce your 2004-05 payments on account. Make sure you enter the **reduced** amount of your first payment in box 18.7. Then, in the 'Additional information' box, box 23.5 on page 9, say why you are making a claim

  18.6

- Your first payment on account for 2004-05 *(include the pence)*

  18.7 £

- Any 2004-05 tax you are reclaiming now

  18.8 £

Q19 Do you want to claim a repayment if you have paid too much tax? *(If you do not tick 'Yes' or the tax you have overpaid is below £10, I will use the amount you are owed to reduce your next tax bill.)*

YES

If yes, tick this box and then fill in boxes 19.1 to 19.12 as appropriate.
If not applicable, go to Question 20.

Should the repayment be sent:

- to your bank or building society account?
  Tick box 19.1 and fill in boxes 19.3 to 19.7   19.1

or

- to your nominee's bank or building society account? **Tick box 19.2 and fill in boxes 19.3 to 19.12**   19.2

*We prefer to make repayment direct into a bank or building society account. (But tick box 19.8A **or** box 19.8B if you would like a cheque to be sent to you or your nominee.)*

Name of bank or building society
19.3

Branch sort code
19.4

Account number
19.5

Name of account holder
19.6

Building society reference
19.7

If you would like a cheque to be sent to:

- you, at the address on page 1, **tick box 19.8A**   19.8A

or

- your nominee, **tick box 19.8B**   19.8B

If your nominee is your agent, **tick box 19.9A**   19.9A

Agent's reference for you (if your nominee is your agent)
19.9

I authorise

Name of your nominee/agent
19.10

Nominee/agent address
19.11

Postcode

to receive on my behalf the amount due

19.12 *This authority must be signed by you. A photocopy of your signature will not do.*

Signature

BS 12/2002net   Tax Return: page 8

OTHER INFORMATION *for the year ended 5 April 2004, continued*

Q20 Have you already had any 2003-04 tax refunded or set off
by your Inland Revenue office or the Benefits Agency
(in Northern Ireland, the Social Security Agency)?
Read the notes on page 32 of your Tax Return Guide.

| YES | | If yes, tick this box and then enter the amount of the refund in box 20.1. |

20.1 £

Q21 Is your name or address on the front of the Tax Return *wrong*?
*If you are filling in an approved substitute Tax Return, see the notes on
page 32 of the Tax Return Guide.*

| YES | | If yes, please tick this box and make any corrections on the front of the form. |

Q22 Please give other personal details in boxes 22.1 to 22.7. *This information helps us to be more efficient and effective.*

Your daytime telephone number

22.1

Your agent's telephone number

22.2

and their name and address

22.3

Postcode

Your first two forenames

22.4

Say if you are single, married, widowed, divorced or separated

22.5

Your date of birth (If you were born before 6 April 1938, you may
get a higher age-related allowance.)

22.6 / /

Your National Insurance number
(if known and not on page 1 of your Tax Return)

22.7

Q23 Please tick boxes 23.1 to 23.4 if they apply. Provide any additional information in box 23.5 below
(continue on page 10, if necessary).

Tick box 23.1 if you do **not** want any tax you owe for 2003-04 collected through your tax code.

23.1

Please tick box 23.2 if this Tax Return contains figures that are provisional because you do not yet have final figures.
Pages 32 and 33 of the Tax Return Guide explain the circumstances in which provisional figures may be used and asks for
some additional information to be provided in box 23.5 below.

23.2

Tick box 23.3 if you are claiming relief now for 2004-05 trading, or certain capital, losses. Enter in box 23.5 the
amount and year.

23.3

Tick box 23.4 if you are claiming to have post-cessation or other business receipts taxed as income of an earlier
year. Enter in box 23.5 the amount and year.

23.4

23.5 *Additional information*

OTHER INFORMATION *for the year ended 5 April 2004, continued*

23.5 *Additional information continued*

Q24 ▶ **Declaration**

I have filled in and am sending back to you the following pages:

Tick

*In the second box enter the number of **complete sets** of supplementary Pages enclosed*

	Tick	Number of sets		Tick	Number of sets		Tick
1 TO 10 OF THIS FORM							
EMPLOYMENT	✓		PARTNERSHIP			TRUSTS, ETC	
SHARE SCHEMES		Number of sets	LAND & PROPERTY			CAPITAL GAINS	
SELF-EMPLOYMENT			FOREIGN			NON-RESIDENCE, ETC	

Before you send your completed Tax Return back to your Inland Revenue office, you must sign the statement below.
If you give false information or conceal any part of your income or chargeable gains, you may be liable to financial penalties and/or you may be prosecuted.

24.1 The information I have given in this Tax Return is correct and complete to the best of my knowledge and belief.

Signature   Date

There are very few reasons why we accept a signature from someone who is not the person making this Return but if you are signing for someone else please read the notes on page 33 of the Tax Return Guide, and:

- enter the capacity in which you are signing (for example, as executor or receiver)

24.2

- enter the name of the person you are signing for

24.3

- please **PRINT** your name and address in box 24.4

24.4

Postcode

BS 12/2002net   TAX RETURN: PAGE 10

Income for the year ended 5 April 2004

Inland Revenue

EMPLOYMENT

Fill in these boxes first

Name
JOHN WATSON

Tax reference
427/8901

If you want help, look up the box numbers in the Notes.

Details of employer

Employer's PAYE reference - may be shown under 'Inland Revenue office number and reference' on your P60 or 'PAYE reference' on your P45

1.1 427/8901

Employer's name
1.2 JDJ CHEMICAL

Date employment started (only if between 6 April 2003 and 5 April 2004)
1.3 / /

Date employment finished (only if between 6 April 2003 and 5 April 2004)
1.4 / /

Employer's address
1.5 12 HIGH ST ANYTOWN

Postcode

Tick box 1.6 if you were a director of the company
1.6

and, if so, tick box 1.7 if it was a close company
1.7

Income from employment

■ *Money - see Notes, page EN3*

• Payments from P60 (or P45)   Before tax
1.8 £ 29 250

• Payments not on P60, etc. - tips
1.9 £

  - other payments (excluding expenses entered below and lump sums and compensation payments or benefits entered overleaf)
1.10 £

• **Tax deducted** in the UK from payments in boxes 1.8 to 1.10   Tax deducted
1.11 £ 9,059

■ *Benefits and expenses - see Notes, pages EN3 to EN6. If any benefits connected with termination of employment were received, or enjoyed, after that termination and were from a **former** employer you need to complete Help Sheet IR204, available from the Orderline. Do not enter such benefits here.*

	Amount			Amount
• Assets transferred/ payments made for you	**1.12** £		• Vans	**1.18** £
• Vouchers, credit cards and tokens	**1.13** £		• Taxable cheap loans *see Note for box 1.19, page EN5*	**1.19** £
• Living accommodation	**1.14** £		*box 1.20 is not used*	
• Excess mileage allowances and passenger payments	**1.15** £		• Private medical or dental insurance	**1.21** £ 656
• Company cars	**1.16** £ 2253		• Other benefits	**1.22** £ 130
• Fuel for company cars	**1.17** £ 2592		• Expenses payments received and balancing charges	**1.23** £ 3229

SA101

BS 12/2002net

TAX RETURN ■ EMPLOYMENT: PAGE E1

Please turn over

71

Income from employment continued

■ *Lump sums and compensation payments or benefits including such payments and benefits from a former employer*
Note that 'lump sums' here includes any contributions which your employer made to an unapproved retirement benefits scheme

You must read page EN6 of the Notes **before** filling in boxes 1.24 to 1.30

Reliefs

- £30,000 exemption — **1.24** £
- Foreign service and disability — **1.25** £
- Retirement and death lump sums — **1.26** £

Taxable lump sums

- From box B of *Help Sheet IR204* — **1.27** £
- From box K of *Help Sheet IR204* — **1.28** £
- From box L of *Help Sheet IR204* — **1.29** £

- Tax deducted from payments in boxes 1.27 to 1.29 - *leave blank if this tax is included in the box 1.11 figure.* — Tax deducted **1.30** £

■ *Foreign earnings not taxable in the UK in the year ended 5 April 2004 - see Notes, page EN6* — **1.31** £

■ *Expenses you incurred in doing your job - see Notes, pages EN7 to EN8*

- Travel and subsistence costs — **1.32** £ 1255
- Fixed deductions for expenses — **1.33** £
- Professional fees and subscriptions — **1.34** £
- Other expenses and capital allowances — **1.35** £ 1492
- Tick box 1.36 if the figure in box 1.32 includes travel between your home and a permanent workplace — **1.36**

■ *Foreign Earnings Deduction* (seafarers only) — **1.37** £

■ *Foreign tax for which tax credit relief not claimed* — **1.38** £

Student Loans

■ *Student Loans repaid by deduction by employer - see Notes, page EN8* — **1.39** £

- Tick box 1.39A if your income is under Repayment of Teachers' Loans Scheme — **1.39A**

1.40 *Additional information*

Now fill in any other supplementary Pages that apply to you.
Otherwise, go back to page 2 in your Tax Return and finish filling it in.

Full Exam based Assessments

PRACTICE EXAM PAPER 1

TECHNICIAN STAGE – NVQ4

Unit 19

Preparing personal tax computations (PTC)

DO NOT OPEN THIS PAPER UNTIL YOU ARE READY TO START UNDER EXAM CONDITIONS

INSTRUCTIONS

This examination paper is in TWO sections.

You have to show competence in BOTH sections.

You should therefore attempt and aim to compete EVERY task in EACH section.

You should spend about 60 minutes on Section 1 and 120 minutes on Section 2.

COVERAGE OF PERFORMANCE CRITERIA

The following performance criteria are covered in this exam.

Element	PC Coverage
19.1	**Calculate income from employment**
A	Prepare accurate computations of emoluments, including benefits
B	List allowable expenses and deductions
C	Record relevant details of income from employment accurately and legibly in the tax return
D	Make computations and submissions in accordance with current tax law and take account of current Revenue practice
19.2	**Calculate property and investment income**
B	Prepare schedules of property income and determine profits and losses
D	Apply deductions and reliefs and claim loss set-offs
E	Record relevant details of property and invest income accurately and legibly in the tax return
F	Make computations and submissions are made in accordance with current tax law and take account of current Inland Revenue practice
19.3	**Prepare Income Tax Computations**
A	List general income, savings income and dividend income and check for completeness
B	Calculate and deduct charges and personal allowance
C	Calculate Income Tax payable
D	Record income and payments legibly and accurately in the tax return
E	Make computations and submissions are made in accordance with current tax law and take account of current Revenue practice
19.4	**Prepare capital gains tax computations**
A	Identify and value disposed-of chargeable assets
C	Calculate chargeable gains and allowable losses
D	Apply reliefs and exemptions correctly
E	Calculate Capital Gains Tax payable
F	Record details of gains and the Capital Gains Tax payable legibly and accurately in the tax return
G	More computations and submissions are made in accordance with current tax law and take account of current Revenue practice

Section 1

DATA

Mrs Austen has been one of Mole and Co's clients for a number of years. She is employed as a director of a local company and also has rental income. Mrs Austen has provided you with the attached P60, P11D and property income statement for 2003/04.

Mrs Austen had given you the following additional information.

Date of birth: 31 March 1969

Employment: Director of Book Supplies Limited

In receipt of salary (see Form P60) and benefits (see Form P11D). Note that some of the information that would normally be on the P11D (cash equivalent of benefits) has been omitted for exam purposes.

Entertaining expenditure is generally all deductible as an employment expense.

Task 1.1

Prepare a calculation of taxable earnings for 2003/04.

Task 1.2

Prepare a computation of Schedule A rental income for 2003/04.

Task 1.3

Complete the extracts from Mrs Austen's self assessment income tax return for 2003/04.

Task 1.4

Calculate Mrs Austen's taxable income for 2003/04.

Task 1.5

Calculate income tax payable for 2003/04. Mrs Austen did not make any payments on account in respect of her 2003/04 tax.

Section 2

DATA

Mrs Austen sold two of her rental properties on 30 April 2003. Mrs Austen held the freehold interest in both properties. The sale proceeds, costs of sale and original cost of both properties were as follows:

	Property 1	Property 2
Sale Proceeds	£300,000	£100,200
Costs of sale (Toad & Co's fees)	£1,500	£2,000
Original cost of building on 31 March 1982/25 June 1994	£125,000	£25,000

In 2002/03 Mrs Austen had capital losses of £10,000, unused and available to carry forward against future capital gains.

The addresses of the two properties sold were 1 High Street and 2 High Street respectively.

Tasks to be completed on Mrs Jane Austen's capital gains tax liability.

Task 2.1

Calculate the capital gains before taper relief on the two disposals for 2003/04.

Task 2.2

Calculate the capital gains tax payable for 2003/04.

Task 2.3

Complete the section of the self assessment income tax return for 2003/04 in respect of capital gains.

Task 2.4

Write a covering letter to Mrs Austen, enclosing the income tax computation, capital gains tax computation and self assessment return, and advising her of the amount of tax to be paid and of the due date by which payment should be made.

P60 *End of Year Certificate*

Tax Year to 5 April 2004

To the employee:

Please keep this certificate in a safe place as you will not be able to get a duplicate. **You will need it if you have to fill in a Tax Return.**

You can also use it to check that your employer is deducting the right rate of National Insurance contributions for you and using your correct National Insurance number.

By law you are required to tell the Inland Revenue about any income that is not fully taxed, even if you are not sent a Tax Return.

INLAND REVENUE

Employee's details

Surname	Austen
Forenames or initials	Jane

National Insurance number: N B 4 0 2 0 3 0 E

Works/payroll number:

Pay and Income Tax details

	Pay £ p	Tax deducted £ p
In previous employment(s)		

	Pay	Tax deducted *if refund mark 'R'*
In this employment	41,000 00	15,000 00

Figures shown here should be used for your Tax Return, if you get one

Final tax code

	£ p
Employee's Widows & Orphans/Life Assurance contributions in this employment	

National Insurance contributions in this employment

NIC table letter	Earnings up to and including the Earnings Threshold (where earnings are equal to or exceed the Lower Earnings Limit) £	Earnings above the Earnings Threshold, up to and including the Upper Earnings Limit £	Employee's contributions payable on earnings in previous column £ p

Employee's contributions above to be reduced by this amount of NIC rebate £ p

This applies only to employees in contracted-out occupational pension schemes

Employee's contributions are payable on earnings above the 'Earnings Threshold', up to and including the 'Upper Earnings Limit'

Other details

	£
Student Loan Deductions in this employment	

	£ p
Tax Credits in this employment	

To Employee

Employer's full name and address (including Postcode)

Book Supplies Ltd
121 High Street
Anytown

Employer's PAYE reference: B 452

Certificate by Employer/Paying Office:

This form shows your total pay for Income Tax purposes in this employment for the year. Any overtime, bonus, commission etc, statutory sick pay or statutory maternity pay is included. It also shows, for this employment, total Income Tax and National Insurance contributions deducted (less any refunds), Student Loan deductions made, and Tax Credits paid to you.

Inland Revenue

P11D EXPENSES AND BENEFITS 2003-04

Note to employer
Complete this return for a director, or an employee who earned at a rate of £8,500 a year or more during the year 6 April 2003 to 5 April 2004. Do not include expenses and benefits covered by a dispensation or PAYE settlement agreement. Read the P11D Guide and booklet 480, Chapter 24, before you complete the form. Send the completed P11D and form P11D(b) to the Inland Revenue office by 6 July 2004. You must give a copy of this information to the director or employee by the same date. The term employee is used to cover both directors and employees throughout the rest of this form.

Note to employee
Your employer has filled in this form. Keep it in a safe place as you may not be able to get a duplicate. You will need it for your tax records and to complete your 2003-04 Tax Return if you get one. Your tax code may need to be adjusted to take account of the information given on this P11D. The box numbers on this P11D have the same numbering as the Employment Pages of the Tax Return, for example, 1.12. Include the total figures in the corresponding box on the Tax Return, unless you think some other figure is more appropriate.

Employer's details
Employer's name

Book Supplies Ltd

PAYE tax reference

B452

Employee's details
Employee's name

Jane Austen

If a director tick here ✓

Works number/department

National Insurance number

NB 40 20 30 E

Employers pay Class 1A National Insurance contributions on most benefits. These are shown in boxes which are brown and have a **1A** indicator

A **Assets transferred (cars, property, goods or other assets)**

| Description of asset | Cost/Market value £ | Amount made good or from which tax deducted – £ | Cash equivalent = **1.12** £ | **1A** |

B **Payments made on behalf of employee**

| Description of payment | | **1.12** £ |

Tax on notional payments not borne by employee within 30 days of receipt of each notional payment   **1.12** £

C **Vouchers or credit cards**

| | Gross amount | Amount made good or from which tax deducted | Cash equivalent | |
| Value of vouchers and payments made using credit cards or tokens | £ | – £ | = **1.13** £ | |

D **Living accommodation**

| | Cash equivalent |
| Cash equivalent of accommodation provided for employee, or his/her family or household | **1.14** £ **1A** |

E **Mileage allowance**

| | Gross amount | Amount made good or from which tax deducted | Taxable payment | |
| Car and mileage allowances paid for employee's car | £ | – £ | = **1.15** £ | |

F **Cars and car fuel** If more than two cars were made available, either at the same time or in succession, please give details on a separate sheet

	Car 1	Car 2
Make and Model	Vauxhall Vectra	
Dates car was available *Only enter a 'from' or 'to' date if the car was first made available and/or ceased to be available in 2003-04*	From / / to / /	From / / to / /
Enter CO$_2$ emissions data for the car	205 g/km	g/km
Tick type of fuel	Petrol ✓ Diesel ☐	Petrol ☐ Diesel ☐
List price of car *If there is no list price, or if it is a classic car, employers see booklet 480; employees see leaflet IR172*	£ 19,000	£
Price of optional accessories fitted when car was first made available to the employee	£	£
Price of accessories added after the car was first made available to the employee	£	£
Capital contributions (maximum £5,000) the employee made towards the cost of car or accessories	£	£
Amount paid by employee for private use of the car	£ 600	£
Cash equivalent of each car	£	£

| Total cash equivalent of all cars available in 2003-04 | | | **1.16** £ **1A** |

| Cash equivalent of fuel for each car | £ | £ | |

| Total cash equivalent of fuel for all cars available in 2003-04 | | **1.17** £ **1A** |

G Vans

Cash equivalent of all vans made available for private use | **1.18** £ | 1A

H Interest-free and low interest loans

If the total amount outstanding on all loans does not exceed £5,000 at any time in the year, there is no need for details in this section.

	Loan 1	Loan 2
Number of joint borrowers *(if applicable)*		
Amount outstanding at 5 April 2003 or at date loan was made if later	£	£
Amount outstanding at 5 April 2004 or at date loan was discharged if earlier	£	£
Maximum amount outstanding at any time in the year	£	£
Total amount of interest paid by the borrower in 2003-04 – *enter "NIL" if none was paid*	£	£
Date loan was made in 2003-04 if applicable	/ /	/ /
Date loan was discharged in 2002-03 if applicable	/ /	/ /
Cash equivalent of loans after deducting any interest paid by the borrower	**1.19** £ 1A	**1.19** £ 1A

I Private medical treatment or insurance

	Cost to you	Amount made good or from which tax deducted	Cash equivalent
Private medical treatment or insurance	£ 965	– £	= **1.21** £ 965 1A

J Qualifying relocation expenses payments and benefits

Non-qualifying benefits and expenses go in N and O below

Excess over £8,000 of all qualifying relocation expenses payments and benefits for each move | **1.22** £ | 1A

K Services supplied

	Cost to you	Amount made good or from which tax deducted	Cash equivalent
Services supplied to the employee	£	– £	= **1.22** £ 1A

L Assets placed at the employee's disposal

	Annual value plus expenses incurred	Amount made good or from which tax deducted	Cash equivalent
Description of asset *Video recorder (made available 1.7.03 - cost £1,500)*	£	£	**1.22** £ 225 1A

M Shares

Tick the box if during the year there have been share-related benefits for the employee | ☐

N Other items (including subscriptions and professional fees)

	Cost to you	Amount made good or from which tax deducted	Cash equivalent
Description of other items	£	– £	= **1.22** 1A
Description of other items	£	– £	= **1.22** £

		Tax paid
Income tax paid but not deducted from director's remuneration		**1.22**

O Expenses payments made to, or on behalf of, the employee

	Cost to you	Amount made good or from which tax deducted	Taxable payment
Travelling and subsistence payments	£	– £	= **1.23** £
Entertainment *(trading organisations read P11D Guide and then enter a tick or a cross as appropriate here)* ☐	£ 3,500	– £	= **1.23** £ 3,500
General expenses allowance for business travel ✓	£	– £	= **1.23** £
Payments for use of home telephone	£	– £	= **1.23** £
Non-qualifying relocation expenses *(those not shown in sections J or N)*	£	– £	= **1.23** £
Description of other expenses	£	– £	= **1.23** £

Property Rental Agencies Limited

Rental income and expenditure statement

Client: Mrs Jane Austen
Dates: 6 April 2003 to 5 April 2004

Furnished property let	1	2	3	4
Rental Income	4,000	3,000	2,000	6,500
Less expenses				
Management fees	400	300	200	650
Buildings insurance	100	100	100	100
Contents insurance	50	50	50	50
Cleaning	260	260	260	260
Repairs	100	250	3,000	50
Council Tax	450	350	200	350
Total remitted to client in year	2,640	1,690	(1,810)	5,040

Total				£7,560

Please note: all properties were fully let all year and are fully furnished.

Property Rental Agencies Limited
12 Another Street
Anytown

Margaret Jones
Tax Manager
Mole and Co Chartered Accountants
24 Main Street
Anytown

Dear Ms Jones

Mrs Jane Austen – Property rental statement for 2003/04

Further to your recent letter concerning the repairs expenditure shown on the above statement, we are able to provide the following additional information:

Property	Amount	Description
1	£100	Repainting the doors and windows
2	£250	Repairing a chimney damaged by bad weather
3	£3,000	Building a kitchen extension
4	£50	Repainting the front door

I hope this is enough information, but should you require any more details please contact us.

Yours sincerely

John Smith

Property Letting Consultant

TAXATION TABLES

Capital gains tax

Annual Exemption 2003/04   £7,900

Indexation Allowance:

Retail Price Index (RPI) for:

| March 1982 | 79.4 | April 1998 | 162.6 |
| June 1994 | 144.7 | April 2003 | 174.2 |

Income tax – 2003/04

Personal allowance	£4,615
Taxed at 10%	£1,960
Taxed at 22% (next)	£28,540
Taxed at 40%	The balance

Savings (excl. dividend) income that falls in the basic rate band is taxed at 20%. Any dividend income in the starting or basic rate band is taxed at 10% and dividend income that exceeds the higher rate threshold is taxed at 32.5%.

Fuel benefit

Flat rate, £14,400

Inland Revenue

Income for the year ended 5 April 2004

LAND AND PROPERTY

Fill in these boxes first

Name

Tax reference

If you want help, look up the box numbers in the Notes.

Are you claiming Rent a Room relief for gross rents of £4,250 or less?
(Or £2,125 if the claim is shared?)
Read the Notes on page LN2 to find out
- **whether you can claim Rent a Room relief; and**
- **how to claim relief for gross rents over £4,250**

Yes

If 'Yes', tick box. If this is your only income from UK property, you have finished these Pages

Is your income from furnished holiday lettings?
If not applicable, please turn over and fill in Page L2 to give details of your property income

Yes

If 'Yes', tick box and fill in boxes 5.1 to 5.18 before completing Page L2

Furnished holiday lettings

- Income from furnished holiday lettings — **5.1** £

- *Expenses* (furnished holiday lettings only)

- Rent, rates, insurance, ground rents etc. — **5.2** £
- Repairs, maintenance and renewals — **5.3** £
- Finance charges, including interest — **5.4** £
- Legal and professional costs — **5.5** £
- Costs of services provided, including wages — **5.6** £
- Other expenses — **5.7** £

total of boxes 5.2 to 5.7
5.8 £

Net profit (put figures in brackets if a loss)

box 5.1 *minus* box 5.8
5.9 £

- *Tax adjustments*

- Private use — **5.10** £
- Balancing charges — **5.11** £

box 5.10 + box 5.11
5.12 £

- Capital allowances — **5.13** £

- Tick box 5.13A if box 5.13 includes enhanced capital allowances for environmentally friendly expenditure — **5.13A**

boxes 5.9 + 5.12 *minus* box 5.13
5.14 £

Profit for the year (copy to box 5.19). If loss, enter '0' in box 5.14 and put the loss in box 5.15

Loss for the year (if you have entered '0' in box 5.14)

boxes 5.9 + 5.12 *minus* box 5.13
5.15 £

- *Losses*

- Loss offset against 2003-04 total income — **5.16** £

- Loss carried back —
see Notes, page LN4
5.17 £

- Loss offset against other income from property (copy to box 5.38) —
see Notes, page LN4
5.18 £

SA105

BS 12/2002net

TAX RETURN ■ LAND AND PROPERTY: PAGE L1

Please turn over

Other property income

■ *Income*

copy from box 5.14

- Furnished holiday lettings profits **5.19** £

Tax deducted

- Rents and other income from land and property **5.20** £ | **5.21** £

- Chargeable premiums **5.22** £

boxes 5.19 + 5.20 + 5.22 + 5.22A

- Reverse premiums **5.22A** £ | **5.23** £

■ *Expenses* (do not include figures you have already put in boxes 5.2 to 5.7 on Page L1)

- Rent, rates, insurance, ground rents etc. **5.24** £ *19950*
- Repairs, maintenance and renewals **5.25** £
- Finance charges, including interest **5.26** £
- Legal and professional costs **5.27** £
- Costs of services provided, including wages **5.28** £
- Other expenses **5.29** £

total of boxes 5.24 to 5.29

5.30 £ *19990*

box 5.23 *minus* box 5.30

Net profit (put figures in brackets if a loss) **5.31** £

■ *Tax adjustments*

- Private use **5.32** £

box 5.32 + box 5.33

- Balancing charges **5.33** £ | **5.34** £

- Rent a Room exempt amount **5.35** £
- Capital allowances **5.36** £

- Tick box 5.36A if box 5.36 includes a claim for 100% capital allowances for flats over shops **5.36A**

- Tick box 5.36B if box 5.36 includes enhanced capital allowances for environmentally friendly expenditure **5.36B**

- 10% wear and tear **5.37** £ *1415*

boxes 5.35 to box 5.38

- Furnished holiday lettings losses (from box 5.18) **5.38** £ | **5.39** £ *1415*

boxes 5.31 + 5.34 *minus* box 5.39

Adjusted profit (if loss enter '0' in box 5.40 and put the loss in box 5.41) **5.40** £

boxes 5.31 + 5.34 *minus* box 5.39

Adjusted loss (if you have entered '0' in box 5.40) **5.41** £

- Loss brought forward from previous year **5.42** £

box 5.40 *minus* box 5.42

Profit for the year **5.43** £

■ *Losses etc*

- Loss offset against total income (read the note on page LN8) **5.44** £
- Loss to carry forward to following year **5.45** £
- Tick box 5.46 if these Pages include details of property let jointly **5.46**
- Tick box 5.47 if **all** property income ceased in the year to 5 April 2004 **and** you don't expect to receive such income again, in the year to 5 April 2005 **5.47**

Now fill in any other supplementary Pages that apply to you.
Otherwise, go back to page 2 of your Tax Return and finish filling it in.

BS 12/2002net

TAX RETURN ■ LAND AND PROPERTY: PAGE L2

PROFESSIONAL EDUCATION

Income for the year ended 5 April 2004

Inland Revenue

EMPLOYMENT

Name

Tax reference

Fill in these boxes first

If you want help, look up the box numbers in the Notes.

Details of employer

Employer's PAYE reference - may be shown under 'Inland Revenue office number and reference' on your P60 or 'PAYE reference' on your P45

1.1

Employer's name

1.2

Date employment started
(only if between 6 April 2003 and 5 April 2004)

1.3 /   /

Employer's address

1.5

Date employment finished
(only if between 6 April 2003 and 5 April 2004)

1.4 /   /

Postcode

Tick box 1.6 if you were a director of the company

1.6

and, if so, tick box 1.7 if it was a close company

1.7

Income from employment

■ *Money* - see Notes, page EN3

Before tax

● Payments from P60 (or P45)   **1.8** £ 11,000

● Payments not on P60, etc.   - tips   **1.9** £

  - other payments (excluding expenses entered below and lump sums and compensation payments or benefits entered overleaf)   **1.10** £

Tax deducted

● **Tax deducted** in the UK from payments in boxes 1.8 to 1.10   **1.11** £ 15,000

■ *Benefits and expenses* - *see Notes, pages EN3 to EN6. If any benefits connected with termination of employment were received, or enjoyed, after that termination and were from a **former** employer you need to complete Help Sheet IR204, available from the Orderline. Do not enter such benefits here.*

Amount

● Assets transferred/ payments made for you   **1.12** £

● Vans   **1.18** £

Amount

● Vouchers, credit cards and tokens   **1.13** £

● Taxable cheap loans *see Note for box 1.19, page EN5*   **1.19** £

Amount

● Living accommodation   **1.14** £

box 1.20 is not used

Amount

● Excess mileage allowances and passenger payments   **1.15** £

● Private medical or dental insurance   **1.21** £ 465

Amount

● Company cars   **1.16** £ 4,150

● Other benefits   **1.22** £

Amount

● Fuel for company cars   **1.17** £ 3600

● Expenses payments received and balancing charges   **1.23** £

SA101

Income from employment continued

■ *Lump sums and compensation payments or benefits including such payments and benefits from a former employer*
Note that 'lump sums' here includes any contributions which your employer made to an unapproved retirement benefits scheme

You must read page EN6 of the Notes before filling in boxes 1.24 to 1.30

Reliefs

- £30,000 exemption | **1.24** £
- Foreign service and disability | **1.25** £
- Retirement and death lump sums | **1.26** £

Taxable lump sums

- From box B of *Help Sheet IR204* | **1.27** £
- From box K of *Help Sheet IR204* | **1.28** £
- From box L of *Help Sheet IR204* | **1.29** £
- Tax deducted from payments in boxes 1.27 to 1.29 - *leave blank if this tax is included in the box 1.11 figure.* | Tax deducted **1.30** £

■ *Foreign earnings not taxable in the UK in the year ended 5 April 2004 - see Notes, page EN6* | **1.31** £

■ *Expenses you incurred in doing your job - see Notes, pages EN7 to EN8*

- Travel and subsistence costs | **1.32** £
- Fixed deductions for expenses | **1.33** £
- Professional fees and subscriptions | **1.34** £
- Other expenses and capital allowances | **1.35** £ 3500
- Tick box 1.36 if the figure in box 1.32 includes travel between your home and a permanent workplace | **1.36**

■ *Foreign Earnings Deduction* (seafarers only) | **1.37** £

■ *Foreign tax for which tax credit relief not claimed* | **1.38** £

Student Loans

■ *Student Loans repaid by deduction by employer - see Notes, page EN8* | **1.39** £

- Tick box 1.39A if your income is under Repayment of Teachers' Loans Scheme | **1.39A**

1.40 *Additional information*

Now fill in any other supplementary Pages that apply to you.
Otherwise, go back to page 2 in your Tax Return and finish filling it in.

BS 12/2002net

TAX RETURN ■ EMPLOYMENT: PAGE E2

Inland Revenue

CAPITAL GAINS

For the year ended 5 April 2004

Name

Fill in these boxes first

Tax reference

Only use this Page if **all** your transactions were in quoted shares or other securities unless taper relief is due on any of them, or any were held at 31 March 1982, or you are claiming a relief, for example, Enterprise Investment Scheme deferral relief. Otherwise you cannot use this page and must use Pages CG2 to CG6 to work out **all** of your capital gains or allowable losses.

A Enter details of quoted shares or other securities disposed of	B Tick box if estimate or valuation used	C Enter the date of disposal	D Disposal proceeds	E Gain or loss after indexation allowance, if due (enter loss in brackets)	F Further information, including any elections made
1		/ /	£	£	
2		/ /	£	£	
3		/ /	£	£	
4		/ /	£	£	
5		/ /	£	£	
6		/ /	£	£	
7		/ /	£	£	
8		/ /	£	£	

Total gains **F1** £ — Total your gains in column E and enter the amount in box F1

Total losses **F2** £ — Total your losses in column E and enter the amount in box F2

Net gain/(loss) **F3** £ box F1 minus box F2 — If your net gains are below £7,900 **or** you have a net loss, there is no liability. If you have a net loss, please fill in the losses summary on Page CG8 otherwise carry on to box F4

minus income losses set against gains **F4** £

F5 £ box F3 minus box F4 — If your gains are now below £7,900, there is no liability; copy box F5 to box F7 and complete Page CG8. Otherwise, carry on to box F6

minus losses brought forward **F6** £ — Enter losses brought forward up to the **smaller** of either the total losses brought forward or the figure in box F5 **minus** £7,900

Total taxable gains **F7** £ box F5 minus box F6 — Copy this figure to box 8.7 on Page CG8 (if F7 is blank because there is no liability, leave 8.7 blank).

Go to Page CG8

Tax Return ■ Capital Gains: page CG1

Note:
This Page is only for transactions in quoted shares or other securities.
See the definition on page CGN3 of the Notes on Capital Gains.

BS 12/2002net

SA108

Your 2003-04 Capital Gains Tax liability

A Brief description of asset	AA* Type of disposal. Enter Q, U, L, T or O	B Tick box if estimate or valuation used	C Tick box if asset held at 31 March 1982	D Enter the later of date of acquisition and 16 March 1998	E Enter the date of disposal	F Disposal proceeds	G Enter details of any elections made, reliefs claimed or due and state amount (£)
Gains on assets which are either wholly business or wholly non-business							
1 1 HIGH STREET	L		✓	16/8/98	30/4/03	£ 298,500	
2 2 HIGH STREET.	L			16/8/98	30/4/03	£ 915,200	
3				/ /	/ /	£	
4				/ /	/ /	£	
5				/ /	/ /	£	
6				/ /	/ /	£	
7				/ /	/ /	£	
8				/ /	/ /	£	
Gains on assets which are partly business and partly non-business (see the notes on page CGN4)							
9				/ /	/ /	£	
10				/ /	/ /	£	

* Column **AA**: for
  - quoted shares or other securities, (see the definition on page CGN3 of the Notes) enter **Q**
  - other shares or securities, enter **U**
  - land and property, enter **L**
  - amounts attributable to settlor (see page CGN4) enter **T**
  - other assets (for example, goodwill), enter **O**

Complete Pages CG4 to CG6 for all U, L and O transactions

Losses

Description of asset	Type of * disposal. Enter Q, U, L or O	Tick box if estimate or valuation used	Tick box if asset held at 31 March 1982	Enter the later of date of acquisition and 16 March 1998	Enter the date of disposal	Disposal proceeds	Enter details of any elections made, reliefs claimed or due and state amount (£)
13				/ /	/ /	£	
14				/ /	/ /	£	
15				/ /	/ /	£	
16				/ /	/ /	£	

Total losses of

PROFESSIONAL EDUCATION

H Chargeable Gains after reliefs but before losses and taper	I Enter 'Bus' if business asset	J Taper rate	K Losses deducted			L Gains after losses	M Tapered gains (gains from column L x % in column J)
			K1 Allowable losses of the year	K2 Income losses of 2003-04 set against gains	K3 Unused losses b/f from earlier years		
£ 42 500	Bus (crossed)	80 %	£	£	£10,000	£ 32 500	£ 26,000
£ 70 100	Bus (crossed)	80%	£	£	£	£ 70 100	£ 56 080
£		%	£	£	£	£	£
£		%	£	£	£	£	£
£		%	£	£	£	£	£
£		%	£	£	£	£	£
£		%	£	£	£	£	£
£		%	£	£	£	£	£
£	Bus	%	£	£	£	£	£
£		%	£	£	£	£	£
£	Bus	%	£	£	£	£	£
£		%	£	£	£	£	£

Total 8.1 £ 112600
Total column H

8.5 £
Total column K2

8.6 £ 10,000
Total column K3

8.3 £ 82,080
Total column M

11 **Attributed gains from UK resident trusts where no election has been made for the set off of personal losses** (see page CGN4) *(enter the name of the Trust on Page CG7)* £

Losses arising	

12 **Attributed gains from non UK resident trusts where no election has been made for the set off of personal losses** (see page CGN4) *(enter the name of the Trust on Page CG7)* £

Total of attributed gains where no election has been made (total of rows 11 and 12) 8.4 £

box 8.3 + box 8.4

Total taxable gains (after allowable losses and taper relief) £ 82,080

Copy to box 8.7 on Page CG8 and complete Pages CG4 to CG6 for all U, L and O transactions

	Losses arising
	£
	£
	£
	£

year 8.2 £

Other shares or securities (U) - further information

Please give details of each transaction of this type of asset in the boxes below. If you have more than two of these transactions to return, please photocopy this Page before completion. (Please also complete Pages CG2 and CG3.)

1st transaction

Description of shares or securities - including name of company, company registration number (if known), number, class and nominal value of shares. Also, if possible, give a history of the shares disposed of, for instance, if there has been a reorganisation or takeover (give details of the original company and shares held in that company)

Tick box if you have already submitted form CG34

State any connection between you and the person from whom you acquired the asset, or to whom you disposed of the asset (see Notes, page CGN14)

If you have used an estimate or valuation in your capital gains computation but have not submitted form CG34, please enter the date to which the valuation relates, the amount (£) and the reason for the estimate or valuation. Please also attach a copy of any valuation obtained

2nd transaction

Description of shares or securities - including name of company, company registration number (if known), number, class and nominal value of shares. Also, if possible, give a history of the shares disposed of, for instance, if there has been a reorganisation or takeover (give details of the original company and shares held in that company)

Tick box if you have already submitted form CG34

State any connection between you and the person from whom you acquired the asset, or to whom you disposed of the asset (see Notes, page CGN14)

If you have used an estimate or valuation in your capital gains computation but have not submitted form CG34, please enter the date to which the valuation relates, the amount (£) and the reason for the estimate or valuation. Please also attach a copy of any valuation obtained

BS 12/2002net

TAX RETURN ■ CAPITAL GAINS: PAGE CG4

Land and property disposals (L) - further information

Please give details of each transaction of this type of asset in the boxes below. If you have more than two of these transactions to return, please photocopy this Page **before** completion. (Please also complete Pages CG2 and CG3.)

1st transaction

Full address of land/property affected (attach a copy of any plan if this helps identification)

Description of land/property disposed of, including details of your ownership, for example freehold/leasehold and any tenancies affecting your ownership and the date of transaction or any other date for which a valuation has been made.

Tick box if you have already submitted form CG34

State any connection between you and the person from whom you acquired the asset, or to whom you disposed of the asset (see Notes, page CGN14)

If you have used an estimate or valuation in your capital gains computation but have not submitted form CG34, please enter the date to which the valuation relates, the amount (£) and the reason for the estimate or valuation. Please also attach a copy of any valuation obtained.

2nd transaction

Full address of land/property affected (attach a copy of any plan if this helps identification)

Description of land/property disposed of, including details of your ownership, for example freehold/leasehold and any tenancies affecting your ownership and the date of transaction or any other date for which a valuation has been made.

Tick box if you have already submitted form CG34

State any connection between you and the person from whom you acquired the asset, or to whom you disposed of the asset (see Notes, page CGN14)

If you have used an estimate or valuation in your capital gains computation but have not submitted form CG34, please enter the date to which the valuation relates, the amount (£) and the reason for the estimate or valuation. Please also attach a copy of any valuation obtained.

BS 12/2002net   Tax Return ■ Capital Gains: page CG5   *continued over*

Other assets (O) - further information

Please give details of any transaction involving any other type of asset in the boxes below. If you have more than two of these transactions to return, please photocopy this Page **before** completion. (Please also complete Pages CG2 and CG3.)

1st transaction

Full description of the asset (other than shares or land/property) affected and any other information which helps identify the asset.

Tick box if you have already submitted form CG34

State any connection between you and the person from whom you acquired the asset, or to whom you disposed of the asset (see Notes, page CGN14)

If you have used an estimate or valuation in your capital gains computation but have not submitted form CG34, please enter the date to which the valuation relates, the amount (£) and the reason for the estimate or valuation. Please also attach a copy of any valuation obtained.

2nd transaction

Full description of the asset (other than shares or land/property) affected and any other information which helps identify the asset

Tick box if you have already submitted form CG34

State any connection between you and the person from whom you acquired the asset, or to whom you disposed of the asset (see Notes, page CGN14)

If you have used an estimate or valuation in your capital gains computation but have not submitted form CG34, please enter the date to which the valuation relates, the amount (£) and the reason for the estimate or valuation. Please also attach a copy of any valuation obtained.

BPP
PROFESSIONAL EDUCATION

Chargeable gains and allowable losses

Once you have completed Page CG1, or Pages CG2 to CG6, fill in this Page.

Have you 'ticked' any row in Column B, 'Tick box if estimate or valuation used' on Pages CG1 or CG2 or in Column C on Page CG2 'Tick box if asset held at 31 March 1982'? **YES**

Have you given details in Column G on Pages CG2 and CG3 of any Capital Gains reliefs claimed or due? **YES**

Are you claiming, and/or using, any clogged losses (see Notes, page CGN11)? **YES**

Enter from Page CG1 or column AA on Page CG2:

- the number of transactions in quoted shares or other securities **box Q**
- the number of transactions in other shares or securities **box U**
- the number of transactions in land and property **box L** 2
- the number of gains attributed to settlors **box T**
- the number of other transactions **box O**

Total taxable gains (from Page CG1 **or** Page CG3) **8.7** £ 82080

Your taxable gains *minus* the annual exempt amount of £7,900 (leave blank if '0' or negative) — box 8.7 minus £7,700 — **8.8** £ 74180

Additional liability in respect of non-resident or dual resident trusts (see Notes, page CGN6) **8.9** £

Capital losses

(If your loss arose on a transaction with a connected person, see page CGN14, you can only set that loss against gains you make on disposals to that same connected person. See the notes on clogged losses on page CGN11.)

■ *This year's losses*

- Total (normally from box 8.2 on Page CG3 or box F2 on Page CG1. But, if you have clogged losses, see Notes, page CGN10) **8.10** £
- Used against gains (total of column K1 on Page CG3, or the smaller of boxes F1 and F2 on Page CG1) **8.11** £
- Used against earlier years' gains (generally only available to personal representatives, see Notes, page CGN11) **8.12** £
- Used against income (only losses of the type described on page CGN9 can be used against income) **8.13A** £ *amount claimed against income of 2003-04* / **8.13B** £ *amount claimed against income of 2002-03* — box 8.13A + box 8.13B **8.13** £
- This year's unused losses — box 8.10 minus (boxes 8.11 + 8.12 + 8.13) **8.14** £

■ *Summary of earlier years' losses*

- Unused losses of 1996-97 and later years **8.15** £ 10,000
- Used this year (losses from box 8.15 are used in priority to losses from box 8.18) (column K3 on Page CG3 or box F6 on Page CG1) **8.16** £ 10,000
- Remaining unused losses of 1996-97 and later years — box 8.15 minus box 8.16 **8.17** £
- Unused losses of 1995-96 and earlier years **8.18** £
- Used this year (losses from box 8.15 are used in priority to losses from box 8.18) (column K3 on Page CG3 or box F6 on Page CG1) — box 8.6 minus box 8.16 (or box F6 minus box 8.16) **8.19** £ Nil

■ *Total of unused losses to carry forward*

- Carried forward losses of 1996-97 and later years — box 8.14 + box 8.17 **8.20** £
- Carried forward losses of 1995-96 and earlier years — box 8.18 minus box 8.19 **8.21** £

BS 12/2002net   TAX RETURN ■ CAPITAL GAINS: PAGE CG8

 95

PRACTICE EXAM PAPER 2

TECHNICIAN STAGE – NVQ4

Unit 19

Preparing personal tax computations (PTC)

DO NOT OPEN THIS PAPER UNTIL YOU ARE READY TO START UNDER EXAM CONDITIONS

COVERAGE OF PERFORMANCE CRITERIA

The following performance criteria are covered in this exam.

Element	PC Coverage
19.1	**Calculate income from employment**
A	Prepare accurate computations of emoluments, including benefits
B	List allowable expenses and deductions
C	Record relevant details of income from employment accurately and legibly in the tax return
D	Make computations and submissions are made in accordance with current tax law and take account of current Revenue practice
G	Maintain client confidentiality at all times
19.2	**Calculate property and investment income**
A	Prepare schedules of dividends and interest received on all shares and securities
B	Prepare schedules of property income and determine profits and losses
D	Apply deductions and reliefs and claim loss set offs
E	Record relevant details of property and investment income accurately and legibly in the tax return
F	Make computations and submissions are made in accordance with current tax law and take account of current Revenue practice
I	Maintain client confidentiality at all times
19.3	**Prepare income tax computations**
A	List general income, savings income and dividend income and check for completeness
B	Calculate and deduct charges and personal allowances
C	Calculate Income Tax payable
D	Record income and payments legibly and accurately in the tax return
E	Make computations and submissions in accordance with current tax law and take account of current Revenue practice
H	Maintain client confidentiality

Element	PC Coverage
19.4	**Prepare capital gains tax computations**
A	Identify and value disposed-of chargeable personal assets
B	Identify shares disposed of by individuals
C	Calculate chargeable gains and allowable losses
D	Apply reliefs and exemptions correctly
E	Calculate capital gains tax payable
G	Make computations and submissions in accordance with current tax law and take account of current Revenue practice
J	Maintain client confidentiality at all times

INSTRUCTIONS

This examination paper is in TWO sections.

You have to show competence in BOTH sections.

You should therefore attempt and aim to compete EVERY task in BOTH sections.

You should spend about 120 minutes on Section 1 and 60 minutes on Section 2.

Section 1

DATA

E-MAIL

To: Accounting Technician
From: Mr Smith, Production Director
Date: 31 August 2004

I am in the process of obtaining a mortgage and the bank has requested that I provide them with full details of my income and gains for the tax year 2003/04. They have suggested that I provide them with a copy of my tax return for that year.

Background

My income comprises my salary of £40,000 per annum and benefits from employment together with dividends and interest which I receive from investments which I hold. I also receive rental income from a furnished flat which I let out through a letting agent. Tax of £8,114 was deducted from my salary in 2003/04 under the PAYE system.

The following benefits were received from my employment during 2003/2004.

- I was provided with a space in a multi-storey car park next to the office. The season ticket costs Global plc £2,000 for the year.   *Exempt*

- I do not have a company car nor am I provided with any fuel. I am permitted, however to submit a claim for business mileage undertaken in my Mercedes. I submitted a claim for 15,000 business miles and was reimbursed at a flat rate of 50p per mile. I make a claim for tax purposes using the statutory mileage rates.

- Throughout the year I had use of a home entertainment system which was bought by Global plc at a cost of £10,000.   *20%*

- I am provided with a mobile phone which I use for both business and personal purposes.   *Exempt*

- Some years ago I received a loan from Global plc in the amount of £20,000. The loan is interest free. The loan was outstanding throughout the year.

- The company paid my subscription of £225 to the Institute of Production Management. This is an Inland Revenue approved Institute.

- I often work from home and during 2003/04 I received £104 from my employer towards the costs of working from home.

INCOME FROM INVESTMENTS

	£
Interest received	
£20,000 10% Exchequer Stock 2007	
Cash received 30.04.2003	800.00
Cash received 31.10.2003	800.00
Total cash received	1,600.00

20%

	£
Building Society Account	
Per statement:	
Gross interest	1,200.00
Tax deducted	240.00
Net interest	960.00

20%

	£
Dividends received	
Body Shack Enterprises plc	
Cash received 30.06.2003	270.00
Cash received 30.12.2003	450.00
Total cash received	720.00

10%

RENTAL INCOME AND EXPENSES

The furnished flat, which I acquired during March 2003, was let out throughout the year. I changed tenant mid-way through the year but there was no gap in letting and the rent from each tenant was unchanged at £24,000 per annum.

I used a letting agent who provided me with the following statement for the year ended 5 April 2004:

THE PROPERTY AGENCY
'We will let you if you will let us'

Statement for Mr Smith
Year ended 5 April 2004

Rental income received		£24,000
Expenses incurred:		
Letting Agent's Commission	2,400	
Advertising for tenant	250	
Repair kitchen	125	
Council tax	900	
		(3,675)
Net Rental Income due to you		20,325

EXTRACT FROM PERMANENT FILE

Robert Smith

Date of birth: 18 June 1959

Employment details: Production director of Global plc

General: Mr Smith pays £3,900 (net) into a personal pension scheme each year.

He pays £1,560 per annum (net) to his local church under the gift aid scheme.

He has had no underpayments of tax up to and including the tax year 2002/03.

5,000

£26 3,000.

7,000

Tasks

Task 1.1

Prepare a calculation of taxable earnings for 2003/04.

Task 1.2

Prepare schedules showing taxable dividend and interest income for 2003/04.

Task 1.3

Prepare a calculation of rental income for 2003/04.

Task 1.4

Prepare Mr Smith's income tax computation for 2003/04.

Task 1.5

Complete the income tax return for 2003/04. You should complete the supplementary employment and land and property pages.

Task 1.6

State the latest date by which the 2003/04 tax return can be submitted together with details of the due dates for payment of the tax. Please also advise of any other payments of income tax which Mr Smith has to make on any of the dates. Mr Smith is aware that you correspond with the Inland Revenue on his behalf. He is a bit concerned that others may be able to obtain his details from the Inland Revenue – state whether this could happen.

Section 2

DATA

Another client, Mr Jones, made three capital disposals during the year as follows:

1   **£20,000 10% Exchequer Stock 2007**

Date sold	31.01.2004
Proceeds received	£28,000
Date purchased	30.09.2001
Purchase cost	£20,000

2   **15,000 £1 Ordinary shares in Body Shack Enterprises plc**

Date sold	31.12.2003
Proceeds received (15,000 @ £1.60)	£24,000

Dates of costs and acquisition:

Date	No. of shares	Cost
30.06.02	10,000	9,000
30.11.92	15,000	15,000

3   **10,000 £1 Ordinary shares in JOL plc**

Mr Jones gave shares in JOL plc to his sister on 31 December 2003 at which time they had a market value of £50,000. He subscribed for these shares at their nominal value of £1 per share on 30 June 1990. These shares are a non-business asset for the purposes of taper relief.

Mr Jones had a capital loss of £13,500 brought forward from 2002/03.

Tasks

Task 2.1

Calculate any chargeable gains arising on the disposals.

Task 2.2

Calculate any capital gains tax payable for 2003/04 and state the payment date. Assume that Mr Jones is a higher rate tax payer.

TAXATION TABLES

Income tax

Tables

Starting rate	£1 – 1,960	10%
Basic rate	£1,961 – £30,500	22%
Higher rate	£30,501 and above	40%

Note: Savings (excl. dividend) income that falls in the basic rate band is taxed at 20%. UK dividends are taxed at 10% when they fall within the starting and basic rate bands and at 32.5% thereafter.

Personal allowances

Personal allowance   £4,615

Mileage allowances – Authorised mileage rates

Up to 10,000 miles	40p
Over 10,000 miles	25p

Official rate of interest

Throughout the year ended 5 April 2004   5%

Capital gains tax

Indexation Factors

June 1990	126.7
November 1992	139.7
April 1998	162.6

Tapering reliefs for capital gains tax

The percentage of the gain chargeable is as follows

No of complete tax years after 5 April 1998	Gains on Non-business assets
0	100.0
1	100.0
2	100.0
3	95.0
4	90.0
5	85.0
6	80.0
7	75.0
8	70.0
9	65.0
10 or more	60.0

Annual exemption

Individuals   £7,900

INCOME AND CAPITAL GAINS *for the year ended 5 April 2004*

Step 1

Answer Questions 1 to 9 below to check if you need supplementary Pages to give details of particular income or capital gains. Pages 6 and 7 of your Tax Return Guide will help.

(Ask the Orderline for a Guide if I haven't sent you one with your Tax Return, and you want one.)

If you answer 'Yes' ask the Orderline for the appropriate supplementary Pages and Notes.

Ring the Orderline on 0845 9000 404, or fax on 0845 9000 604 for any you need (closed Christmas Day, Boxing Day and New Year's Day).

If you do need supplementary Pages, tick the boxes below when you've got them.

Q1 Were you an employee, or office holder, or director, or agency worker or did you receive payments or benefits from a former employer (excluding a pension) in the year ended 5 April 2004?
If you were a non-resident director of a UK company but received no remuneration, see the notes to the Employment Pages, page EN3, box 1.6.
YES ✓ — EMPLOYMENT ✗

Q2 Did you have any taxable income from share options, shares or share related benefits in the year? (This does not include
- dividends, **or**
- dividend shares ceasing to be subject to an Inland Revenue approved share incentive plan within three years of acquisition they go in Question 10.)
YES — SHARE SCHEMES

Q3 Were you self-employed (but not in partnership)?
(You should also tick 'Yes' if you were a Name at Lloyd's.)
YES — SELF-EMPLOYMENT

Q4 Were you in partnership?
YES — PARTNERSHIP

Q5 Did you receive any rent or other income from land and property in the UK?
YES ✓ — LAND & PROPERTY ✓

Q6 Did you have any taxable income from overseas pensions or benefits, or from foreign companies or savings institutions, offshore funds or trusts abroad, or from land and property abroad or gains on foreign insurance policies?
YES
Have you or could you have received, or enjoyed directly or indirectly, or benefited in any way from, income of a foreign entity as a result of a transfer of assets made in this or earlier years?
YES
Do you want to claim foreign tax credit relief for foreign tax paid on foreign income or gains?
YES — FOREIGN

Q7 Did you receive, or are you deemed to have, income from a trust, settlement or the residue of a deceased person's estate?
YES — TRUSTS ETC

Q8 Capital gains - read the guidance on page 7 of the Tax Return Guide.
- If you have disposed of your only or main residence do you need the Capital Gains Pages?
YES
- Did you dispose of other chargeable assets worth more than £31,600 in total?
YES
- Were your total chargeable gains more than £7,900 or do you want to make a claim or election for the year?
YES — CAPITAL GAINS

Q9 Are you claiming that you were not resident, or not ordinarily resident, or not domiciled, in the UK, or dual resident in the UK and another country, for all or part of the year?
YES — NON-RESIDENCE ETC

Step 2 **Fill in any supplementary Pages BEFORE going to Step 3.**
Please use blue or black ink to fill in your Tax Return and please do not include pence. Round down your income and gains. Round up your tax credits and tax deductions. Round to the nearest pound.
When you have filled in all the supplementary Pages you need, tick this box. ☑

Step 3 Fill in Questions 10 to 24. If you answer 'Yes', fill in the relevant boxes. If not applicable, go to the next question.

BS 12/2002net   TAX RETURN: PAGE 2

INCOME *for the year ended 5 April 2004*

Q10 **Did you receive any income from UK savings and investments?**   YES ✓   *If yes,* tick this box and then fill in boxes 10.1 to 10.26 as appropriate. Include only your share from any joint savings and investments.
If not applicable, go to Question 11.

■ *Interest*

● Interest from UK banks, building societies and deposit takers (interest from UK Internet accounts must be included) - *if you have more than one bank or building society etc. account enter **totals** in the boxes.*

- enter any bank, building society etc. interest that **has not** had tax taken off. (Most interest is taxed by your bank or building society etc. so make sure you should be filling in box 10.1, rather than boxes 10.2 to 10.4)

	Taxable amount
	10.1 £

- enter details of your **taxed** bank or building society etc. interest. *The Working Sheet on page 10 of your Tax Return Guide will help you fill in boxes 10.2 to 10.4.*

Amount **after** tax deducted	Tax deducted	Gross amount **before** tax
10.2 £ 2560	**10.3** £ 640	**10.4** £ 3200

● Interest distributions from UK authorised unit trusts and open-ended investment companies (dividend distributions go below)

Amount **after** tax deducted	Tax deducted	Gross amount **before** tax
10.5 £	**10.6** £	**10.7** £

● National Savings & Investments (other than First Option Bonds and Fixed Rate Savings Bonds and the first £70 of interest from an Ordinary Account)

	Taxable amount
	10.8 £

● National Savings & Investments First Option Bonds and Fixed Rate Savings Bonds

Amount **after** tax deducted	Tax deducted	Gross amount **before** tax
10.9 £	**10.10** £	**10.11** £

● Other income from UK savings and investments (except dividends)

Amount **after** tax deducted	Tax deducted	Gross amount **before** tax
10.12 £	**10.13** £	**10.14** £

■ *Dividends*

● Dividends and other qualifying distributions from UK companies

Dividend/distribution	Tax credit	Dividend/distribution **plus** credit
10.15 £ 720	**10.16** £ 80	**10.17** £ 800

● Dividend distributions from UK authorised unit trusts and open-ended investment companies

Dividend/distribution	Tax credit	Dividend/distribution **plus** credit
10.18 £	**10.19** £	**10.20** £

● Scrip dividends from UK companies

Dividend	Notional tax	Dividend **plus** notional tax
10.21 £	**10.22** £	**10.23** £

● Non-qualifying distributions and loans written off

Distribution/Loan	Notional tax	Taxable amount
10.24 £	**10.25** £	**10.26** £

INCOME *for the year ended 5 April 2004, continued*

Q11 **Did you receive a taxable UK pension, retirement annuity or Social Security benefit?**
Read the notes on pages 13 to 15 of the Tax Return Guide.

YES ☒ If yes, tick this box and then fill in boxes 11.1 to 11.14 as appropriate.
If not applicable, go to Question 12.

■ *State pensions and benefits*

Taxable amount for 2003-04

- State Retirement Pension - *enter the **total** of your entitlements for the year* | **11.1** £
- Widow's Pension or Bereavement Allowance | **11.2** £
- Widowed Mother's Allowance or Widowed Parent's Allowance | **11.3** £
- Industrial Death Benefit Pension | **11.4** £
- Jobseeker's Allowance | **11.5** £
- Invalid Care Allowance | **11.6** £
- Statutory Sick Pay, Statutory Maternity Pay and Statutory Paternity Pay paid by the Inland Revenue | **11.7** £

	Tax deducted	Gross amount **before** tax
• Taxable Incapacity Benefit	**11.8** £	**11.9** £

■ *Other pensions and retirement annuities*

- Pensions (other than State pensions) and retirement annuities - *if you have more than one pension or annuity, please add together and complete boxes 11.10 to 11.12. Provide details of each one in box 11.14*

Amount after tax deducted	Tax deducted	Gross amount **before** tax
11.10 £	**11.11** £	**11.12** £

11.14

- Deduction - *see the note for box 11.13 on page 15 of your Tax Return Guide*

Amount of deduction
11.13 £

Q12 **Did you make any gains on UK life insurance policies, life annuities or capital redemption policies or receive refunds of surplus funds from additional voluntary contributions?**

YES ☐ If yes, tick this box and then fill in boxes 12.1 to 12.12 as appropriate.
If not applicable, go to Question 13.

- Gains on UK annuities and friendly societies' life insurance policies where no tax is treated as paid

Number of years		Amount of gain(s)
12.1		**12.2** £

- Gains on UK life insurance policies etc. on which tax is treated as paid - *read pages 15 to 18 of your Tax Return Guide*

Number of years	Tax treated as paid	Amount of gain(s)
12.3	**12.4** £	**12.5** £

- Gains on life insurance policies in ISAs that have been made void

Number of years	Tax deducted	Amount of gain(s)
12.6	**12.7** £	**12.8** £

- Corresponding deficiency relief

Amount
12.9 £

- Refunds of surplus funds from additional voluntary contributions

Amount received	Notional tax	Amount plus notional tax
12.10 £	**12.11** £	**12.12** £

Q13 **Did you receive any other taxable income which you have not already entered elsewhere in your Tax Return?**
Fill in any supplementary Pages before answering Question 13. (Supplementary Pages follow page 10, or are available from the Orderline.)

YES ☐ If yes, tick this box and then fill in boxes 13.1 to 13.6 as appropriate.
If not applicable, go to Question 14.

- Other taxable income – also provide details in box 23.5 - *read the notes on pages 18 to 20 of your Tax Return Guide*

Amount **after** tax deducted	Tax deducted	Amount **before** tax
13.1 £	**13.2** £	**13.3** £

- Tick box 13.1A if box 13.1 includes enhanced capital allowances for environmentally friendly expenditure

13.1A ☐

	Losses brought forward	Earlier years' losses used in 2003-04
	13.4 £	**13.5** £

2003-04 losses carried forward
13.6 £

BS 12/2002net

Tax Return: page 4

RELIEFS *for the year ended 5 April 2004*

Q14 **Do you want to claim relief for your pension contributions?** | YES | If yes, tick this box and then fill in boxes 14.1 to 14.11 as appropriate.
If not appliable, go to Question 15.

*Do not include contributions deducted from your pay by your employer to their pension scheme or associated AVC scheme, because tax relief is given automatically. But **do include** your contributions to personal pension schemes and Free-Standing AVC schemes.*

■ *Payments to your retirement annuity contracts - only fill in boxes 14.1 to 14.5 for policies taken out before 1 July 1988.*
See the notes on pages 20 and 21 of your Tax Return Guide.

| Qualifying payments made in 2003-04 | **14.1** £ | 2003-04 payments used in an earlier year | **14.2** £ | Relief claimed
box 14.1 *minus* (boxes 14.2 and 14.3, but not 14.4) |
| 2003-04 payments now to be carried back | **14.3** £ | Payments brought back from 2004-05 | **14.4** £ | **14.5** £ |

■ *Payments to your personal pension (including stakeholder pension) contracts - enter the amount of the payment you made with the basic rate tax added (the **gross** payment). See the note for box 14.6 on page 22 of your Tax Return Guide.*

| Gross qualifying payments made in 2003-04 | **14.6** £ 5,000 | |
| 2003-04 gross payments carried back to 2002-03 | **14.7** £ | Relief claimed
box 14.6 *minus* box 14.7 (but not 14.8) |
| Gross qualifying payments made between 6 April 2004 and 31 January 2005 brought back to 2003-04 - *see page 22 of your Tax Return Guide* | **14.8** £ | **14.9** £ 5,000 |

■ *Contributions to other pension schemes and Free-Standing AVC schemes*

● Amount of contributions to employer's schemes **not deducted** at source from pay | **14.10** £

● Gross amount of Free-Standing Additional Voluntary Contributions paid in 2003-04 | **14.11** £

Q15 **Do you want to claim any of the following reliefs?**
If you have made any annual payments, after basic rate tax, answer 'Yes' to Question 15 and fill in box 15.9. If you have made any gifts to charity go to Question 15A. | YES | If yes, tick this box and then fill in boxes 15.1 to 15.12, as appropriate.
If not applicable, go to Question 15A

● Interest eligible for relief on qualifying loans | **15.1** £

● Maintenance or alimony payments you have made under a court order, Child Support Agency assessment or legally binding order or agreement | Amount claimed up to £2,150
15.2 £

To claim this relief, either you or your former spouse must have been 65 or over on 5 April 2000. So, if **your** date of birth, which is entered in box 22.6, is after 5 April 1935 then you must enter your former **spouse's** date of birth in box 15.2A - *see pages 23 and 24 of your Tax Return Guide* | Former spouse's date of birth
15.2A / /

● Subscriptions for Venture Capital Trust shares (up to £100,000) | Amount on which relief is claimed
15.3 £

● Subscriptions under the Enterprise Investment Scheme (up to £150,000) - *also provide details in box 23.5, see page 24 of your Tax Return Guide* | Amount on which relief is claimed
15.4 £

● Community Investment Tax relief - invested amount relating to previous tax year(s) and on which relief is due | **15.5** £ | Total amount on which relief is claimed
box 15.5 + box 15.6

● Community Investment Tax relief - invested amount for current tax year | **15.6** £ | **15.7** £

● Post-cessation expenses, pre-incorporation losses brought forward and losses on relevant discounted securities, etc. - *see pages 24 and 25 of your Tax Return Guide* | Amount of payment
15.8 £

● Annuities and annual payments | Payments made
15.9 £

● Payments to a trade union or friendly society for death benefits | Half amount of payment
15.10 £

● Payment to your employer's compulsory widow's, widower's or orphan's benefit scheme - *available in some circumstances – **first** read the notes on page 25 of your Tax Return Guide* | Relief claimed
15.11 £

● Relief claimed on a qualifying distribution on the **redemption** of bonus shares or securities. | Relief claimed
15.12 £

BS 12/2002net | Tax Return: page 5 | *Please turn over* ▶

ALLOWANCES for the year ended 5 April 2004

Q15A **Do you want to claim relief on gifts to charity?**
If you have made any Gift Aid payments answer 'Yes' to Question 15A. You should include Gift Aid payments to Community Amateur Sports Clubs here. You can elect to include in this Return Gift Aid payments made between 6 April 2004 and the date you send in this Return. See page 26 in the Tax Return Guide and the leaflet enclosed on Gift Aid.

YES

If yes, tick this box and then read page 26 of your Tax Return Guide. Fill in boxes 15A.1 to 15A.5 as appropriate. If not applicable, go to Question 16.

- Gift Aid and payments under charitable covenants made between 6 April 2003 and 5 April 2004 | **15A.1** £ *1560*

- Enter in box 15A.2 the total of any 'one off' payments included in box 15A.1 | **15A.2** £

- Enter in box 15A.3 the amount of Gift Aid payments made after 5 April 2004 but treated as if made in the tax year 2003-04 | **15A.3** £

- Gifts of qualifying investments to charities – shares and securities | **15A.4** £

- Gifts of qualifying investments to charities – real property | **15A.5** £

Q16 **Do you want to claim blind person's allowance, married couple's allowance or the Children's Tax Credit?**

YES

If yes, tick this box and then read pages 26 to 31 of your Tax Return Guide. Fill in boxes 16.1 to 16.33 as appropriate. If not applicable, go to Question 17.

*You get your personal allowance of £4,615 automatically. **If you were born before 6 April 1938, enter your date of birth in box 22.6** - you may get a higher age-related personal allowance.*

■ *Blind person's allowance*

Date of registration (if first year of claim) **16.1** | **16.2** Local authority (or other register)

■ *Married couple's allowance -* *In 2003-04 married couple's allowance can only be claimed if either you, or your husband or wife, were born **before 6 April 1935**. So you can only claim the allowance in 2003-04 if either of you had reached **65 years of age before 6 April 2000**. Further guidance is given beginning on page 27 of your Tax Return Guide.*

*If **both** you and your husband or wife were born after 5 April 1935 you cannot claim; **do not** complete boxes 16.3 to 16.13.*

If you can claim fill in boxes 16.3 and 16.4 if you are a married man or if you are a married woman and you are claiming half or all of the married couple's allowance.

- Enter your date of birth (if born before 6 April 1935) | **16.3** / /

- Enter your spouse's date of birth (**if born before 6 April 1935 and** if older than you) | **16.4** / /

Then, if you are a married man fill in boxes 16.5 to 16.9. If you are a married woman fill in boxes 16.10 to 16.13.

- Wife's full name | **16.5** | ● Date of marriage (if after 5 April 2003) | **16.6** / /

- Tick box 16.7, or box 16.8, if you or your wife have allocated half, or all, of the minimum amount of the allowance to her | Half **16.7** | All **16.8**

- Enter in box 16.9 the date of birth of any previous wife with whom you lived at any time during 2003-04. *Read 'Special rules if you are a man who married in the year ended 5 April 2004' on page 28 before completing box 16.9.* | **16.9**

- Tick box 16.10, or box 16.11, if you or your husband have allocated half, or all, of the minimum amount of the allowance to you | Half **16.10** | All **16.11**

- Husband's full name | **16.12** | ● Date of marriage (if after 5 April 2003) | **16.13** / /

■ *Child Tax Credit* – even if you have already completed a separate Child's Tax Credit (CTC) claim form and received the relief in your tax code, you should still fill in boxes 16.14 to 16.26, as directed. Any reference to 'partner' in this question means the person you lived with during the year to 5 April 2004 – your husband or wife, or someone you lived with as husband or wife.

Guidance for claiming CTC is on pages 29 to 31 of your Tax Return Guide. Please read the notes before completing your claim, particularly if either you, or your partner, are liable to tax above the basic rate in the year to 5 April 2004.

- Enter in box 16.14 the date of birth of a child living with you who was born on or after 6 April 1986. *If you have a child living with you who was born on or after 6 April 2003 make sure you enter their date of birth in this box in preference to claiming for an older child.* | **16.14** / /

- Tick box 16.15 if the child was your own child or one you looked after at your own expense. If not, you cannot claim CTC – go to box 16.27, if appropriate, or Question 17. | **16.15**

- Tick box 16.16 if the child lived with you **throughout** the year to 5 April 2004. If you ticked box 16.16 and | **16.16**
  - you were a lone or single claimant, you have finished this question; go to Question 17,
  - you have a partner, go to box 16.18.

- If the child lived with you for only **part of the year** you may only be entitled to a proportion of the CTC. Enter in box 16.17 your share in £s that **you have agreed** with any other claimants that you may claim for this child. But leave boxes 16.17 to 16.25 blank if you separated from, or started living with, your partner during the year to 5 April 2004. Special rules apply to work out your entitlement; ask the Orderline for *Help Sheet IR343: Claiming Children's Tax Credit when your circumstances change* which explains how to complete box 16.26. | **16.17** £

BS 12/2002net

TAX RETURN: PAGE 6

(watermark: No longer applicable)

ALLOWANCES *for the year ended 5 April 2004, continued*

■ *Children's Tax Credit,* continued

If you lived with your partner (for CTC this means your husband or wife, or someone you lived with as husband and wife) for the whole of the year to 5 April 2004, fill in boxes 16.18 to 16.25 as appropriate.

- Enter in box 16.18 your partner's surname

  16.18

- Enter in box 16.19 your partner's National Insurance number

  16.19

- Tick
  - box 16.20 if **you** had the higher income in the year to 5 April 2004,

    16.20

  or
  - box 16.21 if **your partner** had the higher income in the year

    16.21

- Tick box 16.22 if either of you were chargeable to tax above the basic rate limit in the year to 5 April 2004. **16.22**

  If you ticked boxes 16.20 and 16.22 your entitlement will be reduced – see page 30 of your Tax Return Guide; **your partner cannot claim CTC** *- go to box 16.28, or Question 17 as appropriate.*

  If you ticked boxes 16.21 and 16.22 your partner's entitlement will be reduced; **you cannot claim CTC** – *go to box 16.27, or Question 17, as appropriate.*

  If **neither** *of you were chargeable above the basic rate and* **you** *had the lower income* **and**
  - *you don't want to claim half of the entitlement to CTC, and*
  - *you didn't make an election for CTC to go to the partner with the lower income*

  you have finished this part of your Return - go to boxes 16.27 or 16.28, or Question 17, as appropriate (your partner should claim CTC if they have not already done so).

  Otherwise, tick one of boxes 16.23 to 16.25 .

- I had the higher income and I am claiming all of our entitlement to CTC **16.23**

- We are both making separate claims for half of our entitlement to CTC **16.24**

- We elected before 6 April 2003, or because of our special circumstances, during the year to 5 April 2004 (see page 31 of your Tax Return Guide), for the partner with the lower income to claim all of our entitlement to CTC **16.25**

- If you separated from, or starting living with, your partner in the year to 5 April 2004, enter in box 16.26 the amount of CTC you are claiming *(following the guidance in Help Sheet IR343: Claiming Children's Tax Credit when your circumstances change).* **16.26** £

■ *Transfer of surplus allowances* - *see page 31 of your Tax Return Guide before you fill in boxes 16.27 to 16.33.*

- Tick box 16.27 if you want your spouse to have your unused allowances **16.27**

- Tick box 16.28 if you want to have your spouse's unused allowances **16.28**

If you want to calculate your tax, enter the amount of the surplus allowance you can have.

- Blind person's surplus allowance **16.31** £

- Married couple's surplus allowance **16.32**

OTHER INFORMATION *for the year ended 5 April 2004*

Q17 **Are you liable to make Student Loan Repayments for 2003-04 on an Income Contingent Student Loan?**
You must read the note on page 31 of your Tax Return Guide before ticking the 'Yes' box.

YES   If yes, tick this box.
If not applicable, go to Question 18.

If yes, and you are calculating your tax enter in Question 18, box 18.2A the amount you work out is repayable in 2003-04

OTHER INFORMATION *for the year ended 5 April 2004, continued*

Q18 **Do you want to calculate your tax and, if appropriate, any Student Loan Repayment?** | **YES** | Use your Tax Calculation Guide then fill in boxes 18.1 to 18.8 as appropriate.

- Unpaid tax for earlier years **included in your tax code for 2003-04** | **18.1** £
- Tax due for 2003-04 included in your tax code for a later year | **18.2** £
- Student Loan Repayment due | **18.2A** £
- Total tax, Class 4 NIC and Student Loan Repayment due for 2003-04 **before** you made any payments on account *(put the amount in brackets if an overpayment)* | **18.3** £
- Tax due for earlier years | **18.4** £
- Tax overpaid for earlier years | **18.5** £
- Tick box 18.6 if you are claiming to reduce your 2004-05 payments on account. Make sure you enter the **reduced** amount of your first payment in box 18.7. Then, in the 'Additional information' box, box 23.5 on page 9, say why you are making a claim | **18.6**
- Your first payment on account for 2004-05 *(include the pence)* | **18.7** £
- Any 2004-05 tax you are reclaiming now | **18.8** £

Q19 **Do you want to claim a repayment if you have paid too much tax?** *(If you do not tick 'Yes' or the tax you have overpaid is below £10, I will use the amount you are owed to reduce your next tax bill.)* | **YES** | If yes, tick this box and then fill in boxes 19.1 to 19.12 as appropriate. If not applicable, go to Question 20.

Should the repayment be sent:

- to your bank or building society account? *Tick box 19.1 and fill in boxes 19.3 to 19.7* | **19.1**

or

- to your nominee's bank or building society account? *Tick box 19.2 and fill in boxes 19.3 to 19.12* | **19.2**

We prefer to make repayment direct into a bank or building society account. (But tick box 19.8A or box 19.8B if you would like a cheque to be sent to you or your nominee.)

Name of bank or building society
19.3

Branch sort code
19.4

Account number
19.5

Name of account holder
19.6

Building society reference
19.7

If you would like a cheque to be sent to:

- you, at the address on page 1, *tick box 19.8A* | **19.8A**

or

- your nominee, *tick box 19.8B* | **19.8B**

If your nominee is your agent, *tick box 19.9A* | **19.9A**

Agent's reference for you (if your nominee is your agent)
19.9

I authorise

Name of your nominee/agent
19.10

Nominee/agent address
19.11

Postcode

to receive on my behalf the amount due

19.12 *This authority must be signed by you. A photocopy of your signature will not do.*

Signature

BS 12/2002net | TAX RETURN: PAGE 8

OTHER INFORMATION *for the year ended 5 April 2004, continued*

Q20 Have you already had any 2003-04 tax refunded or set off by your Inland Revenue office or the Benefits Agency (in Northern Ireland, the Social Security Agency)?
Read the notes on page 32 of your Tax Return Guide.

YES ☐   If yes, tick this box and then enter the amount of the refund in box 20.1.

20.1 £ _____

Q21 Is your name or address on the front of the Tax Return *wrong*?
If you are filling in an approved substitute Tax Return, see the notes on page 32 of the Tax Return Guide.

YES ☐   If yes, please tick this box and make any corrections on the front of the form.

Q22 Please give other personal details in boxes 22.1 to 22.7. *This information helps us to be more efficient and effective.*

Your daytime telephone number
22.1 _____

Your agent's telephone number
22.2 _____

and their name and address
22.3 Mr Smith
_____
_____
Postcode _____

Your first two forenames
22.4 _____

Say if you are single, married, widowed, divorced or separated
22.5 _____

Your date of birth (If you were born before 6 April 1938, you may get a higher age-related allowance.)
22.6 __ / __ / __

Your National Insurance number
(if known and not on page 1 of your Tax Return)
22.7 _____

Q23 Please tick boxes 23.1 to 23.4 if they apply. Provide any additional information in box 23.5 below (continue on page 10, if necessary).

Tick box 23.1 if you do **not** want any tax you owe for 2003-04 collected through your tax code.   **23.1** ☐

Please tick box 23.2 if this Tax Return contains figures that are provisional because you do not yet have final figures. Pages 32 and 33 of the Tax Return Guide explain the circumstances in which provisional figures may be used and asks for some additional information to be provided in box 23.5 below.   **23.2** ☐

Tick box 23.3 if you are claiming relief now for 2004-05 trading, or certain capital, losses. Enter in box 23.5 the amount and year.   **23.3** ☐

Tick box 23.4 if you are claiming to have post-cessation or other business receipts taxed as income of an earlier year. Enter in box 23.5 the amount and year.   **23.4** ☐

23.5 *Additional information*

OTHER INFORMATION *for the year ended 5 April 2004, continued*

23.5 *Additional information continued*

Q24 ▶ Declaration

I have filled in and am sending back to you the following pages:

Tick

*In the second box enter the number of **complete sets** of supplementary Pages enclosed*

1 TO 10 OF THIS FORM	✓	Number of sets					
EMPLOYMENT	✓		**PARTNERSHIP**		Number of sets	**TRUSTS, ETC**	
SHARE SCHEMES	✓	Number of sets	**LAND & PROPERTY**	✓		**CAPITAL GAINS**	
SELF-EMPLOYMENT			**FOREIGN**			**NON-RESIDENCE, ETC**	

Before you send your completed Tax Return back to your Inland Revenue office, you must sign the statement below.
If you give false information or conceal any part of your income or chargeable gains, you may be liable to financial penalties and/or you may be prosecuted.

24.1 The information I have given in this Tax Return is correct and complete to the best of my knowledge and belief.

Signature   *A/c Dueedie*   Date

There are very few reasons why we accept a signature from someone who is not the person making this Return but if you are signing for someone else please read the notes on page 33 of the Tax Return Guide, and:

• enter the capacity in which you are signing (for example, as executor or receiver)

24.2

• enter the name of the person you are signing for

24.3

• please **PRINT** your name and address in box 24.4

24.4

Postcode

BS 12/2002net   TAX RETURN: PAGE 10

Income for the year ended 5 April 2004

Inland Revenue — EMPLOYMENT

Fill in these boxes first

Name: Mr Smith

Tax reference:

If you want help, look up the box numbers in the Notes.

Details of employer

Employer's PAYE reference - may be shown under 'Inland Revenue office number and reference' on your P60 or 'PAYE reference' on your P45

1.1

Employer's name **1.2** GLOBAL PLC

Date employment started (only if between 6 April 2003 and 5 April 2004) **1.3** / /

Date employment finished (only if between 6 April 2003 and 5 April 2004) **1.4** / /

Employer's address **1.5**

Postcode

Tick box 1.6 if you were a director of the company **1.6**

and, if so, tick box 1.7 if it was a close company **1.7**

Income from employment

■ *Money - see Notes, page EN3*

Before tax

• Payments from P60 (or P45) **1.8** £ 40,000

• Payments not on P60, etc. - tips **1.9** £

- other payments (excluding expenses entered below and lump sums and compensation payments or benefits entered overleaf) **1.10** £

Tax deducted

• **Tax deducted** in the UK from payments in boxes 1.8 to 1.10 **1.11** £ 8114

■ *Benefits and expenses - see Notes, pages EN3 to EN6. If any benefits connected with termination of employment were received, or enjoyed, after that termination and were from a **former** employer you need to complete Help Sheet IR204, available from the Orderline. Do not enter such benefits here.*

	Amount		Amount
• Assets transferred/ payments made for you **1.12** £		• Vans **1.18** £	
• Vouchers, credit cards and tokens **1.13** £		• Taxable cheap loans *see Note for box 1.19, page EN5* **1.19** £ 1,000	
• Living accommodation **1.14** £		box 1.20 is not used	
• Excess mileage allowances and passenger payments **1.15** £ 2250		• Private medical or dental insurance **1.21** £	
• Company cars **1.16** £		• Other benefits **1.22** £ 2,000	
• Fuel for company cars **1.17** £		• Expenses payments received and balancing charges **1.23** £	

SA101

BS 12/2002net — TAX RETURN ■ EMPLOYMENT: PAGE E1 — *Please turn over*

115

Income from employment continued

■ *Lump sums and compensation payments or benefits including such payments and benefits from a former employer*
Note that 'lump sums' here includes any contributions which your employer made to an unapproved retirement benefits scheme

*You must read page EN6 of the Notes **before** filling in boxes 1.24 to 1.30*

Reliefs

● £30,000 exemption — **1.24** £

● Foreign service and disability — **1.25** £

● Retirement and death lump sums — **1.26** £

Taxable lump sums

● From box B of *Help Sheet IR204* — **1.27** £

● From box K of *Help Sheet IR204* — **1.28** £

● From box L of *Help Sheet IR204* — **1.29** £

● Tax deducted from payments in boxes 1.27 to 1.29 - ***leave blank** if this tax is included in the box 1.11 figure.* — Tax deducted **1.30** £

■ *Foreign earnings not taxable in the UK in the year ended 5 April 2004* - *see Notes, page EN6* — **1.31** £

■ *Expenses you incurred in doing your job* - *see Notes, pages EN7 to EN8*

● Travel and subsistence costs — **1.32** £

● Fixed deductions for expenses — **1.33** £

● Professional fees and subscriptions — **1.34** £

● Other expenses and capital allowances — **1.35** £

● Tick box 1.36 if the figure in box 1.32 includes travel between your home and a permanent workplace — **1.36**

■ *Foreign Earnings Deduction* (seafarers only) — **1.37** £

■ *Foreign tax for which tax credit relief not claimed* — **1.38** £

Student Loans

■ *Student Loans repaid by deduction by employer* - *see Notes, page EN8* — **1.39** £

● Tick box 1.39A if your income is under Repayment of Teachers' Loans Scheme — **1.39A**

1.40 *Additional information*

Now fill in any other supplementary Pages that apply to you.
Otherwise, go back to page 2 in your Tax Return and finish filling it in.

BS 12/2002net

TAX RETURN ■ EMPLOYMENT: PAGE E2

BPP)))
PROFESSIONAL EDUCATION

Inland Revenue

Income for the year ended 5 April 2004

LAND AND PROPERTY

Name

Tax reference

Fill in these boxes first

If you want help, look up the box numbers in the Notes.

Are you claiming Rent a Room relief for gross rents of £4,250 or less?
(Or £2,125 if the claim is shared?)
Read the Notes on page LN2 to find out
- **whether you can claim Rent a Room relief; and**
- **how to claim relief for gross rents over £4,250**

Yes

If 'Yes', tick box. If this is your only income from UK property, you have finished these Pages

Is your income from furnished holiday lettings?
If not applicable, please turn over and fill in Page L2 to give details of your property income

Yes

If 'Yes', tick box and fill in boxes 5.1 to 5.18 before completing Page L2

Furnished holiday lettings

- **Income from furnished holiday lettings** **5.1** £

- ■ *Expenses* (furnished holiday lettings only)

  - Rent, rates, insurance, ground rents etc. **5.2** £
  - Repairs, maintenance and renewals **5.3** £
  - Finance charges, including interest **5.4** £
  - Legal and professional costs **5.5** £
  - Costs of services provided, including wages **5.6** £
  - Other expenses **5.7** £

  total of boxes 5.2 to 5.7
  5.8 £

Net profit (put figures in brackets if a loss)

box 5.1 minus box 5.8
5.9 £

- ■ *Tax adjustments*

  - Private use **5.10** £
  - Balancing charges **5.11** £

  box 5.10 + box 5.11
  5.12 £

  - Capital allowances **5.13** £

  - Tick box 5.13A if box 5.13 includes enhanced capital allowances for environmentally friendly expenditure **5.13A**

Profit for the year (copy to box 5.19). If loss, enter '0' in box 5.14 and put the loss in box 5.15

boxes 5.9 + 5.12 minus box 5.13
5.14 £

Loss for the year (if you have entered '0' in box 5.14)

boxes 5.9 + 5.12 minus box 5.13
5.15 £

- ■ *Losses*

  - Loss offset against 2003-04 total income **5.16** £

  see Notes, page LN4
  - Loss carried back **5.17** £

  see Notes, page LN4
  - Loss offset against other income from property (copy to box 5.38) **5.18** £

SA105

BS 12/2002net

TAX RETURN ■ LAND AND PROPERTY: PAGE L1

Please turn over

PROFESSIONAL EDUCATION

Other property income

■ Income

		copy from box 5.14
● Furnished holiday lettings profits	**5.19** £	
● Rents and other income from land and property	**5.20** £	Tax deducted **5.21** £
● Chargeable premiums	**5.22** £	
● Reverse premiums	**5.22A** £	boxes 5.19 + 5.20 + 5.22 + 5.22A **5.23** £ 24,000.

■ Expenses (do not include figures you have already put in boxes 5.2 to 5.7 on Page L1)

● Rent, rates, insurance, ground rents etc.	**5.24** £ 900	
● Repairs, maintenance and renewals	**5.25** £ 125	
● Finance charges, including interest	**5.26** £	
● Legal and professional costs	**5.27** £ 2400	
● Costs of services provided, including wages	**5.28** £ 250	
● Other expenses	**5.29** £	total of boxes 5.24 to 5.29 **5.30** £ 3675

Net profit (put figures in brackets if a loss)   box 5.23 *minus* box 5.30 **5.31** £ 20 325

■ Tax adjustments

● Private use	**5.32** £	
● Balancing charges	**5.33** £	box 5.32 + box 5.33 **5.34** £
● Rent a Room exempt amount	**5.35** £	
● Capital allowances	**5.36** £	
● Tick box 5.36A if box 5.36 includes a claim for 100% capital allowances for flats over shops	**5.36A**	
● Tick box 5.36B if box 5.36 includes enhanced capital allowances for environmentally friendly expenditure	**5.36B**	
● 10% wear and tear	**5.37** £ 2310	
● Furnished holiday lettings losses (from box 5.18)	**5.38** £	boxes 5.35 to 5.38 **5.39** £ 18,015

Adjusted profit (if loss enter '0' in box 5.40 and put the loss in box 5.41)   boxes 5.31 + 5.34 *minus* box 5.39 **5.40** £

Adjusted loss (if you have entered '0' in box 5.40)   boxes 5.31 + 5.34 *minus* box 5.39 **5.41** £

● Loss brought forward from previous year	**5.42** £

Profit for the year   box 5.40 *minus* box 5.42 **5.43** £

■ Losses etc

● Loss offset against total income (read the note on page LN8)	**5.44** £
● Loss to carry forward to following year	**5.45** £
● Tick box 5.46 if these Pages include details of property let jointly	**5.46**
● Tick box 5.47 if **all** property income ceased in the year to 5 April 2004 **and** you don't expect to receive such income again, in the year to 5 April 2005	**5.47**

Now fill in any other supplementary Pages that apply to you.
Otherwise, go back to page 2 of your Tax Return and finish filling it in.

BS 12/2002net

TAX RETURN ■ LAND AND PROPERTY: PAGE L2

AAT
Specimen Exam

AAT SPECIMEN EXAM PAPER – 2003 STANDARDS

NVQ/SVQ IN ACCOUNTING, LEVEL 4

UNIT 19

Preparing Personal Tax Computations

This examination paper is in TWO sections.

You have to show competence in BOTH sections.

You should therefore attempt and aim to complete EVERY task in EACH section.

You should spend about 70 minutes on Section 1 and 110 minutes on Section 2.

COVERAGE OF PERFORMANCE CRITERIA

The following performance criteria are covered in this exam.

Element	PC Coverage
19.1	**Calculate income from employment**
A	Prepare accurate computations of emoluments, including benefits
B	List allowable expenses and deductions
C	Record relevant details of income from employment accurately and legibly in the tax return
D	Make computations and submissions in accordance with current tax law and take account of current Revenue practice
G	Maintain client confidentiality at all times
19.2	**Calculate property and investment income**
A	Prepare schedules of dividends and interest received on shares and securities
F	Make computations and submissions in accordance with current tax law and take account of current Revenue practice
I	Maintain client confidentiality at all times
19.3	**Prepare income tax computations**
A	List general income, savings income and dividend income and check for completeness
B	Calculate and deduct charges and personal allowances
C	Calculate Income Tax payable
E	Make computations and submissions in accordance with current tax law and take account of current Revenue practice
H	Maintain client confidentiality at all times
19.4	**Prepare Capital Gains Tax computations**
A	Identify and value disposed-of chargeable personal assets
B	Identify shares disposed of by individuals
C	Calculate chargeable gains and allowance losses
D	Apply reliefs and exemptions correctly
E	Calculate Capital Gains Tax payable
G	Make computations and submissions in accordance with current tax law and take account of current Revenue practice
J	Maintain client confidentiality at all times

Section 1

DATA

The date is May 2004. You work for Autumn Jewels Ltd in its payroll department. One of the employees, Phil Bright, has asked if you could help him complete his 2003/04 tax return.

From the company records, you determine that his taxable earnings comprise:

1   Annual salary of £18,500

2   Throughout the year, he was provided with a 2,500cc petrol-engine company car that had a list price of £28,600 when new. It has an emission rating of 192g/km. The company pays all running costs.

3   In July 2002 he was provided with a company loan of £20,000 on which he pays interest at 2.5% per annum. No capital repayment of the loan has been made.

4   He pays pension contributions to the employer's pension scheme at 5% of his salary.

Phil Bright gives you the following additional information:

1   He is 42 years old

2   He received dividend cheques of £5,400 during 2003/04   600

3   He also received building society interest of £4,160, net

4   He paid an annual subscription to his professional organisation of £250.

Task 1.1

Calculate the total assessable benefits for 2003/04.

....
....
....
....
....
....
....
....
....

Task 1.2

Prepare a schedule of income for 2003/04, clearly showing the distinction between non-savings, savings and dividend income. Phil Bright's personal allowances should be deducted, as appropriate.

....
....
....
....
....
....
....
....
....
....
....
....
....
....

Task 1.3

Calculate the net income tax payable for 2003/04, before deducting PAYE.

....
....
....
....
....
....
....
....

Task 1.4

Another employee, Beryl Simmons, has heard that you are helping Phil Bright sort out his tax. She asks you what you have been doing for Phil, so that she can see if you can also help her.

Discuss how you should reply to this request.

....

....

....

....

....

....

....

....

Task 1.5

Complete the attached tax return for employment income of Phil Bright.

Income for the year ended 5 April 2004

Inland Revenue

EMPLOYMENT

Fill in these boxes first

Name

Tax reference

If you want help, look up the box numbers in the Notes.

Details of employer

Employer's PAYE reference - may be shown under 'inland Revenue office number and reference' on your P60 or 'PAYE reference' on your P45

1.1

Employer's name

1.2

Date employment started
(only if between 6 April 2003 and 5 April 2004)

1.3 / /

Date employment finished
(only if between 6 April 2003 and 5 April 2004)

1.4 / /

Employer's address

1.5

Postcode

Tick box 1.6 if you were a director of the company

1.6

and, if so, tick box 1.7 if it was a close company

1.7

Income from employment

■ *Money* - see Notes, page EN3

- Payments from P60 (or P45)

  Before tax
  1.8 £

- Payments not on P60, etc. - tips

  1.9 £

  - other payments (excluding expenses entered below and lump sums and compensation payments or benefits entered overleaf)

  1.10 £

- **Tax deducted** in the UK from payments in boxes 1.8 to 1.10

  Tax deducted
  1.11 £

■ *Benefits and expenses* - see Notes, pages EN3 to EN6. If any benefits connected with termination of employment were received, or enjoyed, after that termination and were from a **former** employer you need to complete Help Sheet IR204, available from the Orderline. Do not enter such benefits here.

- Assets transferred/ payments made for you

  Amount
  1.12 £

- Vouchers, credit cards and tokens

  Amount
  1.13 £

- Living accommodation

  Amount
  1.14 £

- Excess mileage allowances and passenger payments

  Amount
  1.15 £

- Company cars

  Amount
  1.16 £

- Fuel for company cars

  Amount
  1.17 £

- Vans

  Amount
  1.18 £

- Taxable cheap loans
  see Note for box 1.19, page EN5

  Amount
  1.19 £

  box 1.20 is not used

- Private medical or dental insurance

  Amount
  1.21 £

- Other benefits

  Amount
  1.22 £

- Expenses payments received and balancing charges

  Amount
  1.23 £

SA101

BS 12/2002net

TAX RETURN ■ EMPLOYMENT: PAGE E1

Please turn over

PROFESSIONAL EDUCATION

Income from employment *continued*

■ *Lump sums and compensation payments or benefits including such payments and benefits from a former employer*
Note that 'lump sums' here includes any contributions which your employer made to an unapproved retirement benefits scheme

*You must read page EN6 of the Notes **before** filling in boxes 1.24 to 1.30*

Reliefs

- £30,000 exemption | **1.24** £
- Foreign service and disability | **1.25** £
- Retirement and death lump sums | **1.26** £

Taxable lump sums

- From box B of *Help Sheet IR204* | **1.27** £
- From box K of *Help Sheet IR204* | **1.28** £
- From box L of *Help Sheet IR204* | **1.29** £
- Tax deducted from payments in boxes 1.27 to 1.29 - *leave blank if this tax is included in the box 1.11 figure.* | Tax deducted **1.30** £

■ *Foreign earnings not taxable in the UK in the year ended 5 April 2004 - see Notes, page EN6* | **1.31** £

■ *Expenses you incurred in doing your job - see Notes, pages EN7 to EN8*

- Travel and subsistence costs | **1.32** £
- Fixed deductions for expenses | **1.33** £
- Professional fees and subscriptions | **1.34** £
- Other expenses and capital allowances | **1.35** £
- Tick box 1.36 if the figure in box 1.32 includes travel between your home and a permanent workplace | **1.36**

■ *Foreign Earnings Deduction* (seafarers only) | **1.37** £

■ *Foreign tax for which tax credit relief not claimed* | **1.38** £

Student Loans

■ *Student Loans repaid by deduction by employer - see Notes, page EN8* | **1.39** £

- Tick box 1.39A if your income is under Repayment of Teachers' Loans Scheme | **1.39A**

1.40 *Additional information*

*Now fill in any other supplementary Pages that apply to you.
Otherwise, go back to page 2 in your Tax Return and finish filling it in.*

Section 2

DATA

You work for a firm of Chartered Accountants in the tax department. One of your clients, Jeanette Alsop, has had three capital transactions during the year 2003/04.

1 **Shares**

In January 2004, Jeanette sold all her shares in Purple Ltd for £45,000. These shares do not qualify as business assets. Your records show that her transactions in the shares of Purple Ltd were as follows:

Date	Transaction	No of Shares	£
April 1986	Purchased	300	3,000
May 1990	Purchased	500	8,500
June 1992	Bonus issue	1 for 5	
April 1995	Purchased	1,000	16,000
March 2000	Sold	400	7,600

2 **Motor car**

In November 2003, Jeanette sold a twenty-year old car that she has owned since April 1995. She originally paid £600 for the car, but sold it for £8,500.

3 **Land**

Jeanette bought 10 acres of land as an investment in August 1996 for £80,000. In February 2004, she sold 4 acres of this land to property developer for £71,000. The remaining 6 acres were valued at £95,000 on the date of sale.

Jeanette Alsop also owns a variety of properties that she rents out. The total rent receivable from these properties totalled £4,800 for 2003/04, of which she had received £4,000 by 5th April 2004. Of the remaining £800, £500 was deemed irrecoverable. She also had Schedule A losses brought forward from 2002/03 of £1,600.

Task 2.1

Calculate the taxable gain or loss, after any taper relief, made on the disposal of the shares in Purple Ltd, if applicable.

....
....
....
....
....
....
....
....
....
....
....
....
....
....
....
....
....
....
....
....
....
....
....
....
....
....
....
....
....

Task 2.2

Calculate the taxable gain or loss, after any taper relief, made on the disposal of the car, if applicable.

....
....
....
....
....
....
....

Task 2.3

Calculate the taxable gain or allowable loss, after taper relief, made on the disposal of the land, if applicable.

....
....
....
....
....
....
....
....
....
....
....
....
....
....
....

Task 2.4

Calculate the Schedule A income chargeable to tax for 2003/04.

....
....
....
....

Task 2.5

Assuming Jeanette Alsop has no other income, calculate her tax liability for 2003/04, assuming that she is only entitled to the basic personal allowance.

....
....
....
....
....
....
....
....
....
....
....
....
....
....
....
....

Task 2.6

Jeanette Alsop informs you that when she completed her 2002/03 income tax return,

- She failed to declare £800 received from a building society
- All her other income in that tax year was taxed at basic rate, and totalled £300 short of the 40% tax band.

- As the building society interest had already suffered tax at source, she thought that she did not need to declare it.

She has heard that this was not the right thing to do, and she has sought your advice.

Using the headed paper provided write a memo to Jeanette Alsop advising her of the best course of action to take with regard to her dealings with the Inland Revenue, and the penalties, surcharges and/or interest she may have to pay when her mis-declaration is notified. You do not need to calculate the tax implications of this mistake.

MEMO

To: Jeanette Alsop

From: Accounting Technician

Date: 1 June 2004

Ref: Late declaration of income

TAXATION TABLES FOR PERSONAL TAX

Tax rates and bands

	%		£
Starting rate	10	first	1,960
Basic rate	22	next	28,540
Higher rate	40	over	30,500

Savings income taxed at 10%, 20% and 40%.

Dividends are taxed at 10% and 32.5%.

Personal allowances

Personal allowance	£4,615

Car fuel charge

Set figure £14,400

Inland revenue official rate

5%

Capital gains tax

Annual exemption	£7,900

Indexation factors:

April 1986 to May 1990	0.224
May 1990 to June 1992	0.111
June 1992 to April 1995	0.070
May 1990 to April 1995	0.181
April 1995 to April 1998	0.091
August 1996 to April 1998	0.062

Tapering relief for non-business assets:

Number of years held after 05/04/98	% of gain
2 or less	100
3	95
4	90
5	85
6	80
7	75
8	70

Answers to Practice Activities

Chapter 1 An outline of Income Tax

1 Income tax computation

(a) INCOME TAX COMPUTATION

	Non-savings £	Savings (excl dividend) £	Dividend £	Total £
Salary	45,000			
Dividend £900 × 100/90			1,000	
Schedule D Case III		496		
Bank deposit interest £800 × 100/80		1,000		
	45,000	1,496	1,000	
Less personal allowance	(4,615)			
Taxable income	40,385	1,496	1,000	42,881

(b)

	£
Tax on non-savings income	
£1,960 × 10%	196
£28,540 × 22%	6,279
£6,579 (extended band: see part (c)) × 22%	1,447
£3,306 × 40%	1,322
Tax on savings (excl dividend) income £1,496 × 40%	598
Tax on dividend income £1,000 × 32.5%	325
Tax liability	10,167
Less tax credit on dividend income	(100)
Less tax suffered on bank interest (£1,000 × 20%)	(200)
Less PAYE	(9,500)
Tax payable	367

Tutorial note 1. National Savings Bank interest is received gross.

Tutorial note 2. The basic rate band must be extended by the gross amount of any gift aid donation.

(c) The payment under the gift aid scheme is treated as though it were paid net of basic rate tax. Additional relief is given though the income tax computation: the basic rate band is extended by the gross amount of the gift aid donation. The gross amount of the gift aid donation is £5,132 × 100/78 = £6,579.

2 Mr Betteredge

(a)

	Non-savings	Savings (excl dividend)	Total
	£	£	£
Earnings £(12,105 + 2,960)	15,065		
Schedule D Case III		26	
Bank deposit interest × 100/80		571	
Building society interest × 100/80		500	
National savings certificates: exempt			
Mini cash ISA: exempt			
STI	15,065	1,097	16,162
Less personal allowance	(4,615)		
Taxable income	10,450	1,097	11,547

(b)

	£
Income tax on non-savings income	
£1,960 × 10%	196
£8,490 × 22%	1,868
Income tax on savings (excl dividend) income £1,097 × 20%	219
Income tax liability	2,283

Tutorial note 1. It is important to recognise which types of income are exempt from tax.

3 Selina

(a)

	Non-savings	Dividend	Total
	£	£	£
Salary	18,900		
Dividends × 100/90		331	
STI	18,900	331	19,231
Less personal allowance	(4,615)		
	14,285	331	14,616

(b)

	£
Income tax on non-savings income	
£1,960 × 10%	196
£12,325 × 22%	2,712
Income tax on dividend income	
£331 × 10%	33
Tax liability	2,941

(c) It would not be possible to offset the daughter's personal allowance against the income, because the income will be treated as her mother's until she reaches the age of 18 or marries. (The annual income on £20,000 would clearly exceed the £100 limit for income not to be treated as the parent's income.)

Tutorial note. The rule that income of an unmarried child under 18 arising from a parental disposition is treated as the parent's income is designed precisely to stop the use of a child's personal allowance in the way suggested in the question. However, it does not apply to income on gifts from other people.

4 Mrs Rogers

(a)

	Non-savings £	Savings (excl dividends) £	Dividends £	Total £
Salary	17,776			
Dividends (10,000 × £1.35 × 100/90)			15,000	
Interest on ISA – exempt				
Schedule D Case III		150		
Building society interest × 100/80		1,875		
STI	17,776	2,025	15,000	34,801
Less personal allowance	(4,615)			
Taxable income	13,161	2,025	15,000	30,186

Tutorial note 1. It is important to be aware of which items are exempt from income tax.

(b)

	£
Income tax on non-savings income	
£1,960 × 10%	196
£11,201 × 22%	2,464
Savings (excl dividend) income	
£2,025 × 20%	405
Dividend income	
£15,000 × 10%	1,500
	4,565
Less: tax deducted at source	
Tax credit on dividends	(1,500)
BSI	(375)
PAYE	(3,000)
Income tax repayable	(310)

5 Mrs Butcher

(a)   INCOME TAX COMPUTATION

	Non-savings £	Savings £	Dividends £	Total £
Pension	7,204			
Schedule A	5,776			
Interest on government stock		490		
Dividends £270 × 100/90			300	
Building society Interest £4,000 × 100/80		5,000		
STI	12,980	5,490	300	18,770
Less personal allowance	(4,615)	0		
Taxable income	8,365	5,490	300	14,155

Tutorial note 1. Don't forget to gross up any amounts that are received net of tax.

Tutorial note 2. Premium bond prizes are tax free.

(b)

Income tax payable:

	£
Starting rate: £1,960 × 10%	196
Basic rate (non-savings): £6,405 × 22%	1,409
Basic rate (savings): £5,490 × 20%	1,098
Basic rate (dividends): £300 × 10%	30
Tax liability	2,733
Less tax suffered:	
Tax credit on dividend income (£300 × 10%)	(30)
Tax deducted at source on building society interest (£5,000 × 20%)	(1,000)
Tax payable	1,703

6 Eric Wright

(a)   Eric

	Non-savings £	Savings (excl dividends) £	Dividends £	Total £
Sch DII	26,060			
BI £1,600 × 100/80		2,000		
STI	26,060	2,000	Nil	28,060
Less: PA	(4,615)			(4,615)
Taxable income	21,445	2,000	Nil	23,445

(b)   *Tax on non-savings income*

	£
£1,960 × 10%	196
£19,485 × 22%	4,287

Tax on savings (excluding dividend) income

	£
£2,000 × 20%	400
	4,883
Less: tax deducted at source	(400)
Tax due	4,483

Tutorial note. Eric will have paid the gift aid donation net of basic rate tax. As Eric is only a basic rate taxpayer the donation will have no further effect on the income tax computation.

(c)   Doreen

	Non-savings £	Dividends £	Total £
Pension	4,027		
Dividends (×$^{100}/_{90}$)		2,020	
STI	4,027	2,020	6,047
Less: PA	(4,027)	(588)	(4,615)
Taxable income	Nil	1,432	1,432

(d)

	£
£1,432 × 10%	143
Less: Tax Credit on dividends	(143)
Income tax payable (repayable)	–

Tutorial note. The tax credit on the dividends can be deducted to bring the tax payable down to £nil. However the excess tax credit (£202 – £143 = £59) cannot be rapaid.

7 Melanie Wong

(a)

	Non-savings £	Savings (excl dividends) £	Dividends £	Total £
Earnings	40,000			
Dividends £4,500 × 100/90			5,000	
NS Certificates interest – exempt				
STI	40,000	Nil	5,000	45,000
Less: PA	(4,615)			(4,615)
Taxable income	35,385	Nil	5,000	40,385

Tutorial note. Interest on the National Savings Certificate is exempt from income tax.

(b)   *Tax on non-savings income*

	£
£1,960 × 10%	196
£28,540 × 22%	6,279
(£1,170 × 10/78) = £1,500 × 22% (gift aid)	330
£3,385 × 40%	1,354
Tax on dividend income	
£5,000 × $32\frac{1}{2}$%	1,625
	9,784
Less: PAYE	(8,429)
dividend tax credit	(500)
Tax due	855

Tutorial note. The basic rate band is extended by the gross amount of the gift aid donation.

Chapter 2 The taxation of employment income

8 Cars and lunches

(a)   TOTAL ASSESSABLE BENEFITS

	£
Luncheon vouchers 50 × (£5 – 15p)	243
Meals in staff canteen	0
Car £25,000 × 25%	6,250
Fuel £14,400 × 25%	3,600
Assessable benefits	10,093

Tutorial note. As the staff canteen is open to all employees there is no taxable benefit in respect of the meals taken there.

Workings

1   *Taxable Percentage for car and fuel benefits*

Cars CO_2 emissions = 205g/km.

Amount above baseline 205 – 155 = 50g/km.

Divide by 5 = 10.

Taxable percentage = 15% + 10% = 25%.

(b)   The annual tax cost of the fuel benefit is £3,600 × 40% = £1,440.

The annual cost of petrol for private use would be 65p × 4,000/5 = £520.

Mr Sherman should therefore pay for all private petrol, saving £920 a year.

Tutorial note. The key here is to consider by how much in total Mr Sherman would be out of pocket under each of the two methods. He is clearly liable to tax at 40% in any case.

9 Directors

(a) **The use of a private house which cost £120,000**

Two calculations are required.

(i) The living accommodation benefit

	£
Annual value	2,000
Less contribution by director	(2,000)
	0

(ii) The additional charge for expensive accommodation

£(120,000 − 75,000) × 5%   £2,250

The total benefit is £2,250.

(b) **The purchase of a company asset at an undervalue**

The **benefit is the greater** of:

(i) The **asset's current market value**, and

(ii) The **asset's market value when first provided, less the total benefits taxed during the period of use**.

The acquisition price paid by the director is deducted from whichever of (i) and (ii) is used.

	£	£
Market value when first provided		3,500
Less: taxed in 1999/00 (20% of market value)	700	
taxed in 2000/01 (20% of market value)	700	
taxed in 2001/02 (20%)	700	
taxed in 2002/03 (20%)	700	
		(2,800)
		700

The figure of £700 is taken (as greater than the current market value of £600).

Benefit taxed in 2003/04

	£
Initial market value minus benefits already taxed	700
Less amount paid by director	(600)
Benefit	100

(c) **Taxable cheap loan to a director**

Using the average method produces a taxable benefit of £350.

$$\frac{£40,000 + £30,000}{2} \times (5\% - 4\%) = £350$$

Using the strict method the benefit would be.

£40,000 × 8/12 (5% − 4%) + £30,000 × 4/12 (5% − 4%) = £367

The Revenue usually only insist on the strict method being used when the average method is being deliberately exploited

(d) **The provision of medical insurance**

Under the residual charge, the taxable amount of a benefit for an employee earning £8,500 or more a year or a director is the cost to the employer of providing it. The benefit is thus £800.

(e) **Mercedes car**

The car was available for only seven months of the year so the benefit must be on a time basis.

£24,000 × 35% (W) × 7/12   £4,900

(f) **Computer**

	£
£3,900 × 20%	780
Less: de minimis	(500)
	280

Working

1   *Taxable percentage for car benefit*

CO_2 emissions = 255g/km
Emissions over baseline figure 255 − 155 = 100g/km
Divide by 5 = 20. Taxable % = 15 + 20 = 35%.

10 Taxable and exempt benefits

(a) As the loan to Zoë Dexter does not exceed £5,000, this is not a taxable loan.

(b) The annual value of the computer equipment lent to Victoria Eustace is 20% × £2,000 = £400. The first £500 of any annual benefit that would otherwise arise in respect of the private use of a computer by an employee is exempt. This means there is no taxable benefit.

(c) The taxable benefit arising in respect of the car and fuel is:

	£
Car (£17,250 × 15%) × 10/12	2,156
Fuel (£14,400 × 15%) × 10/12	1,800
	3,956

Tutorial note 1. The car and fuel benefits are both multiplied by 10/12 as the car was available for only ten months throughout 2003/04.

Tutorial note 2. The car benefit is based on the original cost of the car, not the market value when first provided to Amanda.

Tutorial note 3. As the car emits CO_2 of 155g/km the taxable percentage used for calculating the car and fuel benefit is 15%.

(d)   The taxable amount in respect of the car and fuel is:

	£
Car (£16,000 × 30%)	4,800
Fuel (£14,400 × 30%)	4,320
	9,120

Tutorial note 1. The car emits 230g/km of CO_2, This is 75g/km above the baseline emissions of 155 g/km.

This means the taxable percentage is 15% + 75/5% = 30%. CO_2

Tutorial note 2. The fuel benefit is not reduced by partial reimbursements of the cost of private fuel.

(e)   The private use of a mobile telephone is an exempt benefit.

11 Accommodation

The taxable benefit for Mr Ford will be equal to the annual value of the flat and of the furniture. The company's payment of the council tax will also be a taxable benefit:

	£
Basic accommodation benefit: Rateable value	900
Additional benefit £(100,000 − 75,000) × 5%	1,250
Furniture (20% × £5,000)	1,000
Council tax	500
	3,650

As Charles Rainer's accommodation is job-related he is not taxable on either the accommodation or the council tax paid by the company.

Tutorial note. If accommodation is job related there is no taxable benefit in respect of the accommodation or of any council tax paid by the employer.

12 Rita

	£
Accommodation (W1)	21,200
Relocation (£12,000 − £8,000)	4,000
Loan (£10,000 × 5%)	500
Taxable benefits	25,700

Workings

1   *Accommodation*

		£
Annual value (higher than rent paid)		4,000
Electricity		700
Gas		1,200
Water		500
Council tax		1,300
Repairs		3,500
Furniture (20% × £30,000 × 6/12)		3,000
Purchase (W2)		7,000
		21,200

2   *Purchase of furniture*

Benefit is the higher of:

			£
(i)	Cost		30,000
	Less: taxed		(3,000)
			27,000
	Less: amount paid		(20,000)
			7,000
(ii)	Market value		25,000
	Less: amount paid		(20,000)
			5,000

ie £7,000

13 Sally

(a)   SCHEDULE: DEDUCTIBLE EXPENSES

   (i)   **Expenses other than professional subscriptions**

      Business calls on home telephone   £270

   (ii)   **Professional subscriptions**

      Chartered Institute of Marketing £50

(b)

MEMORANDUM

To: Sally
From: Richard
Date: 12 April 2004
Subject: Tax-deductibility of expenses

The tax treatment of your expenses is as follows.

(i)   Rail fare: no deduction, because the cost of travelling from home to work is the cost of your ordinary commuting to work. If you were only working at the new location on a temporary basis (up to 24 months), the cost would be deductible.

(ii)   Telephone bill: the cost of business calls is deductible. However, it is not possible to apportion the line rental between business and private use and claim a deduction for the business proportion.

(iii)   Subscription to the Chartered Institute of Marketing: this is deductible under a special rule relating to subscriptions to professional bodies relevant to your job. The fact that you are a member in order to put yourself in a position to perform your duties better does not matter.

(iv)   Subscriptions to professional journals: not deductible, because you read them in order to put yourself in a position to perform your duties better. You do not read them in performing your duties.

(v)   Subscription to a London club: not deductible, because the subscription is not necessary in order to enable you to perform your duties.

14 Bill Wilson

(a)   **Bill Wilson – Taxable income 2003/04**

	Non-savings income £	Savings (excl. dividends) income £	Dividend income £	Total income £
Salary	29,750			
Car benefit (W2)	3,300			
Fuel benefit (W3)	2,376			
Job seekers allowance	1,025			
Dividends £1,350 × 100/90			1,500	
Interest £360 × 100/80		450		
National Savings Bank – received gross		110		
3.5% War Loan – received gross		250		
STI	36,451	810	1,500	38,761
Less: PA	(4,615)			(4,615)
Taxable income	31,836	810	1,500	34,146

(b)   **Tax payable 2003/04**

		£
Non-savings income		
£1,960 × 10%		196
£28,540 × 22%		6,279
£400 × 22% (Gift Aid)		88
£(31,836 − 30,500 − 400) = £936 × 40%		374
Savings (excluding dividends) income		
£810 × 40%		324
Dividend income		
£1,500 × 32.5%		488
Tax liability		7,749
Less: tax on dividends £1,500 × 10%		(150)
tax on bank interest £450 × 20%		(90)
Tax payable (before PAYE)		7,509

Workings

1   *Taxable car and fuel %*

CO$_2$ emissions above baseline

190 g/km(rounded down to nearest below) − 155 g/km = 35 g/km

Divide by 5 = 35/5 = 7

% = 15% + 7% = 22%

2   *Car benefit*

22% (W1) × £20,000 × 9/12 =   £3,300

3   *Fuel benefit*

£14,400× 22% (W1) × 9/12 =   £2,376

(c)   **Amounts left out of calculation**

(i)   Dividends from ISA investments – not taxable.

(ii)   Interest from ISA – not taxable.

(iii) Termination payment – not provided under a contractual obligation and less than £30,000.

(d)   **Four expenses deductible from employment income**

Any four from:

(i)   Contributions (within certain limits) to an approved occupational pension scheme

(ii)   Subscriptions to professional bodies if relevant to occupation

(iii) Payments for certain liabilities and insurance against them

(iv)   Mileage allowance relief

(v)   Qualifying travel expenses

(vi)   Other expenses incurred wholly, exclusively and necessarily in the performance of the duties of the employment

(vii)   Amounts given under the payroll giving scheme.

Chapter 3 Employment income: Additional aspects

15 Ian Warburton

	£
Salary (£1,365 × 100/105 × 4) + (£1,365 × 8)	16,120
Car benefit £11,000 × 25% (W)	2,750
Petrol benefit (partial contribution ignored) £14,400 × 25% (W)	3,600
Bonus	1,000
	23,470
Less pension contributions £16,120 × 3%	(484)
Taxable earnings	22,986

Tutorial note. Contributions to occupational pension schemes can be deducted in arriving at taxable income. Contributions to personal pension plans on the other hand, extend the basic rate income tax band.

Working

1   *Taxable percentage for car and fuel benefits*

CO_2 emissions = 205g/km (Rounded down to nearest 5 below)
Above baseline 205 − 155 = 50g/km
Divide by 5 = 10
Taxable percentage = 15% + 10% = 25%

16 David

David Rogers Esq
1 High Street
Marlow
Bucks

20 April 2004

Dear Mr Rogers

Personal pension contributions

Further to your query regarding personal pensions I have set out below the rules which now apply in respect of personal pension contributions.

With the exception of some members of company pension schemes, anyone who is under the age of 75 can make contributions to a stakeholder pension plan. Any individual can contribute up to £3,600 (gross) in any tax year to a pension scheme regardless of the level of their earnings. It is worth noting that, this means that £3,600 could be paid into a pension scheme for your wife Sue, regardless of the fact that she has no earnings. If contributions are to be higher than £3,600 (gross) per tax year the maximum contribution that can be paid depends on your age at the start of the tax year and, broadly, the level of your self employed earnings in the current tax year or any one of the five previous tax years as shown in the table below.

Age on 6 April in tax year	Maximum % of net relevant earnings that may be paid
35 or under	17$\frac{1}{2}$%
36 – 45	20%
46 – 50	25%
51 – 55	30%
56 – 60	35%
61 or over	40%

Any contributions made to a personal pension scheme are paid net of basic rate (22%) income tax. If you remain a basic rate income tax payer there will be no need for you to take any further action in respect of your pension contributions. If you become a higher rate (40%) taxpayer you will be able to claim additional tax relief on your pension contributions through your income tax return.

There is some flexibility in which year tax relief is claimed for a pension contribution. Provided you pay a contribution before 31 January in a tax year, and elect at the same time to carry it back, the contribution can be treated as though it were paid (and therefore eligible to tax relief) in the previous tax year.

I hope the above is helpful. If you have any further queries please do not hesitate to contact me.

Yours sincerely

A N Accountant

17 Stakeholder pensions

(a) Maximum contributions

Tax year	Age at start of tax year	Basis year	%	Maximum contribution £
2003/04	42	2003/04	20	5,000
2004/05	43	2004/05	20	16,000
2005/06	44	2004/05	20	16,000
2006/07	45	2004/05	20	16,000
2007/08	46	2004/05	25	20,000
2008/09	47	2004/05	25	20,000
2009/10	48	2004/05	25	20,000
2010/11	49	2007/08	25	18,750

Note. The % depends on age at *start of the tax year of contribution* not on age at the start of the basis year.

(b) **Personal pension contributions are paid net of basic rate tax**. This means that for a basic rate taxpayer tax relief is given at source and there is no need to take any further action.

Higher rate taxpayers obtain additional relief through their personal tax computation. The basic rate band is extended by the gross amount of the pension contribution.

18 Roger Thesaurus

(a) **Income tax computation**

	Non-savings £	Savings (excl. dividend) £	Dividend £	Total £
Schedule D Case I	57,000			
Dividend (£900 × 100/90)			1,000	
Bank interest £1,197 × 100/80		1,496		
	57,000	1,496	1,000	
Less charges: copyright royalty	(6,000)			
STI	51,000	1,496	1,000	53,496
Less personal allowance	(4,615)			
	46,385	1,496	1,000	48,881

Tutorial note. In Unit 19 you will not be expected to compute Schedule D Case I income but you may, as here, be expected to include it in the income tax computation.

£

Tax on non-savings income

£1,960 × 10%	196
£28,540 × 22%	6,279
£15,000 (extended band) × 22%	3,300
£885 × 40%	354

Tax on savings (excl. dividend) income

£1,496 × 40%	598

Tax on dividend income

£1,000 × 32.5%	325
Tax liability	11,052
Less tax suffered on bank interest £1,496 × 20%	(299)
tax credit on dividends £1,000 × 10%	(100)
Tax payable	10,653

(b) As 1998/99 was the basis year, the maximum gross pension premium relievable in 2003/04 is 20% × £80,000, ie £16,000.

The basic rate band is extended by the gross amount of the premium actually paid, £15,000 (£11,700 × $^{100}/_{78}$).

The copyright royalty qualifies for tax relief as a charge on income. The royalty is paid gross.

Tutorial note. Note that the % for personal pension purposes depends on Mr Thesaurus' age at the **start** of 2003/04.

19 PAYE forms

(a) Following the end of each tax year, the employer must send the Revenue:

(i) by 19 May:

- **End of year Returns P14** (showing the same details as the P60);
- **Form P35** (summary of tax and NI deducted).

(ii) by 6 July:

- **Forms P11D** (benefits etc for directors and employees paid £8,500+ pa);
- **Forms P9D** (benefits etc for other employees).

(b) At the end of each tax year, the employer must provide each employee with a form P60. This shows total taxable emoluments for the year, tax deducted, code number, NI number and the employer's name and address. The P60 must be provided by 31 May following the year of assessment.

(c) When an employee leaves, a certificate on form P45 (particulars of Employee Leaving) must be prepared. This form shows the employee's code and details of his income and tax paid to date and is a four part form. One part is sent to the Revenue, and three parts handed to the employee. One of the parts (part 1A) is the employee's personal copy. If the employee takes up a new employment, he must hand the other two parts of the form P45 to the new employer. The new employer will fill in details of the new employment and send one part to the Revenue, retaining the other. The details on the form are used by the new employer to calculate the PAYE due on the next payday.

20 Frederick Fuse

Task 1

TAXABLE EARNINGS 2003/04

		£	£
Salary			41,000
Benefits:			
	Car £14,003 × 25% (W1)	3,501	
	Fuel £14,400 × 25% (W1)	3,600	
	Private medical insurance	965	
	Entertainment	3,000	
	Home telephone: (£100 + £600)	700	
	Computer (£10,000 × 20% × 4/12 – £500)	167	
			11,933
			52,933
Less:	Claim for expenses wholly, exclusively and necessarily in the course of employment		
	Telephone calls (50% × £600)	300	
	Entertaining	2,900	
			(3,200)
Taxable earnings			49,733

Tutorial notes

1   The employee is taxed on the cost to the employer of providing the private medical insurance.

2   An employee is taxable of any amount reimbursed for expenses, such as in respect of entertaining or the use of a home telephone. However, he can then claim tax relief for any expense incurred wholly, exclusively and necessarily in the course of the employment. The rental of a home phone line cannot be the subject of such a claim although the charge for business calls can.

3   For assets made available for private use there is, in general, a taxable benefit of 20% per annum of the asset's market value when it was first made available. However, the first £500 of any such benefit calculated in respect of the private use of a computer is exempt from tax.

Working

1   *Car and fuel taxable percentage*
     CO_2 emissions = 205g/km (rounded down to nearest 5)
     Excess over baseline figure 205 – 155 = 50g/km
     Divide by × 5 = 10
     Taxable percentage = 15 + 10 = 25%

Task 2

	Non-savings	Savings (excl dividend)	Dividend	Total
	£	£	£	£
Earnings (Part (a))	49,733			
Savings income:				
Dividends			3,700	
Buildings society interest		5,625		
ISA – exempt		0		
Bank interest		1,375		
National Savings Bank		95		
STI	49,733	7,095	3,700	60,528
Less: Personal allowance	(4,615)			
	45,118	7,095	3,700	55,913

Task 3

		£
Income tax on non-savings income		
£1,960 × 10%		196
£28,540 × 22%		6,279
£2,538 × 22% (extended basic rate band)		558
£12,080 × 40%		4,832
Income tax on savings (excl dividend) income		
£7,095 × 40%		2,838
Income tax on dividend income		
£3,700 × 32.5%		1,203
		15,906
Less: Tax credit on dividend income	370	
PAYE	13,600	
Savings income	1,400	
		(15,370)
Tax payable		536

Tutorial note 1. National Savings Bank interest is received gross.

Tutorial note 2. The basic rate band is extended by the gross amount of the personal pension contribution, £2,538, (£165 × 12 × 100/78).

Task 4

If Mr Fuse contributes £100 per month towards the private use of his car, the taxable value of the car benefit will be reduced by £100 a month.

There will be no reduction of the taxable value of the fuel benefit unless Mr Fuse pays the full cost of the private fuel. Therefore, if he contributes £10 a month towards the private fuel there will be no reduction in the taxable value of the fuel benefit.

21 The Benns

(a) INCOME TAX COMPUTATION FOR MR BENN

	Non-savings £	Savings (excl dividends) £	Dividends £	Total £
Taxable earnings £(40,720 + 5,000)	45,720			
Building society interest × 100/80		400		
Dividends (given gross)			230	
Bank interest £(51 + 56) × 100/80		134		
STI	45,720	534	230	46,484
Less personal allowance	(4,615)	0	0	
Taxable income	41,105	534	230	41,869

Tutorial note. Interest arising on the ISA account is ignored as it is exempt.

(b) Income tax

	£
Non-savings income	
£1,960 × 10%	196
£28,540 × 22%	6,279
£10,605 (W1) × 22%	2,333
Savings (excl dividend) income	
£534 (W1) × 20%	107
Dividend income	
£15 (W1) × 10%	2
£215 × 32.5%	70
	8,987

Tax liability

Working

1 **Basic rate band**

The basic rate band is extended by the gross amount of the pension contribution made by Mr Benn:

£8,700 × 100/78 = £11,154

(c)   INCOME TAX COMPUTATION FOR MRS BENN

	Non-savings £	Dividends £	Total £
Schedule D Case I	9,800		
Dividends (given gross)		100	
	9,800	100	
Less: Charge on income (£780 × 100/78)	(1,000)		
	8,800	100	8,900
Less personal allowance	(4,615)	0	
Taxable income	4,185	100	4,285

Tutorial note. Patent royalties are paid net of basic rate tax and so must be grossed up by multiplying $^{100}/_{78}$ in the income tax box.

(d)   **Income tax liability**   £

Non-savings income

Starting rate band £1,960 × 10%   196

Basic rate band: non-savings income £2,225 × 22%   490

Dividend income

£100 × 10%   10

                                                                                                              696

Chapter 4 Investments and land

22 Tax rates

Tutorial note. A fairly simple explanation was appropriate, as the question clearly came from a layman.

Technicians & Co
14 Duke Street
Notown
NT4 5AZ

A Smith Esq
23 Charles Street
Anytown
AN1 4BQ

3 October 2003

Dear Anthony

Thank you for your letter of 1 October.

You are correct in your statement that dividends are received net of a 10% tax credit and building society interest is received net of 20% tax. However, although it may seem rather odd, there are special rules for taxing dividend and interest income which means that only higher rate taxpayers have to pay extra tax on of these types of income.

Any dividend income received must be grossed up by multiplying it by 100/90. The gross dividend is then included in the income tax computation and the gross amount is either taxed at 10% or at 32.5%. Higher rate taxpayers have to pay tax on dividend income at 32.5%. However, other taxpayers such as yourself, pay tax on dividend income at 10% which means that the tax liability is exactly matched by the 10% tax credit and there is no extra tax to pay.

Building society interest must be grossed up by multiplying it by 100/80. The gross amount is included in the income tax computation and is taxed at 10%, 20% or at 40%. Higher rate taxpayers pay tax at 40%, basic rate taxpayers pay tax at 20% and starting rate taxpayers pay tax at 10%. Again, for a basic rate taxpayer such as yourself this means that the tax liability is exactly matched by the tax deducted at source. A starting rate taxpayer would receive a tax repayment.

This may be best illustrated by the following example.

Suppose that four individuals, W, X, Y and Z each receive dividend income of £90 and building society interest of £80 (net). The other income of these four individuals is as follows:

Individual	Other income £	Personal allowance £	Marginal tax rate %
W	0	4,615	0
X	5,400	4,615	10
Y	15,000	4,615	22
Z	60,000	4,615	40

The tax positions of the four individuals are as follows.

W: a non-taxpayer

W cannot reclaim the tax credit of £10 attached to the dividend but he can reclaim the £20 tax suffered on the building society interest. Overall W gets £190 (£90 + £80 + £20) in his pocket.

X: a 10% taxpayer

X will have to pay tax at 10% on both his gross dividend income and his gross interest. The liability on the dividend income is exactly matched by the tax credit so there is no tax payable by X. However, there will be a repayment of the excess tax suffered on the building society interest. Overall X gets £180 (£90 + £80 + £10) in his pocket.

Y: a 22% taxpayer

Y will have to pay tax at 10% on his gross dividend income and tax at 20% on his gross interest. These liabilities are exactly matched by the tax credit/tax deducted at source so there is no tax to pay by Y. Overall Y gets £170 (£80 + £90) in his pocket.

Z: a 40% taxpayer

Z will have to pay tax at 32.5% on his gross dividend income and at 40% on his gross interest. Relief will be allowed for the tax credit/tax deducted at source

	Dividend £100 £	Interest £100 £
Gross income		
Tax @ 32.5%/40%	32.50	40
Less: tax credit/suffered	(10.00)	(20)
Extra tax to pay	22.50	20

Overall Z will get £127.50 (£90 + £80 – £22.50 – £20) in his pocket.

I hope that this letter explains the position to you, even if it leaves you feeling that the rules are illogical!

Yours sincerely

Hilary Jones

Hilary Jones

23 Dividends

Company	Net dividend £	Tax credit £	Gross dividend £
A plc	520	58	578
B plc	600	67	667
C plc	420	47	467
D plc	1,280	142	1,422

Tutorial notes

1. Faced with this sort of problem, you need to take great care to get the relationship of ex dividend dates to purchase and sale dates right. You may find it helpful to make a list of relevant dates in your workings.

2. The tax credit in each case is 10/90 of the net dividend.

3. The purchase of 10,000 B plc shares was made after the ex dividend date for the dividend paid on 1 December 2003. The total dividend is therefore (2,000 × 6p) + (12,000 × 4p) = £600.

4. A percentage preference dividend (in this case 7%) is a *net* dividend: 24,000 × 25p × 7% = £420. The rate of interest on securities, on the other hand, is quoted *gross*.

5. The sale of 12,000 D plc shares was after the ex dividend date for the dividend paid on 5 September 2003. The total dividend is therefore (25,000 × 2p) + (13,000 × 6p) = £1,280.

24 Peter

PETER: SCHEDULE A INCOME

	£	£	£
First house			
Rent £4,000 × 9/12			3,000
Second house			
Rent £600 × 3		1,800	
Rent £2,100 × 1/3		700	
		2,500	
Less: water rates £390 × 6/12	195		
insurance £440 × 6/11	240		
interest £37,000 × 10% × 6/12	1,850		
repairs: capital	0		
furniture: in 2003/04	0		
		2,285	
			215
Schedule A income			3,215

Tutorial note. Schedule A income is taxed on an accruals basis.

25 Mr and Mrs Faulds

Tutorial note. As you were asked to draft short notes you could write your answer in bullet point form.

Notes for meeting regarding individual savings accounts (ISAs)

- Investments within an ISA are exempt from both income and capital gains tax.

- There is no statutory minimum period for which an ISA must be held. A full or partial withdrawal may be made at any time without loss of the tax exemption.

- To open an ISA an investor must, in general, be aged 18 or over. However, a cash ISA can be held by individuals aged 16 or 17.

- ISAs can be made up of three components.

  - Cash
  - Life insurance
  - Stocks and shares

- There are three distinct types of ISA:

  (a) **Maxi-accounts** which must contain a stocks and shares component and may contain the other two components (either one or both):

  (b) **Mini-accounts** which comprise a single component only; and

  (c) **TESSA only** accounts, which consist of a cash component and can only accept subscriptions by way of transfers from matured tax exempt special savings accounts (TESSAs). The maximum investment is equal to the capital deposited in the TESSA.

- A **'maxi-account'**, must contain a stocks and shares component with or without other components. Subscribing to a maxi-account in one year precludes an investor from also subscribing to a mini-account of any type in that year. Investment in a TESSA only account in the same year is not, however, prohibited. **There is an annual subscription limit for maxi-accounts of £7,000 of which a maximum of £3,000 can be in cash and £1,000 in life insurance.** A husband and wife each have their own limits.

- A **mini-account** comprises a single component only. Once a mini-account, for any component, has been subscribed to for a particular tax year the only other ISAs that may be subscribed to for that year are other mini-accounts comprising different components and a TESSA only account. **The annual subscription limits for mini-accounts are:**

  (a)   Cash component accounts; £3,000
  (b)   Insurance component accounts; £1,000
  (c)   Stocks and shares component accounts; £3,000

26 William Wiles

(a)   (i)   The houses qualify to be treated as a trade under the furnished holiday letting rules, because they were:

(1)   **let furnished on a commercial basis with a view to the realisation of profits.**

(2)   available for commercial letting to the public **for at least 140 days** during 2003/04 (294 days and 224 days respectively).

(3)   **on average let for at least 70 days**. House 2 satisfies this test since the average for the two houses is 77 days.

(4)   **not occupied by the same person for more than 31 days for at least seven months** during 2003/04.

The tax advantages are that:

(1)   **Relief for losses is available as if they were trading losses**, including the facility to set losses against other income. The usual Schedule A loss reliefs do not apply.

(2)   **Capital allowances are available on furniture**.

(3)   **The income qualifies as net relevant earnings for personal pension relief.**

(4)   Capital gains tax **rollover relief, relief for gifts of business assets** and **business assets taper relief are all available.**

(ii) The Schedule A loss on the furnished holiday lets must be calculated separately to the Schedule A loss arising on the other accommodation.

Schedule A loss on furnished holiday lets:

	£	£
Rental income		
House 1 (14 × £375)		5,250
House 2 (8 × £340)		2,720
		7,970
Expenses		
Business rates (£730 + £590)	1,320	
Insurance (£310 + £330)	640	
Advertising (£545 + £225)	770	
Repairs	6,250	
Capital allowances		
House 1 (£6,500 × 40%)	2,600	
House 2 (£6,500 × 40%)	2,600	
Private use (re house 1)		
(£730 + £310 + £2,600) × 10/52	(700)	
		(13,480)
Schedule A loss		(5,510)

Schedule A loss on other lettings:

	£	£
Rental income		
House 3 (£8,600 × 3/12)		2,150
Expenses		
Loan interest	3,200	
Repairs	710	
Wear and tear allowance (£2,150 × 10%)	215	
		(4,125)
Schedule A loss		1,975

Tutorial note. No capital allowance available on lettings other that furnished holiday lettings. In Unit 19 you will not be expected to compute the amount of capital allowances but you may need to deduct capital allowances in arriving at net rental income, as here.

William can claim to have the Schedule A loss of £5,510 arising in respect of furnished holiday accommodation set off as if they were trading losses including the ability to set them off against his total income.

The Schedule A loss of £1,975 will be carried forward and set against the first available Schedule A profits.

Chapters 5 and 6 Capital gains tax

27 Oregon

(a) **The table**

	£
Proceeds	40,000
Less cost	(7,000)
	33,000
Less indexation allowance to April 1998	(5,523)

$$\frac{162.6 - 90.9}{90.9} = 0.789 \times £7,000$$

Chargeable gain before taper relief	27,477

The table is a non-business asset which has been owned for six years for taper relief purposes, so the taxable gain after taper relief is £21,982 (£27,477 × 80%)

Tutorial note. Non business assets qualify for an additional year for taper relief purposes if they were owned on 17 March 1998.

(b) **The picture**

	£
Proceeds	75,000
Less cost	(37,000)
	38,000
Less indexation allowance to April 1998	(38,776)

$$\frac{162.6 - 79.4}{79.4} = 1.048 \times £37,000$$

	nil

The chargeable gain is nil. Indexation cannot convert a gain into a loss.

(c) **The land**

	£
Proceeds	120,000
Less expenses of sale	(2,500)
	117,500
Less: cost	(57,000)
expenditure in 2000	(4,000)
expenditure in May 2002	(3,800)
	52,700

The chargeable gain before taper relief is £52,700. This is a non-business asset which has been held for five years, so the taxable gain after taper relief is £44,795 (£52,700 × 85%).

(d)

	£
Table (part (a))	21,982
Picture (part (b))	Nil
Land (part (c))	44,795
Chargeable gains	66,777
Less annual exemption	(7,900)
Taxable gains	58,877

(e)

Capital gains tax liability £58,877 × 40%	£23,551

Tutorial note. With income of £80,000, Oregon is clearly a higher rate tax payer and will, therefore, pay CGT at 40%.

28 John Lewis

(a)   JOHN LEWIS: TAXABLE GAINS

	£
Motor car: exempt asset	0
Gain on investment property (W1)	35,000
	35,000
Less allowable loss on part disposal (W2)	(300)
	34,700
Less loss brought forward (W3)	(1,500)
Net taxable gains before taper relief	33,200

(b)

	£
Gain after taper relief (95%) (see note)	31,540
Less annual exemption	(7,900)
Taxable gains	23,640

Tutorial note 1. Taper relief reduces the gain on the investment property to 95% of the amount chargeable. There are three complete years of ownership post 5.4.1998.

Tutorial note 2. Taper relief applies to chargeable gains after deduction of any losses of the same tax year and any losses carried forward from earlier years.

(c)   (i)   CGT with income of £6,000

The income will be partly covered by the personal allowance, with the rest £1,385 (£6,000 − £4,615) taxable at the starting rate of tax. £575 (£1,960 − £1,385) of the gains fall within the starting rate band and are taxable at 10%. The rest fall within the basic rate band, and are taxable at 20%.

The capital gains tax liability will be as follows.

	£
£575 × 10%	58
£23,065 × 20%	4,613
	4,671

(ii)   CGT with income of £34,480

	£
Income	34,480
Less personal allowance	(4,615)
Taxable income	29,865
Basic rate limit	(30,500)
	(635)

Remaining basic rate band

CGT:	£635 × 20%	127
	£23,005 £(23,640 – 635) × 40%	9,202
Capital gains tax liability		9,329

Workings

1   The disposal of the investment property

	£
Proceeds	60,000
Less cost	(25,000)
Gain before taper relief	35,000

2   The part disposal of the field

	£
Proceeds (£125,000 – £300)	124,700
Less probate value of part disposal $\dfrac{125,000}{125,000+375,000} \times £500,000$	(125,000)
Allowable loss	(300)

3   Losses brought forward

Year	Current year net gains £	Loss brought forward set off £	Annual exemption £
2001/02	7,000	0	7,500
2002/03	8,700	1,000	7,700
		1,000	
Loss brought forward at 6.4.01		2,500	
Loss brought forward to 2003/04		1,500	

29 Wyoming

(a)   TAXABLE INCOME

	Non-savings £
Income	20,150
Less personal allowance	(4,615)
Taxable income	15,535

(b)   INCOME TAX

	£
Non-savings income	
£1,960 × 10%	196
£13,575 × 22%	2,987
15,535	3,183

(c)   CAPITAL GAINS AFTER TAPER RELIEF

	£
Gains	
Picture (80%)	11,600
Shares (80%)	16,000
	27,600
Less annual exemption	(7,900)
Taxable gains	19,700

The picture and the shares are both non-business assets which have been held for 6 years (including the additional year) so 80% of the gains are chargeable after taper relief.

Tutorial note. The motor car and the gilt edged securities are exempt assets so no allowable loss or chargeable gain arises on them.

(d)   CAPITAL GAINS TAX

	£
£14,965 (£30,500 – £15,535) × 20%	2,993
£4,735 × 40%	1,894
19,700	4,887

30 Washington

Tutorial note. Losses carried back on death or carried forward during lifetime never waste the annual exemption.

Before Washington's death, the position would have been as follows.

	£
2000/01	
Gains	2,000
Less losses	(2,000)
Taxable gains	0
Losses carried forward	8,000

2001/02

Gains	32,500
Less current year losses	(4,500)
	28,000
Less losses brought forward	(8,000)
	20,000
Less annual exemption	(7,500)
Taxable gains	12,500

2002/03

Gains	9,900
Less losses	(2,000)
	7,900
Less annual exemption	(7,700)
Taxable gains	200

Following Washington's death, the position would be as follows.

£

2003/04

Gains	15,000
Less losses	(15,000)
Taxable gains	0

Losses to carry back	12,000

Year	Original taxable gains £	Losses brought back £	Final taxable gains £
2000/01	0	0	0
2001/02	12,500	11,800	700
2002/03	200	200	0
		12,000	

31 Alison Garry

Task 1

Cottage 1 £

Proceeds net of fees	92,082
Less cost	(41,000)
	51,082

Less indexation allowance to April 1998 $\frac{162.6-84.8}{84.8}$ = 0.917 × £41,000 (37,597)

Chargeable gain before taper relief 13,485

Task 2

	£
Cottage 2	
Proceeds net of fees £(85,000 − 850 − 1,500)	82,650
Less Cost	(30,000)
Enhancement expenditure (June 1983)	(10,000)
	42,650
Less indexation allowance to April 1998 $\dfrac{162.6 - 79.4}{79.4} = 1.048 \times £30,000$	(31,440)
£10,000 × 0.917 (see task 1)	(9,170)
Chargeable gain before taper relief	2,040

Task 3

	£
Gains after taper relief £(13,485 + 2,040) × 80%	12,420
Less annual exemption	(7,900)
Taxable gains	4,520
CGT £4,520 × 40%	£1,808

Chapter 7 Shares and securities

32 Eleanor

Post 6.4.98 acquisitions are treated as disposed of on a LIFO basis:

   (i)   3.11.01 acquisition

	£
Proceeds (2,000/11,000) × £66,000)	12,000
Less: Cost	(12,800)
Allowable loss	(800)

   (ii)   29.6.00 acquisition

	£
Proceeds (3,000/11,000 × £66,000)	18,000
Less: Cost	(17,500)
Gain	500

No taper relief as the shares had been owned for less that three years for taper relief purposes.

(iii)   The FA 1985 pool

	Shares	Cost £	Indexed cost £
Acquisition 19.9.82	2,000	1,700	1,700
Indexation to April 1985			
$\dfrac{94.8 - 81.9}{81.9} = 0.158 \times £1,700$			269
Acquisition 17.1.85	2,000	6,000	6,000
Indexation to April 1985			
$\dfrac{94.8 - 91.2}{91.2} = 0.039 \times £6,000$			234
	4,000	7,700	8,203
Indexed rise to December 1985			
$\dfrac{96.0 - 94.8}{94.8} \times £8,203$			104
Acquisition 12.12.85	2,000	5,500	5,500
	6,000	13,200	13,807
Indexed rise to April 1998			
$\dfrac{162.6 - 96.0}{96.0} \times £13,807$			9,579
Value when pool closes (5.4.98)	6,000	13,200	23,386
Disposal 17.5.03	(6,000)	(13,200)	(23,386)
	0	0	0

	£
Proceeds $\dfrac{6,000}{11,000} \times £66,000$	36,000
Less cost	(13,200)
	22,800
Less indexation allowance £(23,386 − 13,200)	(10,186)
Chargeable gain before taper relief	12,614

The loss is first deducted from the gain of £500 as this does not qualify for taper relief. The balance of the loss, £300, is then deducted from the above gain before taper relief is applied.

There are six complete years of ownership (including the additional year) post 5 April 1998 so the gain remaining after taper relief but before the annual exemption is £9,851 (80% (£12,614 − £300)).

Tutorial note. Losses should be set against gains where the largest percentage of the gain remains chargeable after taper relief.

33 Yvonne

The sale of Yvonne's shares is initially matched with the shares bought in the next 30 days.

	£
Proceeds (1,000/5,000)	4,600
Less: cost (28.3.04)	(4,400)
Chargeable gain	200

No taper relief.

Next the shares are matched with the post 6.4.98 acquisition.

	£
Proceeds (2,000/5,000)	9,200
Less: cost (19.9.01)	(5,000)
Gain	4,200

No taper relief due.

Finally the shares are matched with the FA1985 pool.

	No	Cost £	Indexed cost £
18.8.95	3,000	6,000	6,000
Index to April 1998			
£6,000 × 0.085			510
Pool at April 1998	3,000	6,000	6,510

	£
Disposal proceeds (2,000/5,000)	9,200
Less: cost (2,000/3,000 × £6,000)	(4,000)
	5,200
Less: indexation (2,000/3,000 (6,510 – 6,000))	(340)
Gain before taper relief	4,860
Gain after taper relief (80%)	£3,888

Yvonne's total gain before the annual exemption is £8,288 (£3,888 + £4,200 + £200).

34 James Ramesty

(a) **Capital gains before taper relief**

Sale of holiday cottage

		£
Proceeds		160,028
Less:	Legal fees	(2,000)
	Estate agent's fees	(1,000)
		157,028
Less cost		(30,000)
		127,028

Less: Indexation allowance to April 1998 £30,000 $\times \dfrac{162.6 - 86.4}{86.4} = (0.882)$ (26,460)

Chargeable gain before taper relief   100,568

For taper relief purposes the holiday cottage was held for 6 years (including the additional year). This means that 80% of the gain remains chargeable after taper relief.

Sale of shares

The disposal of shares is initially matched with the post April 1998 acquisitions on a LIFO basis.

12 July 2001 acquisition

	£
Disposal proceeds ($\dfrac{1,000}{7,300} \times$ £41,010)	5,618
Less: cost	(5,000)
Chargeable gain before taper relief	618

No taper relief is due as these shares have only been owned for two years for taper relief purposes.

7 June 2000 acquisition

	£
Disposal proceeds ($\dfrac{3,000}{7,300} \times$ £41,010)	16,853
Less: cost	(15,000)
Gain before taper relief	1,853

For taper relief purposes, these shares have been owned for 3 years, so 95% of the gain will remain chargeable after taper relief (see below).

FA 1985 Pool shares

	No	Cost £	Indexed cost £
12.3.89	200	400	400
4.5.91			
$£400 \times \dfrac{133.5 - 112.3}{112.3}$			76
			476
Addition	2,000	10,000	10,000
Bonus issue	1,100	–	–
	3,300	10,400	10,476
5.4.98			
$£10,476 \times \dfrac{162.6 - 133.5}{133.5}$			2,284
Value when pool closes (5.4.98)	3,300	10,400	12,760
Less disposal (10.01.04)	(3,300)	(10,400)	(12,760)

	£
Disposal proceeds ($\dfrac{3,300}{7,300} \times £41,010$)	18,539
Less cost	(10,400)
	8,139
Less indexation (£12,760 – £10,400)	(2,360)
Chargeable gain before taper relief	5,779

For taper relief purposes, the share are a non business asset that has been held for 6 years (including the additional year). This means that 80% of the gain is chargeable after taper relief (see below).

Sale of car: Cars are exempt assets so no chargeable gain or allowable loss arises.

(b)   The losses brought forward should be allocated to the gains, where the highest amount of the gain remains chargeable after taper relief:

Shares

12.7.01 Acquisition	618
Less: loss brought forward	(618)
Gain after taper relief	–
7.6.00 Acquisition	1,853
Less: loss b/f (£1,000 – £618)	(382)
	1,471
Gain after taper relief (95%)	1,397
FA 1985 pool	
Gain after taper relief (80%)	4,623
Cottage (80%)	80,454
	86,474
Less: annual exemption	(7,900)
	78,574

(c)   Capital gains tax liability @ 40%   £31,430

35 Nigel, Kay and Shirley

(a)

	£
Proceeds	75,000

Less: $£20,000 \times \dfrac{P16.5}{P30}$

$£20,000 \times \dfrac{64.116 + \frac{1}{2}(66.47 - 64.116)}{87.33}$ (14,953)

	60,047

Less: Indexation to April 1998

$£14,953 \times \dfrac{162.6 - 126.2}{126.2} = (0.288)$ (4,306)

	55,741

This non-business asset has been owned for six years (including the additional year) so the gain after taper relief is £44,593 (80% × £55,741).

(b)

	£
Proceeds	21,600

Less: Part cost $£40,000 \times \dfrac{21,600}{21,600 + 72,000}$ (9,231)

	12,369

Less: indexation to April 1998

$£9,231 \times \dfrac{162.6 - 136.3}{136.3}$ (0.193)   (1,782)

	10,587

Gain after taper relief £8,470 (80% × £10,587)

	£
Taxable gain	8,470
Less: Annual exemption	(7,900)
Chargeable gain	570

(c)   Shares are matched with post April 1998 acquisitions first:

Shares acquired November 2003

	No	Cost
		£
Bought	3,000	24,000
Bonus issue	1,500	–
	4,500	24,000

	£
Proceeds (4,500/7,000 × £56,000)	36,000
Less: cost	(24,000)
Gain	12,000

No taper relief on non-business asset.

1985 Pool

	Number	Cost	Indexed cost
		£	£
January 1997	4,000	18,000	18,000
April 1998 – Pool closes $\frac{162.6-154.4}{154.4}$			956
	4,000	18,000	18,956
March 2000 rights issue	1,000	7,000	7,000
	5,000	25,000	25,956
January 2004			
Bonus issue	2,500	–	–
	7,500	25,000	25,956
March 2004			
Sale	(2,500)	(8,333)	(8,652)
C/f	5,000	16,667	17,304

	£
Proceeds (56,000 × $\frac{2,500}{7,000}$)	20,000
Less: cost	(8,333)
	11,667
Less: Indexation (£8,652 – £8,333)	(319)
	11,348

Gain after taper relief £9,078 (£11,348 × 80%)

Shirley's taxable gain before the annual exemption is £21,078 (£12,000 + £9,078).

Chapter 8 CGT: additional aspects

36 Michelle

	£
Proceeds	10,000
Less sales commission	(1,000)
Net proceeds	9,000
Less cost	(4,000)
Unindexed gain	5,000
Less indexation allowance to April 1998	(4,192)

$$\frac{162.6 - 79.4}{79.4} = 1.048 \times £4,000$$

	808

The maximum gain is 5/3 × £(10,000 − 6,000) = £6,667.

The chargeable gain before taper relief is therefore £808.

The gain after taper relief is £646 (£808 × 80%)

Tutorial note. The gross proceeds are used in the formula for calculating the maximum gain on a chattel.

37 A cottage, shares and a chattel

(a)   The cottage

	£	£
Proceeds £(100,000 − 800)		99,200
Cost	25,000	
expenditure 1.12.83	8,000	
		(33,000)
Unindexed gain		66,200
Less indexation allowance to April 1998		

$$\frac{162.6 - 79.4}{79.4} = 1.048 \times £25,000 \quad 26,200$$

$$\frac{162.6 - 86.9}{86.9} = 0.871 \times £8,000 \quad 6,968$$

		(33,168)
Gain before taper relief		33,032

The gain after taper relief is £26,426 (£33,032 × 80%).

Tutorial note 1. Enhancement expenditure is deductible if it is reflected in the state or nature of an asset at the time of disposal.

(b) The disposal of shares in JVD Products plc

The shares are on a LIFO basis:

	£
2 August 2003 acquisition	
Proceeds (2,800/4,000 × £20,000)	14,000
Less: Cost	(13,900)
Gain	100

No taper relief

	£
10 March 2001 acquisition	
Proceeds (500/4,000 × £20,000)	2,500
Less: Cost	(800)
Gain	1,700

No taper relief

	£
6 June 2000 acquisition	
Proceeds (500/4,000 × £20,000)	2,500
Less: Cost	(400)
Gain before taper relief	2,100

The shares have been owned for three years so the gain after taper relief is £1,995 (£2,100 × 95%).

FA 1985 Pool

	£
Proceeds (200/4,000 × £20,000)	1,000
Less: Cost (200/2,000 × £1,500)	(150)
	850

Less: Indexation to April 1998

$$\frac{162.6 - 156.9}{156.9} \times £150$$

	£
	(5)
Gain before taper relief	845

Gain after taper relief £676 (£845 × 80%)

The total chargeable gain on the sale of the shares is £4,471 (£100 + £1,700 + £1,995 + £676).

(c) The oil painting

	£
Proceeds (market value)	7,000
Less cost	(10,000)
Loss	(3,000)

The loss on the disposal to John's sister, being on a disposal to a connected person, can only be set against a chargeable gain on a disposal to the same connected person while still connected. This loss must therefore be carried forward.

Tutorial note. A disposal to a connected person must be treated as though it were made at market value. Any loss arising can only be offset against gains made on disposal to the same connected person.

(d)   The tax liabilities

	Non-savings £
Salary/ STI	21,000
Less personal allowance	(4,615)
Taxable income	16,385

	£
Income tax on non-savings income	
£1,960 × 10%	196
£14,425 × 22%	3,174
Tax liability	3,370

	£
Gain on cottage	26,426
Gain on shares	4,471
	30,897
Less annual exemption	(7,900)
Taxable gains	22,997

Capital gains tax		£
£14,115	£(30,500 – 16,385) × 20%	2,823
£8,882	× 40%	3,553
22,997		6,376

38 Geoff Williams

	£	£
1 Ming vase		
Proceeds	10,000	
Less selling expenses	(500)	
	9,500	
Less cost (£2,400 + £100)	(2,500)	
	7,000	
Less indexation allowance to April 1998 0.171 × £2,500	(428)	
	6,572	
Compared to:		
Marginal relief (£10,000 – 6,000) × 5/3	6,666	
Lowest gain taken		6,572

2   Painting

Proceeds	20,000	
Less cost $\dfrac{20,000}{20,000+90,000} \times £40,000$	(7,273)	
	12,727	
Less indexation allowance to April 1998 0.596 × £7,273	(4,335)	
	8,392	
		8,392
Picture - exempt as proceeds and cost < £6,000		Nil
Gains before taper relief		14,964
Gains after taper relief (6 April 1998 – 5 April 2003 = 5 years plus additional year = 6 years) 80% × £14,964		£11,971

39 Miss Wolf

(a)   *The lease*

	£
Proceeds	30,750
Less $\dfrac{64.116\,(16\ years)}{80.361\,(24\frac{1}{2}\ years)} \times £8,000$	(6,383)
Unindexed gain	24,367
Less indexation allowance (January 1995 to April 1998)	
$\dfrac{162.6 - 146.0}{146.0} = (0.114) \times £6,383$	(728)
Gain before taper relief	23,639

The percentage for 24½ years is 79.622 + (81.100 − 79.622) × 6/12 = 80.361.

Taper relief period is six years (6.4.98 − 5.4.03 = 5 years plus additional year).

(b)   *The racehorse*

This is a wasting chattel and is therefore exempt.

(c)   *Painting*

	£
Proceeds	9,000
Less: costs of sale	(900)
	8,100
Less: cost	(2,200)
Gain	5,900

Gain restricted to 5/3 x £(9,000 − 6,000) = £5,000

Taper relief period is 10.9.99 to 9.9.02 = 3 years

(d)   *Summary*

The loss brought forward should be set against the gain on the painting as this has least taper relief.

	Non business 6 years £	Non business 3 years £
Gains	23,639	5,000
Loss: loss b/f		(2,203)
Net gains	23,639	2,797
Taper relief percentages	80%	95%
	£	£
Gains after taper relief	18,911	2,657
Total gains		21,568
Less: annual exemption		(7,900)
		13,668

CGT £13,668 @ 40%   £5,467

40 Mr Fox

Gain on sale

	£
Proceeds	180,000
Less: cost	(50,000)
Unindexed gain	130,000
Less: indexation allowance	
$\dfrac{162.6 - 95.5}{95.5}$ (= 0.703) x £50,000	(35,150)
Indexed gain	94,850

Principal private residence relief then applies to exempt part of the gain:

	Exempt years	Chargeable years
1.8.85 – 31.7.88 (actual occupation)	3	
1.8.88 – 31.7.92 (up to 4 yrs due to place of work – *not* employed abroad)	4	
1.8.92 – 31.7.93 (up to 3 years any other reason)	1	
1.8.93 – 31.1.94 (actual occupation)	½	
1.2.94 – 31.7.00 (note)		6½
1.8.00 – 31.7.03 (last 3 years)	3	
Totals	11½	6½

Gain exempt is 11 ½ out of 18 years x £94,850   60,599

Gain left in charge £(94,850 − 60,599) 34,251

Gain after taper relief (6 years)
80% x £34,251 £27,401

Tutorial note. As Mr Fox did not return to live in the house, no part of the period 1.2.94 to 31.7.00 is exempt.

41 John Harley

(a) **John Harley – Gain on house**

	£
Proceeds	120,000
Less: cost	(40,000)
Unindexed gain	80,000
Less: indexation allowance	
0.808 × £40,000	(32,320)
Indexed gain	47,680
Less: PPR exemption (W)	
179/(53 + 179) × 47,680	(36,788)
Gain left in charge	10,892
Gain after taper relief (6.4.98 – 5.4.03 = 5 years plus additional year = 6 years)	
£10,892 × 80%	8,714

Working

	Chargeable months	Exempt months
1.8.84 – 31.5.85 – actual residence		10
1.6.85 – 31.7.89 – employed abroad any period		50
1.8.89 – 31.7.93 – up to 4 years required to live elsewhere		48
1.8.93 – 31.10.95 – up to 3 years any reason		27
1.11.95 – 30.6.96 – actual residence		8
1.7.96 – 30.11.00 – absent	53	
1.12.00 – 30.11.03 – last 3 years ownership		36
Totals	53	179

No relief is given for any part of the last period of absence (eg rest of 3 years for any reason) as it is not followed by a period of actual residence.

(b) **Peter Robinson CGT payable 2003/04**

Summary of gains

	£
Wasting asset £24,319 × 80% (W1)	19,455
Chandelier (W2)	2,500
	21,955
Less: annual exemption	(7,900)
Taxable gains	14,055

CGT payable

£(30,500 − 27,500) = 3,000 × 20%		600
£(14,055 − 3,000) = 11,055 × 40%		4,422
CGT payable		5,022

1

		£
Proceeds		37,000
Less: cost		
£21,000 ×		
$\dfrac{\text{12 years life remaining}}{\text{25 years total life}}$		(10,080)
Unindexed gain		26,920
Less: indexation allowance		
0.258 × £10,080		(2,601)
Indexed gain		24,319

Taper relief period 6.4.98 to 5.4.03 is 5 years plus additional year makes 6 years.

2

	£
Proceeds	7,500
Less: cost	(4,000)
Gain	3,500
Cannot exceed £(7,500 − 6,000) × 5/3 =	2,500

Taper relief period less than 3 years so no taper relief available.

Chapter 9 Administration

42 Mr Brown

Tutorial note. A claim to reduce the payments on account by £1,500 each was made but as these reduced amounts finally become payable they each carry interest from the due dates for the payments on account concerned.

(a) **Returns**

A tax return, which includes a section allowing for the computation of income and capital gains tax liabilities, must be submitted by 31 January following the tax year concerned. Thus an individual's return for 2003/04 must be delivered by 31 January 2005. However, if the notice requiring the return is served after 31 October following the tax year, the filing date becomes three months after the notice. Thus, if notice to deliver the return for 2003/04 were given, say, on 1 December 2004, it must be delivered by 28 February 2005.

Where a taxpayer fails to file a tax return by the filing date, he is liable to a penalty up to a maximum of £100. The Commissioners may impose a further penalty of up to £60 for each day for which the return remains outstanding after the taxpayer is notified of the penalty, although it cannot be imposed after the failure had been remedied.

If no application is made by the Inspector to the Commissioners and the failure continues for more than six months after the filing date, the taxpayer is liable to a further maximum penalty of £100 subject to a right of appeal on the grounds of reasonable excuse. If the failure continues after the first anniversary of the filing date and the return shows that there is an outstanding liability to tax, the taxpayer is liable to a penalty equal to that outstanding tax liability.

Any penalty will be limited to the amount of tax outstanding for the year and this will be mitigable.

As an alternative to completing their own calculation, the taxpayer can request Revenue assistance and submit a return by 30 September following the tax year (or, if later, two months from the date of the notice requiring delivery of a return). The Inspector must then raise an assessment, also called a self-assessment, in accordance with the information contained in the return and provide the taxpayer with a copy of the assessment.

Payments of tax

Although an individual is not normally required to file a return until 31 January following the tax year, payments on account are required on 31 January in the tax year and on 31 July following it. These payments are required where an individual has either made a self-assessment or been assessed to tax following submission of his tax return for the previous tax year and the amount of the assessment exceeded the tax which was deducted at source: This excess is known as the relevant amount. The taxpayer is required to pay 50% of the previous year's relevant amount on each of 31 January in the tax year and 31 July following it.

If the taxpayer believes that the current year's income tax liability will be less than the previous year's amount, he may make a claim to that effect and each payment on account may then be reduced to 50% of the amount which the taxpayer believes will be due. However, if the taxpayer fraudulently or negligently makes a false statement in connection with such a claim, he will be liable to a penalty equal to the amount of tax lost. Interest is charged on the amount by which payments on account are reduced if the reduced amount finally becomes payable. The interest runs from the due date of payment for the payments on account.

The balance of any income tax due, over and above the payments on account, together with the whole of any capital gains tax, must be paid on 31 January in the following year.

Interest on overdue tax is charged on all unpaid tax from the due date. Where the balance of tax (due on 31 January following the year) is unpaid more than 28 days after the due date, a surcharge of 5% of the unpaid amount is also applied. If it remains unpaid more than six months after the due date, there is a further 5% surcharge. The surcharge carries interest from the date imposed to the date paid.

(b) **Mr Brown**

Due dates of tax – 2003/04

Payments made £	Paid	No claim to reduce payments on account £	Due date
4,500	28 February 2004	6,000	31 January 2004
4,500	14 August 2005	6,000	31 July 2004
4,000	13 March 2005	1,000	31 January 2005
13,000		13,000	

Interest due

Payments on account:

	£
£4,500 × 28/365 × 5%	17.26
£4,500 × 14/365 × 5%	8.63
£1,500 × 406/365 × 5%	83.42
£1,500 × 225/365 × 5%	46.23
Final payment:	
£1,000 × 41/365 × 5%	5.62
	161.16

43 John Jefferies

(a) **John Jefferies – Taxable income 2003/04**

	Non-savings income	Savings (excl. dividends) income	Dividend income	Total income
	£	£	£	£
Salary	48,000			
Car benefit (W1)	5,580			
Car fuel (W1)	4,464			
Institute of Management	(140)			
Sports club – not allowable				
Taxable earnings	57,904			
Dividends 1,800 × 100/90			2,000	
NSB a/c interest £(370 – 70)		300		
Schedule A rental (W2)	1,835			
STI	59,739	300	2,000	62,039
Less: PA	(4,615)			(4,615)
Taxable income	55,124	300	2,000	57,424

(b) **John Jefferies – Income tax payable 2003/04**

	£
Non-saving income	
£1,960 @ 10%	196
£(30,500 – 1,960) = 28,540 @ 22%	6,279
£(390 × $^{100}/_{78}$) = 500 + 4,800 = 5,300 @ 22% (Gift aid and pension) (W3)	1,166
£(55,124 – 30,500 – 5,300) = 19,324 @ 40%	7,730
Savings income	
£300 @ 40%	120
Dividend income	
£2,000 @ 32.5%	650
Tax liability	16,141
Less: tax suffered	
dividend £2,000 @ 10%	(200)
Tax payable	15,941

Note. Usually tax on salary and benefits would be collected through the PAYE system.

Workings

1   *Taxable percentage for car and fuel benefit*   £
    List price   18,000

    Taxable % = 235 − 155 = 80 g/km
    Divide by 5 = 16
    % = 15% + 16% = 31%
    Car Benefit £18,000 × 31%   £5,580
    Fuel Benefit £14,400 × 31%   £4,464

2   £   £
    Income from letting   5,400
    Less:council tax   700
         water rates   350
         agents fees   600
         boiler repairs   350   (2,000)
                                                                          3,400

    Less:wear and tear allowance
         10% × (5,400 − 700 − 350)   (435)
                                                                          2,965
    Less:loss b/f   (1,130)
    Assessable for 2003/04   1,835

    Note. No deduction is allowable for the capital expenditure on the window frames. No specific
    allowance is given for the new furniture as this is covered by the wear and tear allowance.

3   Pension contribution £48,000 × 10% = £4,800

(c)   **Tax Advisors**
                                   1 High Street
                                   Anytown

Mr J Jefferies
2, Right Street
Anytown   [Date]

Dear Mr Jefferies

SELF ASSESSMENT

The self assessment system requires you to give details of your income to the Inland Revenue on which
your tax liability is then calculated.

(i)   *Forms and information required*

      You will need form SA 100 plus additional pages for employment and land and property if not
      already included with form SA 100. You should tick the relevant boxes on page 2 of the main form
      to show the supplementary pages are included.

      In relation to your employment, you need to have details of your salary as shown on the form P60
      given to you by your employer. Details of your car and fuel benefits will be as shown on the form

183

P11D also given by your employer to you. Both your salary and benefits should be included on page 1 of the Employment pages.

The Institute of Management will have sent you a payment request showing the fee payable by you. This amount should be shown on page 2 of the Employment pages.

Your pension provider will give you a statement of the contributions made by you during the year. Details should be shown on the main form.

You will have been sent dividend vouchers showing a tax credit attaching to the dividends paid. The actual dividends plus tax credits need to be shown on page 3 of the main form.

Your bank will have given you details of the interest paid and tax deducted. The net amount, tax deducted and gross amount should be shown on page 3 of the main form.

The amount of your Gift Aid payment should be shown on the main form. The actual amount paid should be shown.

You will need to fill in the Land and Property supplementary pages. However, since your property income is less than £15,000 annually, you do not have to list expenses separately. Instead total expenses can be shown.

(ii)   *Time to keep information*

You should keep details of your employment income, bank interest, dividends, pension, gift aid payment and subscription payment for a year after 31 January following the end of the tax year ie until 31 January 2006.

Details of rental income and expenses should be kept for five years after 31 January following the end of the tax year ie until 31 January 2010.

(iii)   *Deadlines*

You must submit the return (and supplementary pages) by 30 September 2004 if you wish the Revenue to calculate your tax liability. However, if you wish to calculate your liability you have until 31 January 2005 to submit the return and your self assessment of tax.

(iv)   *Payment of tax*

The tax payable is due on 31 January 2005.

You may prefer to have your liability collected through your PAYE code. This will be done by the Revenue if the liability is less than £2,000 and your return is submitted by 30 September 2004 or shortly thereafter.

You may also be required to make payments on account of tax for 2004/05. These would be 50% of your tax payable for 2003/04. The instalments would be due on 31 January 2005 and 31 July 2005.

However, you are not required to make payments on account if the previous year's self assessment payment was reasonably small (ie less than £500 or 20% of total tax liability).

Please do not hesitate to contact me if you require any further information.

Yours sincerely

Tax Advisor

44 Kitty Bennett

Task 1

CALCULATION OF SCHEDULE A INCOME FOR 2003/04

	£	£
Rent accrued		
6.4.03 – 30.9.03		
£4,000 × 6/12		2,000
1.10.03 – 5.4.04		
£5,000 × 6/12		2,500
Less: Property management fees	800	
Interest	2,450	
Repairs	400	
		(3,650)
Schedule A income		850

Task 2

CALCULATION OF INVESTMENT INCOME 2003/04

	Received £	Gross £	Tax £	
Dividends				
31.10.03	3,600	4,000	400	10%
31.3.04	2,700	3,000	300	
	6,300	7,000	700	
Building society interest				
30.6.03	2,000	2,500	500	20%
31.12.03	1,680	2,100	420	
	3,680	4,600	920	
Bank interest				
30.9.03	640	800	160	20%
31.03.04	952	1,190	238	
	1,592	1,990	398	

Task 3

INCOME TAX COMPUTATION 2003/04

	Non-savings £	Savings (exc dividend) £	Dividend	Total £
Schedule D Case I	18,716			
Schedule A	850			
Dividends			7,000	
Building society interest		4,600		
Bank interest		1,990		
STI	19,566	6,590	7,000	33,156
Less personal allowance	(4,615)			
Taxable income	14,951	6,590	7,000	28,541

	£
Income tax on non-savings income	
£1,960 × 10%	196
£12,991 × 22%	2,858
Income tax on savings (excl dividend) income	1,318
£6,590 × 20%	
Income tax on dividend income	
£7,000 × 10%	700
	5,072
Tax liability	
Less: tax credit on dividends	(700)
Less: tax suffered on interest £6,590 × 20%	(1,318)
	3,054
Less payments made on account of 2003/04 tax liability	(1,000)
	2,054
Tax payable	

Task 4

Miss Kitty Bennett's income tax payable for 2003/04 after deducting tax suffered at source and the tax credit on dividends for 2003/04 is £3,054. Two payments on account of £500 each have been made in respect of this amount leaving a final payment of £2,054 due to be paid on 31 January 2005.

Two payments on account of Miss Bennett's 2004/05 income tax liability each of £1,527.00 must be made. These will be due for payment on 31 January 2005 and 31 July 2005.

You should have made the following entries.

Task 5

Tax return
Q3: tick Yes Self-employment: tick
Q5: tick Yes Land and property: tick
Step 2: Tick the box
Q10: tick Yes

Interest

Box 10.2: £5,272   Box 10.3: £1,318   Box 10.4: £6,590

Dividends

Box 10.15: £6,300   Box 10.16: £700   Box 10.17: £7,000

Tax computation
Q18: tick Yes
Box 18.3: £3,054
Box 18.7: £1,527.00

Personal details

Box 22.4: Kitty
Box 22.5: Single
Box 22.6: 13 March 1965
Box 22.7: NB 61 72 21 F

Declaration

Q24: Tick the boxes for   1 to 10 of this form
                           Self-employment
                           Land and property

Supplementary – Land and property

Name: Kitty Bennett   Tax reference: 124/8765

Box 5.20: £4,500

                                              Box 5.23: £4,500

Box 5.25: £400
Box 5.26: £2,450
Box 5.27: £800

                                              Box 5.30: £3,650
                                              Box 5.31: £850
                                              Box 5.40: £850
                                              Box 5.43: £850

Supplementary – Self-employment pages

Name: Kitty Bennett   Tax reference: 124/8765
Box 3.1:   Longbourn Gift Shop   Box 3.2: Gift shop
Box 3.3:   Longbourn House
           Meryton
           Herts

           Box 3.4: 1/4/03   Box 3.5: 31/3/04
           Box 3.7: 1/4/01

Income and expenditure

Box 3.29: £124,304
Box 3.49: £65,645

Box 3.46: £58,659
Box 3.51: £25,394
Box 3.52: £9,186
Box 3.35: £130
Box 3.53: £1,886
Box 3.36: £31
Box 3.54: £1,955
Box 3.37: £302
Box 3.55: £1,954
Box 3.58: £3,980
Box 3.60: £1,291
Box 3.44: £2,557
Box 3.62: £2,557
Box 3.63: £1,746
Box 3.64: £49,949
Box 3.65: £15,696

Box 3.66: £3,020
Box 3.69: £3,020
Box 3.73: £18,716

Adjustments
Box 3.74: 1/4/03   Box 3.75 31/3/04   Box 3.76: £18,716
Box 3.83: £18,716
Box 3.84: £0
Box 3.90: £18,716
Box 3.92: £18,716

PROFESSIONAL EDUCATION

45 Mr Watson

Task 1

CALCULATION OF TAXABLE EARNINGS FOR 2003/04

	£
Salary	29,250
Car benefit £15,850 × 18% (W) − £600	2,253
Fuel benefit 18% × £14,400	2,592
Medical insurance	656
Use of video £650 × 20%	130
Telephone £(125 + 595)	720
Travel	1,255
Entertaining	1,254
	38,110
Less: expenses claim	
Travel	(1,255)
Entertaining	(1,254)
Phone (£595 × 40%)	(238)
Taxable earnings	35,363

Workings

1 *Car and fuel taxable percentage*
   CO_2 emissions = 170g/km
   Above baseline 170 − 155 = 15g/km
   Divide by 5 = 3
   Taxable % = 15 + 3 = 18%

Task 2

SCHEDULES OF DIVIDEND AND INTEREST INCOME FOR 2003/04

	Received £	Gross £	Tax £
Building society interest			
30.6.03	4,768	5,960	1,192
31.12.03	4,888	6,110	1,222
Bank interest			
30.9.03	440	550	110
31.3.04	504	630	126
	10,600	13,250	2,650
Dividends			
31.10.03	1,800	2,000	200
31.3.04	900	1,000	100
	2,700	3,000	300

189

Task 3

INCOME TAX COMPUTATION 2003/04

	Non-savings £	Savings (excl dividend) £	Dividend £	Total £
Taxable earnings (Task 1)	35,363			
Dividends			3,000	
Bank and building society interest		13,250		
STI	35,363	13,250	3,000	51,613
Less personal allowance	(4,615)			
Taxable income	30,748	13,250	3,000	46,998

Income tax on non savings income	
£1,960 × 10%	196
£28,540 × 22%	6,279
£248 × 40%	99
Income tax on savings (excl dividend) income	
£13,250 × 40%	5,300
Income tax on dividend income	
£3,000 × 32.5%	975
Tax liability	12,849
Less: Tax credit on dividends	(300)
PAYE	(9,059)
Tax suffered on interest	(2,650)
Tax payable	840

Task 4

You should have made the following entries.

Tax return

Q1: tick Yes
       Employment: tick Yes
Step 2: Tick the box
Q10: tick Yes

Interest

Box 10.2: £10,600   Box 10.3: £2,650   Box 10.4: £13,250

Dividends

Box 10.15: £2,700   Box 10.16: £300   Box 10.17: £3,000

Tax calculation

Q18: tick Yes
Box 18.3: £840
Box 22.4: John
Box 22.5: Married
Box 22.6: 15.12.53
Box 22.7: NC 95 96 14D

Declaration

Q 24: Tick the boxes for: 1 to 10 of this form   Employment

Supplementary – Employment pages

Name: John Watson   Tax reference: 427/8901

Box 1.1: 427/8901   Box 1.2: JDJ Chemicals

Box 1.5: 12 High Street
Anytown
Box 1.8: £29,250
Box 1.11: £9,059

Box 1.16: £2,253
Box 1.17: £2,592
Box 1.21: £656
Box 1.22: £130
Box 1.23: £3,229

Box 1.32: £1,255
Box 1.35: £1,492

Task 5

You cannot, on the whole, choose your status as employed or self-employed. The Revenue consider several different factors in deciding your status, including the following.

     (a)   Indicators of employment

         (i)   You must accept further work when the current task is completed.
         (ii)   You have a right to further work.
         (iii)   You get paid holidays and sick pay.
         (iv)   You must obey normal office rules.

     (b)   Indicators of self-employment

         (i)   You provide your own equipment.
         (ii)   You can hire your own staff to help you.
         (iii)   You invest your own capital and can increase your profits by sound management.

Answers to Full Exam based Assessments

PRACTICE EXAM PAPER 1: ANSWERS

DO NOT TURN THIS PAGE UNTIL YOU HAVE COMPLETED THE EXAM

SECTION 1

ANSWERS (Task 1.1)

Taxable earnings for 2003/04

		£
Salary		41,000
Car benefit		
(£19,000 × 25%(W))	4,750	
Contribution towards private use of the car	(600)	
		4,150
Fuel benefit (£14,400 × 25%)		3,600
Private medical insurance		965
Entertainment	3,500	
Less claim for expenses incurred wholly, exclusively		
and necessarily in the course of employment	(3,500)	
		Nil
Asset made available for private use		
(£1,500 × 20% × 9/12)		225
Taxable earnings		49,940

Workings

1 **Taxable percentage for car and fuel benefit**

   CO_2 emissions 205g/km (rounded down to nearest 5 below)
   205 – 155 = 50g/km
   Divided by 5 = 10
   Taxable % = 15 + 10 = 25%

ANSWERS (Task 1.2)

Computation of Schedule A rental income for 2003/04

Property	1	2	3	4	Total
	£	£	£	£	£
Rental Income	4,000	3,000	2,000	6,500	15,500
Less allowable expenses:					
Management fees	400	300	200	650	1,550
Buildings Insurance	100	100	100	100	400
Contents Insurance	50	50	50	50	200
Cleaning	260	260	260	260	1,040
Repairs	100	250	nil	50	400
Council tax	450	350	200	350	1,350
Wear and tear allowance					
(10% rent-council tax)	355	265	180	615	1,415
	2,285	1,425	1,010	4,425	9,145

Total Schedule A income £9,145

Tutorial note The repairs expenditure on property 3 is not allowable as it is a capital item.

ANSWERS (Task 1.3)

Inland Revenue

Income for the year ended 5 April 2004

LAND AND PROPERTY

Name: *Jane Austen* (Fill in these boxes first)

Tax reference: *B 452*

If you want help, look up the box numbers in the Notes.

Are you claiming Rent a Room relief for gross rents of £4,250 or less?
(Or £2,125 if the claim is shared?)
Read the Notes on page LN2 to find out
- whether you can claim Rent a Room relief; and
- how to claim relief for gross rents over £4,250

Yes — If 'Yes', tick box. If this is your only income from UK property, you have finished these Pages

Is your income from furnished holiday lettings?
If not applicable, please turn over and fill in Page L2 to give details of your property income

Yes — If 'Yes', tick box and fill in boxes 5.1 to 5.18 before completing Page L2

Furnished holiday lettings

- Income from furnished holiday lettings — **5.1** £

Expenses (furnished holiday lettings only)

- Rent, rates, insurance, ground rents etc. — **5.2** £
- Repairs, maintenance and renewals — **5.3** £
- Finance charges, including interest — **5.4** £
- Legal and professional costs — **5.5** £
- Costs of services provided, including wages — **5.6** £
- Other expenses — **5.7** £

total of boxes 5.2 to 5.7 — **5.8** £

Net profit (put figures in brackets if a loss) — box 5.1 minus box 5.8 — **5.9** £

Tax adjustments

- Private use — **5.10** £
- Balancing charges — **5.11** £

box 5.10 + box 5.11 — **5.12** £

- Capital allowances — **5.13** £

- Tick box 5.13A if box 5.13 includes enhanced capital allowances for environmentally friendly expenditure — **5.13A**

Profit for the year (copy to box 5.19). If loss, enter '0' in box 5.14 and put the loss in box 5.15 — boxes 5.9 + 5.12 minus box 5.13 — **5.14** £

Loss for the year (if you have entered '0' in box 5.14) — boxes 5.9 + 5.12 minus box 5.13 — **5.15** £

Losses

- Loss offset against 2003-04 total income — **5.16** £
- Loss carried back — see Notes, page LN4 — **5.17** £
- Loss offset against other income from property (copy to box 5.38) — see Notes, page LN4 — **5.18** £

SA105

BS 12/2002net

TAX RETURN ■ LAND AND PROPERTY: PAGE L1

Please turn over

BPP PROFESSIONAL EDUCATION **197**

Other property income

■ Income

copy from box 5.14

- Furnished holiday lettings profits | **5.19** £

- Rents and other income from land and property | **5.20** £ *15,500* | Tax deducted **5.21** £

- Chargeable premiums | **5.22** £

- Reverse premiums | **5.22A** £

boxes 5.19 + 5.20 + 5.22 + 5.22A
5.23 £ *15,500*

■ Expenses (do not include figures you have already put in boxes 5.2 to 5.7 on Page L1)

- Rent, rates, insurance, ground rents etc. | **5.24** £ *1,950*

- Repairs, maintenance and renewals | **5.25** £ *400*

- Finance charges, including interest | **5.26** £

- Legal and professional costs | **5.27** £ *1,550*

- Costs of services provided, including wages | **5.28** £ *1,040*

- Other expenses | **5.29** £

total of boxes 5.24 to 5.29
5.30 £ *4,940*

Net profit (put figures in brackets if a loss)

box 5.23 *minus* box 5.30
5.31 £ *10,560*

■ Tax adjustments

- Private use | **5.32** £

- Balancing charges | **5.33** £

box 5.32 + box 5.33
5.34 £

- Rent a Room exempt amount | **5.35** £

- Capital allowances | **5.36** £

- Tick box 5.36A if box 5.36 includes a claim for 100% capital allowances for flats over shops | **5.36A**

- Tick box 5.36B if box 5.36 includes enhanced capital allowances for environmentally friendly expenditure | **5.36B**

- 10% wear and tear | **5.37** £ *1,415*

- Furnished holiday lettings losses (from box 5.18) | **5.38** £

boxes 5.35 to 5.38
5.39 £ *1,415*

Adjusted profit (if loss enter '0' in box 5.40 and put the loss in box 5.41)

boxes 5.31 + 5.34 *minus* box 5.39
5.40 £ *9,145*

Adjusted loss (if you have entered '0' in box 5.40)

boxes 5.31 + 5.34 *minus* box 5.39
5.41 £

- Loss brought forward from previous year | **5.42** £

Profit for the year

box 5.40 *minus* box 5.42
5.43 £ *9,145*

■ Losses etc

- Loss offset against total income (read the note on page LN8) | **5.44** £

- Loss to carry forward to following year | **5.45** £

- Tick box 5.46 if these Pages include details of property let jointly | **5.46**

- Tick box 5.47 if **all** property income ceased in the year to 5 April 2004 **and** you don't expect to receive such income again, in the year to 5 April 2005 | **5.47**

Now fill in any other supplementary Pages that apply to you. Otherwise, go back to page 2 of your Tax Return and finish filling it in.

BS 12/2002net

Tax Return ■ Land and property: page L2

	Income for the year ended 5 April 2004

Inland Revenue

EMPLOYMENT

Fill in these boxes first

Name Jane Austen

Tax reference B 452

If you want help, look up the box numbers in the Notes.

Details of employer

Employer's PAYE reference - may be shown under 'Inland Revenue office number and reference' on your P60 or 'PAYE reference' on your P45

1.1 B 452 —

1.2 Employer's name: Book Supplies Ltd

Date employment started (only if between 6 April 2003 and 5 April 2004)
1.3 / /

Date employment finished (only if between 6 April 2003 and 5 April 2004)
1.4 / /

1.5 Employer's address: 121 High Street, Anytown

Postcode

Tick box 1.6 if you were a director of the company
1.6 ✓

and, if so, tick box 1.7 if it was a close company
1.7

Income from employment

■ *Money - see Notes, page EN3*

Before tax

- Payments from P60 (or P45) **1.8** £ 41,000
- Payments not on P60, etc. - tips **1.9** £
  - other payments (excluding expenses entered below and lump sums and compensation payments or benefits entered overleaf) **1.10** £
- **Tax deducted** in the UK from payments in boxes 1.8 to 1.10 **1.11** £ 15,000

■ *Benefits and expenses - see Notes, pages EN3 to EN6. If any benefits connected with termination of employment were received, or enjoyed, after that termination and were from a **former** employer you need to complete Help Sheet IR204, available from the Orderline. Do not enter such benefits here.*

	Amount			Amount
• Assets transferred/ payments made for you	**1.12** £		• Vans	**1.18** £
• Vouchers, credit cards and tokens	**1.13** £		• Taxable cheap loans see Note for box 1.19, page EN5	**1.19** £
• Living accommodation	**1.14** £		*box 1.20 is not used*	
• Excess mileage allowances and passenger payments	**1.15** £		• Private medical or dental insurance	**1.21** £ 965
• Company cars	**1.16** £ 4,150		• Other benefits	**1.22** £ 225
• Fuel for company cars	**1.17** £ 3,600		• Expenses payments received and balancing charges	**1.23** £ 3,500

SA101

BS 12/2002net   TAX RETURN ■ EMPLOYMENT: PAGE E1   *Please turn over*

Income from employment continued

■ *Lump sums and compensation payments or benefits including such payments and benefits from a former employer*
Note that 'lump sums' here includes any contributions which your employer made to an unapproved retirement benefits scheme

*You must read page EN6 of the Notes **before** filling in boxes 1.24 to 1.30*

Reliefs

- £30,000 exemption   **1.24** £
- Foreign service and disability   **1.25** £
- Retirement and death lump sums   **1.26** £

Taxable lump sums

- From box B of *Help Sheet IR204*   **1.27** £
- From box K of *Help Sheet IR204*   **1.28** £
- From box L of *Help Sheet IR204*   **1.29** £
- Tax deducted from payments in boxes 1.27 to 1.29 - *leave blank if this tax is included in the box 1.11 figure.*   Tax deducted   **1.30** £

■ *Foreign earnings not taxable in the UK in the year ended 5 April 2004 - see Notes, page EN6*   **1.31** £

■ *Expenses you incurred in doing your job - see Notes, pages EN7 to EN8*

- Travel and subsistence costs   **1.32** £
- Fixed deductions for expenses   **1.33** £
- Professional fees and subscriptions   **1.34** £
- Other expenses and capital allowances   **1.35** £ *3,500*
- Tick box 1.36 if the figure in box 1.32 includes travel between your home and a permanent workplace   **1.36**

■ *Foreign Earnings Deduction* (seafarers only)   **1.37** £

■ *Foreign tax for which tax credit relief not claimed*   **1.38** £

Student Loans

■ *Student Loans repaid by deduction by employer - see Notes, page EN8*   **1.39** £

- Tick box 1.39A if your income is under Repayment of Teachers' Loans Scheme   **1.39A**

1.40 *Additional information*

Now fill in any other supplementary Pages that apply to you.
Otherwise, go back to page 2 in your Tax Return and finish filling it in.

BS 12/2002net   TAX RETURN ■ EMPLOYMENT: PAGE E2

ANSWERS (Task 1.4)

MRS JANE AUSTEN INCOME TAX COMPUTATION 2003/04

	Non-saving income £	Tax deducted at source £
Taxable earnings	49,940	15,000
Schedule A profits	9,145	
	59,085	
Less charges on income	–	
Statutory total income	59,085	
Less personal allowance	(4,615)	
Taxable income	54,470	

ANSWERS (Task 1.5)

	£
£1,960 × 10%	196.00
£28,540 × 22%	6,278.80
£23,970 × 40%	9,588.00
	16,062.80
Less tax suffered	(15,000.00)
Tax payable	1,062.80

Tutorial note. Tax is computed to the nearest pence. This was what the assessor did in the specimen paper and what would be required in practice.

SECTION 2

ANSWERS (Task 2.1)

1 Sale of property 1

	£
Sale proceeds	300,000
Less costs of sale	(1,500)
Less original cost	(125,000)
Unindexed gains	173,500
Less: indexation allowance to April 1998	

$$£125,000 \times \frac{162.6 - 79.4}{79.4} = (1.048)$$

	£
	(131,000)
Gain before taper relief	42,500

2 Sale of property 2

	£
Sale proceeds	100,200
Less costs of sale	(2,000)
Less original cost	(25,000)
Unindexed gain	73,200
Less indexation allowance to April 1998	

$$£25,000 \times \frac{162.6 - 144.7}{144.7} = (0.124)$$

	£
	(3,100)
Chargeable gain before taper relief	70,100

Both properties have been owned for six years for taper relief purposes (including the additional year) so 80% of the gains remain chargeable after taper relief.

ANSWERS (Task 2.2)

	£	£
Property 1	42,500	
Less: Loss b/f	(10,000)	
		32,500
Property 2		70,100
Gains before taper relief		102,600
Gains after taper relief (80%)		82,080
Less: Annual exemption		(7,900)
Taxable gains		74,180

Tax payable £74,180 × 40% = £29,672.00

Tutorial note. As both gains attract the same rate of taper relief, it does not matter how the brought forward loss is offset.

ANSWERS (Task 2.3)

Inland Revenue

For the year ended 5 April 2004

CAPITAL GAINS

Name: Jane Austen

Tax reference: B452

Fill in these boxes first

Only use this Page if **all** your transactions were in quoted shares or other securities unless taper relief is due on any of them, or any were held at 31 March 1982, or you are claiming a relief, for example, Enterprise Investment Scheme deferral relief. Otherwise you cannot use this page and must use Pages CG2 to CG6 to work out **all** of your capital gains or allowable losses.

A Enter details of quoted shares or other securities disposed of	B Tick box if estimate or valuation used	C Enter the date of disposal	D Disposal proceeds	E Gain or loss after indexation allowance, if due (enter loss in brackets)	F Further information, including any elections made
1		/ /	£	£	
2		/ /	£	£	
3		/ /	£	£	
4		/ /	£	£	
5		/ /	£	£	
6		/ /	£	£	
7		/ /	£	£	
8		/ /	£	£	

Total gains **F1** £ — *Total your gains in column E and enter the amount in box F1*

Total losses **F2** £ — *Total your losses in column E and enter the amount in box F2*

box F1 *minus* box F2 **F3** £ — *If your net gains are below £7,900 **or** you have a net loss, there is no liability. If you have a net loss, please fill in the losses summary on Page CG8 otherwise carry on to box F4*

Net gain/(loss) **F4** £ —

minus income losses set against gains **F5** £ box F3 *minus* box F4 — *If your gains are now below £7,900, there is no liability; copy box F5 to box F7 and complete Page CG8. Otherwise, carry on to box F6*

minus losses brought forward **F6** £ — *Enter losses brought forward up to the **smaller** of either the total losses brought forward or the figure in box F5 **minus** £7,900*

Total taxable gains **F7** £ box F5 *minus* box F6 — *Copy this figure to box 8.7 on Page CG8 (if F7 is blank because there is no liability, leave 8.7 blank).*

Go to Page CG8

Note:
This Page is only for transactions in quoted shares or other securities.
See the definition on page CGN3 of the Notes on Capital Gains.

BS 12/2002net

TAX RETURN ■ CAPITAL GAINS: PAGE CG1

SA108

Your 2003-04 Capital Gains Tax liability

A Brief description of asset	AA* Type of disposal. Enter Q, U, L, T or O	B Tick box if estimate or valuation used	C Tick box if asset held at 31 March 1982	D Enter the later of date of acquisition and 16 March 1998	E Enter the date of disposal	F Disposal proceeds	G Enter details of any elections made, reliefs claimed or due and state amount (£)

Gains on assets which are either wholly business or wholly non-business

A	AA*	B	C	D	E	F	G
1 Property	L	✓		16/3/98	30/4/03	£300,000	
2 Property	L	✓		16/3/98	30/4/03	£100,200	
3				/ /	/ /	£	
4				/ /	/ /	£	
5				/ /	/ /	£	
6				/ /	/ /	£	
7				/ /	/ /	£	
8				/ /	/ /	£	

Gains on assets which are partly business and partly non-business (see the notes on page CGN4)

9				/ /	/ /	£	
10				/ /	/ /	£	

* Column AA: for
- quoted shares or other securities, (see the definition on page CGN3 of the Notes) enter **Q**
- other shares or securities, enter **U**
- land and property, enter **L**
- amounts attributable to settlor (see page CGN4) enter **T**
- other assets (for example, goodwill), enter **O**

Complete Pages CG4 to CG6 for all U, L and O transactions

Losses

Description of asset	Type of * disposal. Enter Q, U, L or O	Tick box if estimate or valuation used	Tick box if asset held at 31 March 1982	Enter the later of date of acquisition and 16 March 1998	Enter the date of disposal	Disposal proceeds	Enter details of any elections made, reliefs claimed or due and state amount (£)
13				/ /	/ /	£	
14				/ /	/ /	£	
15				/ /	/ /	£	
16				/ /	/ /	£	

Total losses of

H Chargeable Gains after reliefs but before losses and taper	I Enter 'Bus' if business asset	J Taper rate	K Losses deducted			L Gains after losses	M Tapered gains (gains from column L x % in column J)
			K1 Allowable losses of the year	K2 Income losses of 2003-04 set against gains	K3 Unused losses b/f from earlier years		
£ 42,500		80 %	£	£	£ 10,000	£ 32,500	£ 26,000
£ 70,100		80 %	£	£	£	£ 70,100	£ 56,080
£		%	£	£	£	£	£
£		%	£	£	£	£	£
£		%	£	£	£	£	£
£		%	£	£	£	£	£
£		%	£	£	£	£	£
£		%	£	£	£	£	£
£	Bus	%	£	£	£	£	£
£		%	£	£	£	£	£
£	Bus	%	£	£	£	£	£
£		%	£	£	£	£	£

Total 8.1 £ 112,600
Total column H

8.5 £   8.6 £ 10,000
Total column K2   *Total column K3*

8.3 £ 82,080
Total column M

11 Attributed gains from UK resident trusts where no election has been made for the set off of **personal losses** (see page CGN4) *(enter the name of the Trust on Page CG7)*   £

12 Attributed gains from non UK resident trusts where no election has been made for the set off of **personal losses** (see page CGN4) *(enter the name of the Trust on Page CG7)*   £

Total of attributed gains where no election has been made (total of rows 11 and 12)   8.4 £

Losses arising

£

£

£

£

Total taxable gains (after allowable losses and taper relief)

box 8.3 + box 8.4
£ 82,080

Copy to box 8.7 on Page CG8 and complete Pages CG4 to CG6 for all U, L and O transactions

year 8.2 £

Other shares or securities (U) - further information

Please give details of each transaction of this type of asset in the boxes below. If you have more than two of these transactions to return, please photocopy this Page before completion. (Please also complete Pages CG2 and CG3.)

1st transaction

Description of shares or securities - including name of company, company registration number (if known), number, class and nominal value of shares. Also, if possible, give a history of the shares disposed of, for instance, if there has been a reorganisation or takeover (give details of the original company and shares held in that company)

Tick box if you have already submitted form CG34 ☐

State any connection between you and the person from whom you acquired the asset, or to whom you disposed of the asset (see Notes, page CGN14)

If you have used an estimate or valuation in your capital gains computation but have not submitted form CG34, please enter the date to which the valuation relates, the amount (£) and the reason for the estimate or valuation. Please also attach a copy of any valuation obtained

2nd transaction

Description of shares or securities - including name of company, company registration number (if known), number, class and nominal value of shares. Also, if possible, give a history of the shares disposed of, for instance, if there has been a reorganisation or takeover (give details of the original company and shares held in that company)

Tick box if you have already submitted form CG34 ☐

State any connection between you and the person from whom you acquired the asset, or to whom you disposed of the asset (see Notes, page CGN14)

If you have used an estimate or valuation in your capital gains computation but have not submitted form CG34, please enter the date to which the valuation relates, the amount (£) and the reason for the estimate or valuation. Please also attach a copy of any valuation obtained

BS 12/2002net   TAX RETURN ▪ CAPITAL GAINS: PAGE CG4

Land and property disposals (L) - further information

Please give details of each transaction of this type of asset in the boxes below. If you have more than two of these transactions to return, please photocopy this Page before completion. (Please also complete Pages CG2 and CG3.)

1st transaction

Full address of land/property affected (attach a copy of any plan if this helps identification)

> *1 High Street*
> *High Wycombe*
> *Bucks*

Description of land/property disposed of, including details of your ownership, for example freehold/leasehold and any tenancies affecting your ownership and the date of transaction or any other date for which a valuation has been made.

Tick box if you have already submitted form CG34 ☐

> *Freehold*

State any connection between you and the person from whom you acquired the asset, or to whom you disposed of the asset (see Notes, page CGN14)

If you have used an estimate or valuation in your capital gains computation but have not submitted form CG34, please enter the date to which the valuation relates, the amount (£) and the reason for the estimate or valuation. Please also attach a copy of any valuation obtained.

2nd transaction

Full address of land/property affected (attach a copy of any plan if this helps identification)

> *2 High Street*
> *High Wycombe*
> *Bucks*

Description of land/property disposed of, including details of your ownership, for example freehold/leasehold and any tenancies affecting your ownership and the date of transaction or any other date for which a valuation has been made.

Tick box if you have already submitted form CG34 ☐

> *Freehold*

State any connection between you and the person from whom you acquired the asset, or to whom you disposed of the asset (see Notes, page CGN14)

If you have used an estimate or valuation in your capital gains computation but have not submitted form CG34, please enter the date to which the valuation relates, the amount (£) and the reason for the estimate or valuation. Please also attach a copy of any valuation obtained.

BS 12/2002net   Tax Return ■ Capital Gains: page CG5   *continued over* ➡

Other assets (O) - further information

Please give details of any transaction involving any other type of asset in the boxes below. If you have more than two of these transactions to return, please photocopy this Page before completion. (Please also complete Pages CG2 and CG3.)

1st transaction

Full description of the asset (other than shares or land/property) affected and any other information which helps identify the asset.

Tick box if you have already submitted form CG34 ☐

State any connection between you and the person from whom you acquired the asset, or to whom you disposed of the asset (see Notes, page CGN14)

If you have used an estimate or valuation in your capital gains computation but have not submitted form CG34, please enter the date to which the valuation relates, the amount (£) and the reason for the estimate or valuation. Please also attach a copy of any valuation obtained.

2nd transaction

Full description of the asset (other than shares or land/property) affected and any other information which helps identify the asset

Tick box if you have already submitted form CG34 ☐

State any connection between you and the person from whom you acquired the asset, or to whom you disposed of the asset (see Notes, page CGN14)

If you have used an estimate or valuation in your capital gains computation but have not submitted form CG34, please enter the date to which the valuation relates, the amount (£) and the reason for the estimate or valuation. Please also attach a copy of any valuation obtained.

BS 12/2002net

Chargeable gains and allowable losses

Once you have completed Page CG1, or Pages CG2 to CG6, fill in this Page.

Have you 'ticked' any row in Column B, 'Tick box if estimate or valuation used' on Pages CG1 or CG2 or in Column C on Page CG2 'Tick box if asset held at 31 March 1982'? **YES**

Have you given details in Column G on Pages CG2 and CG3 of any Capital Gains reliefs claimed or due? **YES**

Are you claiming, and/or using, any clogged losses (see Notes, page CGN11)? **YES**

Enter from Page CG1 or column AA on Page CG2:

- the number of transactions in quoted shares or other securities **box Q**
- the number of transactions in other shares or securities **box U**
- the number of transactions in land and property **box L**
- the number of gains attributed to settlors **box T**
- the number of other transactions **box O**

Total taxable gains (from Page CG1 **or** Page CG3) **8.7** £ 82,080

Your taxable gains *minus* the annual exempt amount of £7,900 (leave blank if '0' or negative) | box 8.7 minus £7,700 | **8.8** £ 74,180

Additional liability in respect of non-resident or dual resident trusts (see Notes, page CGN6) **8.9** £

Capital losses

(If your loss arose on a transaction with a connected person, see page CGN14, you can only set that loss against gains you make on disposals to that same connected person. See the notes on clogged losses on page CGN11.)

■ **This year's losses**

- Total (normally from box 8.2 on Page CG3 or box F2 on Page CG1. But, if you have clogged losses, see Notes, page CGN10) **8.10** £

- Used against gains (total of column K1 on Page CG3, or the smaller of boxes F1 and F2 on Page CG1) **8.11** £

- Used against earlier years' gains (generally only available to personal representatives, see Notes, page CGN11) **8.12** £

- Used against income (only losses of the type described on page CGN9 can be used against income) | **8.13A** £ | amount claimed against income of 2003-04 |

  | **8.13B** £ | amount claimed against income of 2002-03 | box 8.13A + box 8.13B **8.13** £

- This year's unused losses | box 8.10 minus (boxes 8.11 + 8.12 + 8.13) **8.14** £

■ **Summary of earlier years' losses**

- Unused losses of 1996-97 and later years **8.15** £ 10,000

- Used this year (losses from box 8.15 are used in priority to losses from box 8.18) (column K3 on Page CG3 or box F6 on Page CG1) **8.16** £ 10,000

- Remaining unused losses of 1996-97 and later years | box 8.15 minus box 8.16 **8.17** £

- Unused losses of 1995-96 and earlier years **8.18** £

- Used this year (losses from box 8.15 are used in priority to losses from box 8.18) (column K3 on Page CG3 or box F6 on Page CG1) | box 8.6 minus box 8.16 (or box F6 minus box 8.16) **8.19** £

■ **Total of unused losses to carry forward**

- Carried forward losses of 1996-97 and later years | box 8.14 + box 8.17 **8.20** £ nil

- Carried forward losses of 1995-96 and earlier years | box 8.18 minus box 8.19 **8.21** £

ANSWERS (Task 2.4)

MOLE AND CO
CHARTERED ACCOUNTANTS
24 MAIN STREET
ANYTOWN
TELEPHONE (0116) 520 9345
TAX (0116) 520 9346

Jane Austen
Book Supplies Limited
121 High Street
Anytown

10 June 2004

Dear Mrs Austen

Self Assessment Income Tax Return and Tax Payable

I enclose copies of your income tax and capital gains tax computations for 2003/04, together with your completed Self Assessment Tax Return Form.

I would be grateful if you would look through the computation and the self assessment tax return, and if you are happy with them, please sign and date the self assessment tax return and return it to me for submission to the Inland Revenue.

The Income Tax Return and computation show that income tax of £1,063 and capital gains tax of £29,672 are due for 2003/04. The total due is £30,375. This should be paid to the Collector of Taxes on or before 31 January 2005. You should have received a payslip and prepaid envelope already, but if you need any assistance in making the payment, please do let me know.

If you have any queries, please do not hesitate to contact me.

Yours sincerely

Margaret Jones

Tax Department Manager

Mole and Co

PRACTICE EXAM PAPER 2: ANSWERS

DO NOT TURN THIS PAGE UNTIL YOU HAVE COMPLETED THE EXAM

SECTION 1

ANSWERS (Task 1.1)

Mr Smith – Taxable earnings

	£
Salary	40,000
Benefits (W1)	5,250
Taxable earnings	45,250

Working

1 **Benefits**

		£
Car parking space (exempt)		–
	£	
Reimbursed mileage allowance (15,000 × 50p)	7,500	
Less tax free: 10,000 × 40p	(4,000)	
5,000 × 25p	(1,250)	
Taxable amount		2,250
Home entertainment system		
£10,000 × 20%		2,000
Mobile phone (exempt)		–
Loan £20,000 × 5%		1,000
Subscription	225	
Less: allowance deduction	(225)	–
Homeworking costs		
		–
		5,250

Tutorial notes

1. The provision of a parking space at or near work is an exempt benefit.

2. The private use of a mobile phone is an exempt benefit

3. The £104 paid by Mr Smith's employer towards his costs of working at home is an exempt benefit. Up to £104 per annum can be paid without supporting evidence

ANSWERS (Task 1.2)

Mr Smith – Investment income

Interest

	Net £	Tax £	Gross £
Exchequer Stock	1,600	400	2,000
Building society interest	960	240	1,200
	2,560	640	3,200

Dividends

	Net £	Tax £	Gross £
	720	80	800

ANSWERS (Task 1.3)

Mr Smith – Rental income

	£	£
Rental income		24,000
Less:		
Commission	2,400	
Advertising	250	
Repair	125	
Council tax	900	
Wear and Tear £(24,000 – 900) × 10%	2,310	
		(5,985)
Schedule A income		18,015

ANSWERS (Task 1.4)

Mr Smith – Income tax computation

	Non-savings £	Savings excl. dividend £	Dividend £	Total £
Taxable earnings (Task 1.1)	45,250			
Schedule A (Task 1.3)	18,015			
Interest (Task 1.2)		3,200		
Dividends			800	
	63,265	3,200	800	67,365
Less: Personal allowance	(4,615)			
	58,650	3,200	800	62,750

Income tax on non-savings income

	£
£1,960 × 10%	196.00
£28,540 × 22%	6,278.80
£7,000 (£2,000 + £5,000) (extended band) × 22%	1,540.00
£21,150 × 40%	8,460.00
	16,474.80

Income tax on savings (excl dividend) income

£3,200 × 40%	1,280.00

Income tax on dividend income

£800 × 32.5%	260.00
	18,014.80

Less:			
	Tax credit on dividend	80	
	PAYE	8,114	
	Tax suffered on building society interest	640	
			(8,834.00)
Tax payable			9,180.80

Tutorial note. The basic rate band is extended by the gross amount of the gift aid donation, £1,560 × 100/78 and the personal pension payments, £3,900 × $^{100}/_{78}$.

Tutorial note. Tax is computed to the nearest pence. This was what the assessor did in the specimen paper and what would be required in practice.

ANSWERS (Task 1.5)

INCOME AND CAPITAL GAINS *for the year ended 5 April 2004*

Step 1

Answer Questions 1 to 9 below to check if you need supplementary Pages to give details of particular income or capital gains. Pages 6 and 7 of your Tax Return Guide will help.

(Ask the Orderline for a Guide if I haven't sent you one with your Tax Return, and you want one.)

If you answer 'Yes' ask the Orderline for the appropriate supplementary Pages and Notes.

Ring the Orderline on 0845 9000 404, or fax on 0845 9000 604 for any you need (closed Christmas Day, Boxing Day and New Year's Day).

If you do need supplementary Pages, tick the boxes below when you've got them.

Q1 Were you an employee, or office holder, or director, or agency worker or did you receive payments or benefits from a former employer (excluding a pension) in the year ended 5 April 2004?
If you were a non-resident director of a UK company but received no remuneration, see the notes to the Employment Pages, page EN3, box 1.6.
YES ✓ — EMPLOYMENT

Q2 Did you have any taxable income from share options, shares or share related benefits in the year? (This does not include
- dividends, or
- dividend shares ceasing to be subject to an Inland Revenue approved share incentive plan within three years of acquisition they go in Question 10.)
YES — SHARE SCHEMES

Q3 Were you self-employed (but not in partnership)?
(You should also tick 'Yes' if you were a Name at Lloyd's.)
YES — SELF-EMPLOYMENT

Q4 Were you in partnership?
YES — PARTNERSHIP

Q5 Did you receive any rent or other income from land and property in the UK?
YES ✓ — LAND & PROPERTY ✓

Q6 Did you have any taxable income from overseas pensions or benefits, or from foreign companies or savings institutions, offshore funds or trusts abroad, or from land and property abroad or gains on foreign insurance policies?
YES
Have you or could you have received, or enjoyed directly or indirectly, or benefited in any way from, income of a foreign entity as a result of a transfer of assets made in this or earlier years?
YES
Do you want to claim foreign tax credit relief for foreign tax paid on foreign income or gains?
YES — FOREIGN

Q7 Did you receive, or are you deemed to have, income from a trust, settlement or the residue of a deceased person's estate?
YES — TRUSTS ETC

Q8 Capital gains - read the guidance on page 7 of the Tax Return Guide.
- If you have disposed of your only or main residence do you need the Capital Gains Pages?
YES
- Did you dispose of other chargeable assets worth more than £31,600 in total?
YES
- Were your total chargeable gains more than £7,900 or do you want to make a claim or election for the year?
YES — CAPITAL GAINS

Q9 Are you claiming that you were not resident, or not ordinarily resident, or not domiciled, in the UK, or dual resident in the UK and another country, for all or part of the year?
YES — NON-RESIDENCE ETC

Step 2
Fill in any supplementary Pages BEFORE going to Step 3.
Please use blue or black ink to fill in your Tax Return and please do not include pence. Round down your income and gains. Round up your tax credits and tax deductions. Round to the nearest pound.

When you have filled in all the supplementary Pages you need, tick this box. ✓

Step 3
Fill in Questions 10 to 24. If you answer 'Yes', fill in the relevant boxes. If not applicable, go to the next question.

BS 12/2002net   TAX RETURN: PAGE 2

215

INCOME *for the year ended 5 April 2004*

Q10 ▶ **Did you receive any income from UK savings and investments?**   YES ✓   *If yes, tick this box and then fill in boxes 10.1 to 10.26 as appropriate. Include only your share from any joint savings and investments. If not applicable, go to Question 11.*

■ *Interest*

● Interest from UK banks, building societies and deposit takers (interest from UK Internet accounts must be included) - *if you have more than one bank or building society etc. account enter **totals** in the boxes.*

- enter any bank, building society etc. interest that **has not** had tax taken off. (Most interest is taxed by your bank or building society etc. so make sure you should be filling in box 10.1, rather than boxes 10.2 to 10.4)

Taxable amount
10.1 £

- enter details of your **taxed** bank or building society etc. interest. *The Working Sheet on page 10 of your Tax Return Guide will help you fill in boxes 10.2 to 10.4.*

Amount **after** tax deducted	Tax deducted	Gross amount **before** tax
10.2 £ 960	**10.3** £ 240	**10.4** £ 1,200

● Interest distributions from UK authorised unit trusts and open-ended investment companies (dividend distributions go below)

Amount **after** tax deducted	Tax deducted	Gross amount **before** tax
10.5 £	**10.6** £	**10.7** £

● National Savings & Investments (other than First Option Bonds and Fixed Rate Savings Bonds and the first £70 of interest from an Ordinary Account)

Taxable amount
10.8 £

● National Savings & Investments First Option Bonds and Fixed Rate Savings Bonds

Amount **after** tax deducted	Tax deducted	Gross amount **before** tax
10.9 £	**10.10** £	**10.11** £

● Other income from UK savings and investments (except dividends)

Amount **after** tax deducted	Tax deducted	Gross amount **before** tax
10.12 £ 1,600	**10.13** £ 400	**10.14** £ 2,000

■ *Dividends*

● Dividends and other qualifying distributions from UK companies

Dividend/distribution	Tax credit	Dividend/distribution **plus** credit
10.15 £ 720	**10.16** £ 80	**10.17** £ 800

● Dividend distributions from UK authorised unit trusts and open-ended investment companies

Dividend/distribution	Tax credit	Dividend/distribution **plus** credit
10.18 £	**10.19** £	**10.20** £

● Scrip dividends from UK companies

Dividend	Notional tax	Dividend **plus** notional tax
10.21 £	**10.22** £	**10.23** £

● Non-qualifying distributions and loans written off

Distribution/Loan	Notional tax	Taxable amount
10.24 £	**10.25** £	**10.26** £

BS 12/2002net   TAX RETURN: PAGE 3   *Please turn over* ▶

BPP PROFESSIONAL EDUCATION

INCOME *for the year ended 5 April 2004, continued*

Q11 ▶ **Did you receive a taxable UK pension, retirement annuity or Social Security benefit?**
Read the notes on pages 13 to 15 of the Tax Return Guide.

YES | If yes, tick this box and then fill in boxes 11.1 to 11.14 as appropriate. If not applicable, go to Question 12.

■ *State pensions and benefits*

Taxable amount for 2003-04

- State Retirement Pension - enter the **total** of your entitlements for the year | **11.1** £
- Widow's Pension or Bereavement Allowance | **11.2** £
- Widowed Mother's Allowance or Widowed Parent's Allowance | **11.3** £
- Industrial Death Benefit Pension | **11.4** £
- Jobseeker's Allowance | **11.5** £
- Invalid Care Allowance | **11.6** £
- Statutory Sick Pay, Statutory Maternity Pay and Statutory Paternity Pay paid by the Inland Revenue | **11.7** £

	Tax deducted	Gross amount **before** tax
- Taxable Incapacity Benefit	**11.8** £	**11.9** £

■ *Other pensions and retirement annuities*

- Pensions (other than State pensions) and retirement annuities - if you have more than one pension or annuity, please add together and complete boxes 11.10 to 11.12. Provide details of each one in box 11.14

Amount after tax deducted	Tax deducted	Gross amount **before** tax
11.10 £	**11.11** £	**11.12** £

11.14

- Deduction - *see the note for box 11.13 on page 15 of your Tax Return Guide*

Amount of deduction
11.13 £

Q12 ▶ **Did you make any gains on UK life insurance policies, life annuities or capital redemption policies or receive refunds of surplus funds from additional voluntary contributions?**

YES | If yes, tick this box and then fill in boxes 12.1 to 12.12 as appropriate. If not applicable, go to Question 13.

- Gains on UK annuities and friendly societies' life insurance policies where no tax is treated as paid

Number of years	Amount of gain(s)
12.1	**12.2** £

- Gains on UK life insurance policies etc. on which tax is treated as paid - *read pages 15 to 18 of your Tax Return Guide*

Number of years	Tax treated as paid	Amount of gain(s)
12.3	**12.4** £	**12.5** £

- Gains on life insurance policies in ISAs that have been made void

Number of years	Tax deducted	Amount of gain(s)
12.6	**12.7** £	**12.8** £

- Corresponding deficiency relief

Amount
12.9 £

- Refunds of surplus funds from additional voluntary contributions

Amount received	Notional tax	Amount plus notional tax
12.10 £	**12.11** £	**12.12** £

Q13 ▶ **Did you receive any other taxable income which you have not already entered elsewhere in your Tax Return?**
*Fill in any supplementary Pages **before** answering Question 13. (Supplementary Pages follow page 10, or are available from the Orderline.)*

YES | If yes, tick this box and then fill in boxes 13.1 to 13.6 as appropriate. If not applicable, go to Question 14.

- Other taxable income – also provide details in box 23.5 - *read the notes on pages 18 to 20 of your Tax Return Guide*

Amount **after** tax deducted	Tax deducted	Amount **before** tax
13.1 £	**13.2** £	**13.3** £

- Tick box 13.1A if box 13.1 includes enhanced capital allowances for environmentally friendly expenditure

13.1A

Losses brought forward	Earlier years' losses used in 2003-04
13.4 £	**13.5** £

2003-04 losses carried forward
13.6 £

BS 12/2002net   TAX RETURN: PAGE 4

RELIEFS *for the year ended 5 April 2004*

Q14 **Do you want to claim relief for your pension contributions?** **YES** ✓

Do not include contributions deducted from your pay by your employer to their pension scheme or associated AVC scheme, because tax relief is given automatically. But do include your contributions to personal pension schemes and Free-Standing AVC schemes.

If yes, tick this box and then fill in boxes 14.1 to 14.11 as appropriate.
If not appliable, go to Question 15.

■ *Payments to your retirement annuity contracts - only fill in boxes 14.1 to 14.5 for policies taken out before 1 July 1988.*
See the notes on pages 20 and 21 of your Tax Return Guide.

Qualifying payments made in 2003-04	**14.1** £	2003-04 payments used in an earlier year **14.2** £	Relief claimed box 14.1 *minus* (boxes 14.2 and 14.3, but not 14.4)
2003-04 payments now to be carried back	**14.3** £	Payments brought back from 2004-05 **14.4** £	**14.5** £

■ *Payments to your personal pension (including stakeholder pension) contracts - enter the amount of the payment you made with the basic rate tax added (the **gross** payment). See the note for box 14.6 on page 22 of your Tax Return Guide.*

Gross qualifying payments made in 2003-04	**14.6** £ **5,000**	
2003-04 gross payments carried back to 2002-03	**14.7** £	Relief claimed box 14.6 *minus* box 14.7 (but not 14.8)
Gross qualifying payments made between 6 April 2004 and 31 January 2005 brought back to 2003-04 - *see page 22 of your Tax Return Guide*	**14.8** £	**14.9** £ **5,000**

■ *Contributions to other pension schemes and Free-Standing AVC schemes*

● Amount of contributions to employer's schemes **not deducted** at source from pay **14.10** £

● Gross amount of Free-Standing Additional Voluntary Contributions paid in 2003-04 **14.11** £

Q15 **Do you want to claim any of the following reliefs?**

If you have made any annual payments, after basic rate tax, answer 'Yes' to Question 15 and fill in box 15.9. If you have made any gifts to charity go to Question 15A.

YES

If yes, tick this box and then fill in boxes 15.1 to 15.12, as appropriate.
If not applicable, go to Question 15A

● Interest eligible for relief on qualifying loans **15.1** £

● Maintenance or alimony payments you have made under a court order, Child Support Agency assessment or legally binding order or agreement
Amount claimed up to £2,150 **15.2** £

To claim this relief, either you or your former spouse must have been 65 or over on 5 April 2000. So, if **your** date of birth, which is entered in box 22.6, is after 5 April 1935 then you must enter your former **spouse's** date of birth in box 15.2A - *see pages 23 and 24 of your Tax Return Guide*
Former spouse's date of birth **15.2A** / /

● Subscriptions for Venture Capital Trust shares (up to £100,000)
Amount on which relief is claimed **15.3** £

● Subscriptions under the Enterprise Investment Scheme (up to £150,000) - *also provide details in box 23.5, see page 24 of your Tax Return Guide*
Amount on which relief is claimed **15.4** £

● Community Investment Tax relief - invested amount relating to previous tax year(s) and on which relief is due **15.5** £

● Community Investment Tax relief - invested amount for current tax year **15.6** £
Total amount on which relief is claimed box 15.5 + box 15.6 **15.7** £

● Post-cessation expenses, pre-incorporation losses brought forward and losses on relevant discounted securities, etc. - *see pages 24 and 25 of your Tax Return Guide*
Amount of payment **15.8** £

● Annuities and annual payments
Payments made **15.9** £

● Payments to a trade union or friendly society for death benefits
Half amount of payment **15.10** £

● Payment to your employer's compulsory widow's, widower's or orphan's benefit scheme - *available in some circumstances – **first** read the notes on page 25 of your Tax Return Guide*
Relief claimed **15.11** £

● Relief claimed on a qualifying distribution on the **redemption** of bonus shares or securities.
Relief claimed **15.12** £

ALLOWANCES *for the year ended 5 April 2004*

Q15A **Do you want to claim relief on gifts to charity?** **YES** ✓
If you have made any Gift Aid payments answer 'Yes' to Question 15A. You should include Gift Aid payments to Community Amateur Sports Clubs here. You can elect to include in this Return Gift Aid payments made between 6 April 2004 and the date you send in this Return. See page 26 in the Tax Return Guide and the leaflet enclosed on Gift Aid.

If yes, tick this box and then read page 26 of your Tax Return Guide. Fill in boxes 15A.1 to 15A.5 as appropriate. If not applicable, go to Question 16.

- Gift Aid and payments under charitable covenants made between 6 April 2003 and 5 April 2004 **15A.1** £ *1,560*
- Enter in box 15A.2 the total of any 'one off' payments included in box 15A.1 **15A.2** £
- Enter in box 15A.3 the amount of Gift Aid payments made after 5 April 2004 but treated as if made in the tax year 2003-04 **15A.3** £
- Gifts of qualifying investments to charities – shares and securities **15A.4** £
- Gifts of qualifying investments to charities – real property **15A.5** £

Q16 **Do you want to claim blind person's allowance, married couple's allowance or the Children's Tax Credit?** **YES**
You get your personal allowance of £4,615 automatically. If you were born before 6 April 1938, enter your date of birth in box 22.6 - you may get a higher age-related personal allowance.

If yes, tick this box and then read pages 26 to 31 of your Tax Return Guide. Fill in boxes 16.1 to 16.33 as appropriate. If not applicable, go to Question 17.

- **Blind person's allowance** Date of registration (if first year of claim) **16.1** / / Local authority (or other register) **16.2**

■ Married couple's allowance - *In 2003-04 married couple's allowance can only be claimed if either you, or your husband or wife, were born before 6 April 1935. So you can only claim the allowance in 2003-04 if either of you had reached 65 years of age before 6 April 2000. Further guidance is given beginning on page 27 of your Tax Return Guide.*

If **both** you and your husband or wife were born after 5 April 1935 you cannot claim; **do not** complete boxes 16.3 to 16.13.

If you can claim fill in boxes 16.3 and 16.4 if you are a married man or if you are a married woman and you are claiming half or all of the married couple's allowance.
- Enter your date of birth (if born before 6 April 1935) **16.3** / /
- Enter your spouse's date of birth (**if** born before 6 April 1935 **and** if older than you) **16.4** / /

Then, if you are a married man fill in boxes 16.5 to 16.9. If you are a married woman fill in boxes 16.10 to 16.13.
- Wife's full name **16.5** Date of marriage (if after 5 April 2003) **16.6** / /
- Tick box 16.7, or box 16.8, if you or your wife have allocated half, or all, of the minimum amount of the allowance to her Half **16.7** All **16.8**
- Enter in box 16.9 the date of birth of any previous wife with whom you lived at any time during 2003-04. *Read 'Special rules if you are a man who married in the year ended 5 April 2004' on page 28 before completing box 16.9.* **16.9** / /
- Tick box 16.10, or box 16.11, if you or your husband have allocated half, or all, of the minimum amount of the allowance to you Half **16.10** All **16.11**
- Husband's full name **16.12** Date of marriage (if after 5 April 2003) **16.13** / /

■ Child Tax Credit – *even if you have already completed a separate Child's Tax Credit (CTC) claim form and received the relief in your tax code, you should still fill in boxes 16.14 to 16.26, as directed. Any reference to 'partner' in this question means the person you lived with during the year to 5 April 2004 – your husband or wife, or someone you lived with as husband or wife.*

Guidance for claiming CTC is on pages 29 to 31 of your Tax Return Guide. Please read the notes before completing your claim, particularly if either you, or your partner, were liable to tax above the basic rate in the year to 5 April 2004.

~~No longer applicable~~

- Enter in box 16.14 the date of birth of a child living with you who was born on or after 6 April 1986. *If you have a child living with you who was born on or after 6 April 2003, make sure you enter their date of birth in this box in preference to claiming for a child.* **16.14** / /
- Tick box 16.15 if the child was your own child or one you looked after at your own expense. If not, you cannot claim CTC – go to box 16.27, if appropriate, or Question 17. **16.15**
- Tick box 16.16 if the child lived with you **throughout** the year to 5 April 2004. **16.16**
  If you ticked box 16.16 and
  - you were a lone or single claimant, you have finished this question; go to Question 17,
  - you have a partner, go to box 16.18.
- If the child lived with you for only **part of the year** you may only be entitled to a proportion of the CTC. Enter in box 16.17 your share in £s that **you have agreed** with any other claimants that you may claim for this child. But leave boxes 16.17 to 16.25 blank if you separated from, or started living with, your partner during the year to 5 April 2004. Special rules apply to work out your entitlement; ask the Orderline for *Help Sheet IR343: Claiming Children's Tax Credit when your circumstances change* which explains how to complete box 16.26. **16.17** £

BS 12/2002net TAX RETURN: PAGE 6

 219

ALLOWANCES *for the year ended 5 April 2004, continued*

■ *Children's Tax Credit, continued*

If you lived with your partner (for CTC this means your husband or wife, or someone you lived with as husband and wife) for the whole of the year to 5 April 2004, fill in boxes 16.18 to 16.25 as appropriate.

- Enter in box 16.18 your partner's surname

  16.18

- Enter in box 16.19 your partner's National Insurance number

  16.19

- Tick
  - box 16.20 if you had the higher income in the year to 5 April 2004,

    16.20

  or
  - box 16.21 if **your partner** had the higher income in that year

    16.21

- Tick box 16.22 if either of you were chargeable to tax above the basic rate limit in the year to 5 April 2004.

  16.22

*If you ticked boxes 16.20 and 16.22 your entitlement will be reduced - see page 30 of your Tax Return Guide; **your partner cannot claim CTC** - go to box 16.28, or Question 17, as appropriate.*

*If you ticked boxes 16.21 and 16.22 your partner's entitlement will be reduced; **you cannot claim CTC** – go to box 16.27, or Question 17, as appropriate.*

If neither of you were chargeable above the basic rate and you had the lower income and
- you don't want to claim half of the entitlement to CTC, and
- you didn't make an election for CTC to go to the partner with the lower income

you have finished this part of your Return - go to boxes 16.27 or 16.28, or Question 17, as appropriate (your partner should claim CTC if they have not already done so).

Otherwise, tick one of boxes 16.23 to 16.25 .

- I had the higher income and I am claiming all of our entitlement to CTC

  16.23

- We are both making separate claims for half of our entitlement to CTC

  16.24

- We elected before 6 April 2003, or because of our special circumstances, during the year to 5 April 2004 (see page 31 of your Tax Return Guide), for the partner with the lower income to claim all of our entitlement to CTC

  16.25

- If you separated from, or starting living with, your partner in the year to 5 April 2004, enter in box 16.26 the amount of CTC you are claiming *(following the guidance in Help Sheet IR343: Claiming Children's Tax Credit when your circumstances change).*

  16.26 £

■ *Transfer of surplus allowances - see page 31 of your Tax Return Guide before you fill in boxes 16.27 to 16.33.*

- Tick box 16.27 if you want your spouse to have your unused allowances

  16.27

- Tick box 16.28 if you want to have your spouse's unused allowances

  16.28

If you want to calculate your tax, enter the amount of the surplus allowance you can have.

- Blind person's surplus allowance

  16.31 £

- Married couple's surplus allowance

  16.32

OTHER INFORMATION *for the year ended 5 April 2004*

Q17 **Are you liable to make Student Loan Repayments for 2003-04 on an Income Contingent Student Loan?**
You must read the note on page 31 of your Tax Return Guide before ticking the 'Yes' box.

YES

If yes, tick this box.
If not applicable, go to Question 18.

If yes, and you are calculating your tax enter in Question 18, box 18.2A the amount you work out is repayable in 2003-04

OTHER INFORMATION *for the year ended 5 April 2004, continued*

Q18 **Do you want to calculate your tax and, if appropriate, any Student Loan Repayment?**

YES ✓

Use your Tax Calculation Guide then fill in boxes 18.1 to 18.8 as appropriate.

- Unpaid tax for earlier years **included in your tax code for 2003-04**

18.1 £

- Tax due for 2003-04 included in your tax code for a later year

18.2 £

- Student Loan Repayment due

18.2A £

- Total tax, Class 4 NIC and Student Loan Repayment due for 2003-04 **before** you made any payments on account *(put the amount in brackets if an overpayment)*

18.3 £ *9,180.80*

- Tax due for earlier years

18.4 £

- Tax overpaid for earlier years

18.5 £

- Tick box 18.6 if you are claiming to reduce your 2004-05 payments on account. Make sure you enter the **reduced** amount of your first payment in box 18.7. Then, in the 'Additional information' box, box 23.5 on page 9, say why you are making a claim

18.6

- Your first payment on account for 2004-05 *(include the pence)*

18.7 £ *4,590.40*

- Any 2004-05 tax you are reclaiming now

18.8 £

Q19 **Do you want to claim a repayment if you have paid too much tax?** *(If you do not tick 'Yes' or the tax you have overpaid is below £10, I will use the amount you are owed to reduce your next tax bill.)*

YES

If yes, tick this box and then fill in boxes 19.1 to 19.12 as appropriate.
If not applicable, go to Question 20.

Should the repayment be sent:

- to your bank or building society account?
  Tick box 19.1 and fill in boxes 19.3 to 19.7   **19.1**

or

- to your nominee's bank or building society account? *Tick box 19.2 and fill in boxes 19.3 to 19.12*   **19.2**

We prefer to make repayment direct into a bank or building society account. (But tick box 19.8A or box 19.8B if you would like a cheque to be sent to you or your nominee.)

Name of bank or building society
19.3

Branch sort code
19.4

Account number
19.5

Name of account holder
19.6

Building society reference
19.7

If you would like a cheque to be sent to:

- you, at the address on page 1, *tick box 19.8A*   **19.8A**

or

- your nominee, *tick box 19.8B*   **19.8B**

If your nominee is your agent, *tick box 19.9A*   **19.9A**

Agent's reference for you (if your nominee is your agent)
19.9

I authorise

Name of your nominee/agent
19.10

Nominee/agent address
19.11

Postcode

to receive on my behalf the amount due

19.12 *This authority must be signed by you. A photocopy of your signature will not do.*

Signature

BS 12/2002net

OTHER INFORMATION *for the year ended 5 April 2004, continued*

Q20 Have you already had any 2003-04 tax refunded or set off by your Inland Revenue office or the Benefits Agency (in Northern Ireland, the Social Security Agency)?
Read the notes on page 32 of your Tax Return Guide.

YES ☐ If yes, tick this box and then enter the amount of the refund in box 20.1.

20.1 £ ☐

Q21 Is your name or address on the front of the Tax Return *wrong*?
If you are filling in an approved substitute Tax Return, see the notes on page 32 of the Tax Return Guide.

YES ☐ If yes, please tick this box and make any corrections on the front of the form.

Q22 Please give other personal details in boxes 22.1 to 22.7. *This information helps us to be more efficient and effective.*

Your daytime telephone number
22.1 ☐

Your agent's telephone number
22.2 ☐

and their name and address
22.3 ☐

Postcode

Your first two forenames
22.4 ☐

Say if you are single, married, widowed, divorced or separated
22.5 ☐

Your date of birth (If you were born before 6 April 1938, you may get a higher age-related allowance.)
22.6 ☐ / /

Your National Insurance number
(if known and not on page 1 of your Tax Return)
22.7 ☐

Q23 Please tick boxes 23.1 to 23.4 if they apply. Provide any additional information in box 23.5 below (continue on page 10, if necessary).

Tick box 23.1 if you do **not** want any tax you owe for 2003-04 collected through your tax code.
23.1 ☐

Please tick box 23.2 if this Tax Return contains figures that are provisional because you do not yet have final figures. Pages 32 and 33 of the Tax Return Guide explain the circumstances in which provisional figures may be used and asks for some additional information to be provided in box 23.5 below.
23.2 ☐

Tick box 23.3 if you are claiming relief now for 2004-05 trading, or certain capital, losses. Enter in box 23.5 the amount and year.
23.3 ☐

Tick box 23.4 if you are claiming to have post-cessation or other business receipts taxed as income of an earlier year. Enter in box 23.5 the amount and year.
23.4 ☐

23.5 *Additional information*

OTHER INFORMATION *for the year ended 5 April 2004, continued*

23.5 *Additional information continued*

Q24 **Declaration**

I have filled in and am sending back to you the following pages:

*In the second box enter the number of **complete sets** of supplementary Pages enclosed*

	Tick			Tick			Tick
1 TO 10 OF THIS FORM	✓	Number of sets					
EMPLOYMENT	✓		PARTNERSHIP		Number of sets	TRUSTS, ETC	
SHARE SCHEMES		Number of sets	LAND & PROPERTY	✓		CAPITAL GAINS	
SELF-EMPLOYMENT			FOREIGN			NON-RESIDENCE, ETC	

Before you send your completed Tax Return back to your Inland Revenue office, you must sign the statement below.
If you give false information or conceal any part of your income or chargeable gains, you may be liable to financial penalties and/or you may be prosecuted.

24.1 The information I have given in this Tax Return is correct and complete to the best of my knowledge and belief.

Signature   Date

There are very few reasons why we accept a signature from someone who is not the person making this Return but if you are signing for someone else please read the notes on page 33 of the Tax Return Guide, and:

- enter the capacity in which you are signing (for example, as executor or receiver)
- please **PRINT** your name and address in box 24.4

24.2

24.4

- enter the name of the person you are signing for

24.3

Postcode

BS 12/2002net   TAX RETURN: PAGE 10

Income for the year ended 5 April 2004

Inland Revenue

EMPLOYMENT

Name

Fill in these boxes first

Tax reference

If you want help, look up the box numbers in the Notes.

Details of employer

Employer's PAYE reference - may be shown under 'Inland Revenue office number and reference' on your P60 or 'PAYE reference' on your P45

1.1

Employer's name

1.2 *Global plc*

Date employment started
(only if between 6 April 2003 and 5 April 2004)

1.3 / /

Date employment finished
(only if between 6 April 2003 and 5 April 2004)

1.4 / /

Employer's address

1.5

Postcode

Tick box 1.6 if you were a director of the company

1.6 ✓

and, if so, tick box 1.7 if it was a close company

1.7

Income from employment

■ *Money* - see Notes, page EN3

		Before tax
• Payments from P60 (or P45)	**1.8** £	40,000
• Payments not on P60, etc. - tips	**1.9** £	
- other payments (excluding expenses entered below and lump sums and compensation payments or benefits entered overleaf)	**1.10** £	

	Tax deducted
• **Tax deducted** in the UK from payments in boxes 1.8 to 1.10	**1.11** £ 8,114

■ *Benefits and expenses - see Notes, pages EN3 to EN6. If any benefits connected with termination of employment were received, or enjoyed, after that termination and were from a **former** employer you need to complete Help Sheet IR204, available from the Orderline. Do not enter such benefits here.*

	Amount			Amount
• Assets transferred/ payments made for you	**1.12** £		• Vans	**1.18** £
• Vouchers, credit cards and tokens	**1.13** £		• Taxable cheap loans see Note for box 1.19, page EN5	**1.19** £ 1,000
• Living accommodation	**1.14** £		box 1.20 is not used	
• Excess mileage allowances and passenger payments	**1.15** £ 2,250		• Private medical or dental insurance	**1.21** £
• Company cars	**1.16** £		• Other benefits	**1.22** £ 2,000
• Fuel for company cars	**1.17** £		• Expenses payments received and balancing charges	**1.23** £ 225

SA101

BS 12/2002net

TAX RETURN ■ EMPLOYMENT: PAGE E1

Please turn over

PROFESSIONAL EDUCATION

Income from employment continued

■ *Lump sums and compensation payments or benefits including such payments and benefits from a former employer*
Note that 'lump sums' here includes any contributions which your employer made to an unapproved retirement benefits scheme

*You must read page EN6 of the Notes **before** filling in boxes 1.24 to 1.30*

Reliefs

- £30,000 exemption **1.24** £
- Foreign service and disability **1.25** £
- Retirement and death lump sums **1.26** £

Taxable lump sums

- From box B of *Help Sheet IR204* **1.27** £
- From box K of *Help Sheet IR204* **1.28** £
- From box L of *Help Sheet IR204* **1.29** £
- Tax deducted from payments in boxes 1.27 to 1.29 - *leave blank if this tax is included in the box 1.11 figure.* Tax deducted **1.30** £

■ *Foreign earnings not taxable in the UK in the year ended 5 April 2004 - see Notes, page EN6* **1.31** £

■ *Expenses you incurred in doing your job - see Notes, pages EN7 to EN8*

- Travel and subsistence costs **1.32** £
- Fixed deductions for expenses **1.33** £
- Professional fees and subscriptions **1.34** £ *225*
- Other expenses and capital allowances **1.35** £
- Tick box 1.36 if the figure in box 1.32 includes travel between your home and a permanent workplace **1.36**

■ *Foreign Earnings Deduction* (seafarers only) **1.37** £

■ *Foreign tax for which tax credit relief not claimed* **1.38** £

Student Loans

■ *Student Loans repaid by deduction by employer - see Notes, page EN8* **1.39** £

- Tick box 1.39A if your income is under Repayment of Teachers' Loans Scheme **1.39A**

1.40 *Additional information*

*Now fill in any other supplementary Pages that apply to you.
Otherwise, go back to page 2 in your Tax Return and finish filling it in.*

TAX RETURN ■ EMPLOYMENT: PAGE E2

Inland Revenue

Income for the year ended 5 April 2004

LAND AND PROPERTY

Name _____

Tax reference _____

Fill in these boxes first

If you want help, look up the box numbers in the Notes.

Are you claiming Rent a Room relief for gross rents of £4,250 or less?
(Or £2,125 if the claim is shared?)

Read the Notes on page LN2 to find out
- whether you can claim Rent a Room relief; and
- how to claim relief for gross rents over £4,250

[Yes]

If 'Yes', tick box. If this is your only income from UK property, you have finished these Pages

Is your income from furnished holiday lettings?

If not applicable, please turn over and fill in Page L2 to give details of your property income

[Yes]

If 'Yes', tick box and fill in boxes 5.1 to 5.18 before completing Page L2

Furnished holiday lettings

- Income from furnished holiday lettings — **5.1** £ _____

- ■ *Expenses* (furnished holiday lettings only)

- Rent, rates, insurance, ground rents etc. — **5.2** £ _____

- Repairs, maintenance and renewals — **5.3** £ _____

- Finance charges, including interest — **5.4** £ _____

- Legal and professional costs — **5.5** £ _____

- Costs of services provided, including wages — **5.6** £ _____

- Other expenses — **5.7** £ _____

  total of boxes 5.2 to 5.7
  5.8 £ _____

Net profit (put figures in brackets if a loss)

box 5.1 *minus* box 5.8
5.9 £ _____

- ■ *Tax adjustments*

- Private use — **5.10** £ _____

- Balancing charges — **5.11** £ _____

  box 5.10 + box 5.11
  5.12 £ _____

- Capital allowances — **5.13** £ _____

- Tick box 5.13A if box 5.13 includes enhanced capital allowances for environmentally friendly expenditure — **5.13A** [ ]

Profit for the year (copy to box 5.19). If loss, enter '0' in box 5.14 and put the loss in box 5.15

boxes 5.9 + 5.12 *minus* box 5.13
5.14 £ _____

Loss for the year (if you have entered '0' in box 5.14)

boxes 5.9 + 5.12 *minus* box 5.13
5.15 £ _____

- ■ *Losses*

- Loss offset against 2003-04 total income — **5.16** £ _____

- Loss carried back —
  see Notes, page LN4
  5.17 £ _____

- Loss offset against other income from property (copy to box 5.38) —
  see Notes, page LN4
  5.18 £ _____

SA105

BS 12/2002net

TAX RETURN ■ LAND AND PROPERTY: PAGE L1

Please turn over ➤

PROFESSIONAL EDUCATION

Other property income

■ *Income*

copy from box 5.14

- Furnished holiday lettings profits | 5.19 £

Tax deducted

- Rents and other income from land and property | 5.20 £ *24,000* | 5.21 £

- Chargeable premiums | 5.22 £

boxes 5.19 + 5.20 + 5.22 + 5.22A

- Reverse premiums | 5.22A £ | 5.23 £ *24,000*

■ *Expenses* (do not include figures you have already put in boxes 5.2 to 5.7 on Page L1)

- Rent, rates, insurance, ground rents etc. | 5.24 £ *900*

- Repairs, maintenance and renewals | 5.25 £ *125*

- Finance charges, including interest | 5.26 £

- Legal and professional costs | 5.27 £ *2,650*

- Costs of services provided, including wages | 5.28 £

total of boxes 5.24 to 5.29

- Other expenses | 5.29 £ | 5.30 £ *3,675*

box 5.23 *minus* box 5.30

Net profit (put figures in brackets if a loss) | 5.31 £ *20,325*

■ *Tax adjustments*

- Private use | 5.32 £

box 5.32 + box 5.33

- Balancing charges | 5.33 £ | 5.34 £

- Rent a Room exempt amount | 5.35 £

- Capital allowances | 5.36 £

- Tick box 5.36A if box 5.36 includes a claim for 100% capital allowances for flats over shops | 5.36A

- Tick box 5.36B if box 5.36 includes enhanced capital allowances for environmentally friendly expenditure | 5.36B

- 10% wear and tear | 5.37 £ *2,310*

boxes 5.35 to box 5.38

- Furnished holiday lettings losses (from box 5.18) | 5.38 £ | 5.39 £ *2,310*

boxes 5.31 + 5.34 *minus* box 5.39

Adjusted profit (if loss enter '0' in box 5.40 and put the loss in box 5.41) | 5.40 £ *18,015*

boxes 5.31 + 5.34 *minus* box 5.39

Adjusted loss (if you have entered '0' in box 5.40) | 5.41 £

- Loss brought forward from previous year | 5.42 £

box 5.40 *minus* box 5.42

Profit for the year | 5.43 £ *18,015*

■ *Losses etc*

- Loss offset against total income (read the note on page LN8) | 5.44 £

- Loss to carry forward to following year | 5.45 £

- Tick box 5.46 if these Pages include details of property let jointly | 5.46

- Tick box 5.47 if **all** property income ceased in the year to 5 April 2004 **and** you don't expect to receive such income again, in the year to 5 April 2005 | 5.47

*Now fill in any other supplementary Pages that apply to you.
Otherwise, go back to page 2 of your Tax Return and finish filling it in.*

BS 12/2002net   TAX RETURN ■ LAND AND PROPERTY: PAGE L2

ANSWERS (Task 1.6)

If Mr Smith calculates his own tax liability the due date for submission of his 2003/04 return is 31 January 2005. If he were to wish the Revenue to calculate his tax liability, the due date for submission of the return would be 30 September 2004.

Payment dates

There are three due dates for the payment of tax:

(1)   31 January in the tax year

(2)   31 July following the tax year

(3)   31 January following the tax year

For any tax year a taxpayer must make payments on account of one half of the amount of tax that he had to pay under self assessment in the previous year.

These payments on account are due in two equal instalments on the dates shown in (1) and (2) above. As Mr Smith did not have to pay any tax for 2002/03 under self assessment, he did not have to make payments on account of his 2003/04 tax.

On 31 January 2005 he will have to pay £9,180.80 under self assessment. This is the balance of the tax he owes for 2003/04.

In addition he will have to make two payments on account of his 2004/05 tax, of £4,590.40; the first on 31 January 2005 and the second on 31 July 2005.

Confidentiality

The Inland Revenue only correspond with those people whom a taxpayer has authorised to deal with his affairs. This ensures that confidentiality is maintained. Taxpayers must sign an authorisation allowing agents to deal with the Inland Revenue on their behalf. The Inland Revenue will not disclose details of a taxpayer's affairs to any other individual.

SECTION 2

ANSWERS (Task 2.1)

Mr Jones – Calculation of chargeable gains

Exchequer Stock

Any gain arising on the disposal of Exchequer Stock is exempt from capital gains tax, hence no chargeable gain arises.

Ordinary shares in Body Shack Enterprises plc

Post 6.4.98 acquisition

	£
Disposal proceeds ($\frac{10,000}{15,000} \times £24,000$)	16,000
Less: cost	(9,000)
Chargeable gain before taper relief	7,000

No taper relief is due as the shares are a non-business asset held for one complete year only.

FA 1985 pool shares

	£
Disposal proceeds ($\frac{5,000}{15,000} \times £24,000$)	8,000
Less: cost ($\frac{5,000}{15,000} \times £15,000$)	(5,000)
	3,000
Less: Indexation $\frac{162.6 - 139.7}{139.7} \times £5,000$	(820)
	2,180

Chargeable gain before taper relief.

The shares are a non-business asset that had been held for 6 years including the additional year.

∴ 80% of the net gain is chargeable after taper relief.

JOL plc ordinary shares

	£
Market value	50,000
Less: cost	(10,000)
	40,000
Less: Indexation	
$\frac{162.6 - 126.7}{126.7} \times £10,000$	(2,833)
	37,167

The shares are a non-business asset that has been held for 6 years including the additional year. ∴ 80% of the net gain will be chargeable after taper relief.

Summary of gains

	£	£
Body Shack plc shares	7,000	
Less: Loss	(7,000)	
		–
Body Shack plc shares (FA 85 pool)	2,180	
Less: Loss	(2,180)	
		–
JOL plc Ordinary shares	37,167	
Less: Loss (£13,500 − £7,000 − £2,180)	(4,320)	
		32,847
		32,847
Gain after taper relief (80%)		26,278
Less: Annual exemption		(7,900)
Chargeable gain		18,378

Tutorial note. The capital loss brought forward is first set against the gains which attract the least amount of taper relief. (i.e. the gains where the highest percentage is chargeable after taper relief).

ANSWERS (Task 2.2)

Chargeable gain   £18,378

CGT @ 40% = £7,351.20

£7,351.20 is due for payment on 31 January 2005.

Answers to AAT Specimen Exam

AAT SPECIMEN EXAM PAPER: ANSWERS

DO NOT TURN THIS PAGE UNTIL YOU HAVE COMPLETED THE EXAM

NOTE: THESE ANSWERS HAVE BEEN PREPARED BY BPP PROFESSIONAL EDUCATION

SECTION 1

ANSWERS (Task 1.1)

	£
Car (£28,600 × 22% (W1))	6,292
Fuel (£14,400 × 22% (W1))	3,168
Loan £20,000 × (5% – 2.5%)(Note)	500
	9,960

Workings

1 **Taxable percentage for car and fuel benefit**
   Emission rating rounded down to the nearest 5 below = 190g/km.
   Amount over baseline figure 190 – 155 = 35g/km
   Divided by 5 = 7
   Taxable percentage = 15% + 7% = 22%

Tutorial note Take care when you read the dates; the loan was available for the whole of the tax year.

ANSWERS (Task 1.2)

	Non-savings £	Savings £	Dividend £	Total £
Salary	18,500			
Less pension @ 5%	(925)			
	17,575			
Less annual subscription	(250)			
	17,325			
Benefits (task 1.1)	9,960			
BSI (gross)		5,200		
Dividends (gross)	–	–	6,000	
	27,285	5,200	6,000	38,485
Less PA	(4,615)			
Total	22,670	5,200	6,000	33,870

Tutorial note. Contributions to an employer's pension scheme are deducted in arriving at taxable income. In contrast, contributions to a personal pension plan are not deducted in computing taxable income. The figure on the P60 issued to Phil Bright will be £(18,500 – 925) = £17,575.

ANSWERS (Task 1.3)

		£
Tax on non-savings income		
£1,960 × 10%		196.00
£20,710 × 22%		4,556.20
£22,670		
Tax on savings income		
£5,200 × 20%		1,040.00
Tax on dividend income		
£2,630 × 10%		263.00
£3,370 × 32.5%		1,095.25
£6,000		7,150.45

Less tax deducted at source	£	
Dividends	600	(1,640.00)
BSI	1,040	
Net tax liability		5,510.45

ANSWERS (Task 1.4)

Protecting client confidentiality is crucial. Under no circumstances should the details of a person's tax situation be discussed with another person. You should politely, but firmly, explain to Beryl that you cannot comply with her request, although you would be happy to assist her individually.

ANSWERS (Task 1.5)

Tax return attached.

Income for the year ended 5 April 2004

Inland Revenue

EMPLOYMENT

Fill in these boxes first

Name

Tax reference

If you want help, look up the box numbers in the Notes.

Details of employer

Employer's PAYE reference - may be shown under 'Inland Revenue office number and reference' on your P60 or 'PAYE reference' on your P45

1.1

1.2 Employer's name
Autumn Jewels Ltd

Date employment started
(only if between 6 April 2003 and 5 April 2004)

1.3 / /

Date employment finished
(only if between 6 April 2003 and 5 April 2004)

1.4 / /

1.5 Employer's address

Postcode

Tick box 1.6 if you were a director of the company

1.6

and, if so, tick box 1.7 if it was a close company

1.7

Income from employment

■ *Money - see Notes, page EN3*

			Before tax
● Payments from P60 (or P45)		**1.8**	£ *17,575*
● Payments not on P60, etc.	- tips	**1.9**	£
	- other payments (excluding expenses entered below and lump sums and compensation payments or benefits entered overleaf)	**1.10**	£

● **Tax deducted** in the UK from payments in boxes 1.8 to 1.10

Tax deducted

1.11 £

■ *Benefits and expenses - see Notes, pages EN3 to EN6. If any benefits connected with termination of employment were received, or enjoyed, after that termination and were from a **former** employer you need to complete Help Sheet IR204, available from the Orderline. Do not enter such benefits here.*

	Amount			Amount
● Assets transferred/ payments made for you	**1.12** £		● Vans	**1.18** £
● Vouchers, credit cards and tokens	**1.13** £		● Taxable cheap loans *see Note for box 1.19, page EN5*	**1.19** £ *500*
● Living accommodation	**1.14** £		*box 1.20 is not used*	
● Excess mileage allowances and passenger payments	**1.15** £		● Private medical or dental insurance	**1.21** £
● Company cars	**1.16** £ *6,292*		● Other benefits	**1.22** £
● Fuel for company cars	**1.17** £ *3,168*		● Expenses payments received and balancing charges	**1.23** £

SA101

BS 12/2002net

Tax Return ■ Employment: page E1

Please turn over

PROFESSIONAL EDUCATION

Income from employment continued

■ *Lump sums and compensation payments or benefits including such payments and benefits from a former employer*
Note that 'lump sums' here includes any contributions which your employer made to an unapproved retirement benefits scheme

*You must read page EN6 of the Notes **before** filling in boxes 1.24 to 1.30*

Reliefs

- £30,000 exemption   **1.24** £
- Foreign service and disability   **1.25** £
- Retirement and death lump sums   **1.26** £

Taxable lump sums

- From box B of *Help Sheet IR204*   **1.27** £
- From box K of *Help Sheet IR204*   **1.28** £
- From box L of *Help Sheet IR204*   **1.29** £
- Tax deducted from payments in boxes 1.27 to 1.29 - **leave blank** if this tax is included in the box 1.11 figure.   Tax deducted   **1.30** £

■ *Foreign earnings not taxable in the UK in the year ended 5 April 2004 - see Notes, page EN6*   **1.31** £

■ *Expenses you incurred in doing your job - see Notes, pages EN7 to EN8*

- Travel and subsistence costs   **1.32** £
- Fixed deductions for expenses   **1.33** £
- Professional fees and subscriptions   **1.34** £ *250*
- Other expenses and capital allowances   **1.35** £
- Tick box 1.36 if the figure in box 1.32 includes travel between your home and a permanent workplace   **1.36**

■ *Foreign Earnings Deduction* (seafarers only)   **1.37** £

■ *Foreign tax for which tax credit relief not claimed*   **1.38** £

Student Loans

■ *Student Loans repaid by deduction by employer - see Notes, page EN8*   **1.39** £

- Tick box 1.39A if your income is under Repayment of Teachers' Loans Scheme   **1.39A**

1.40 *Additional information*

Now fill in any other supplementary Pages that apply to you.
Otherwise, go back to page 2 in your Tax Return and finish filling it in.

BS 12/2002net   TAX RETURN ■ EMPLOYMENT: PAGE E2

SECTION 2

ANSWERS (Task 2.1)

	No	Cost £	Indexed cost £
April 1986 – purchase	300	3,000	3,000
IA to May 1990 (£3,000 × 0.224)			672
			3,672
Purchase	500	8,500	8,500
	800	11,500	12,172
June 1992 – bonus issue	160		
	960		
IA to April 1995 (£12,172 × 0.181)			2,203
			14,375
Purchase	1,000	16,000	16,000
	1,960	27,500	30,375
IA to April 1998 (£30,375 × 0.091)			2,764
			33,139
March 2000 – disposal	(400)	(5,612)	(6,763)
	1,560	21,888	26,376
January 2004 – disposal	(1,560)	(21,888)	(26,376)

	£
Proceeds	45,000
Cost	(21,888)
	23,112
IA (26,376 – 21,888)	(4,488)
Chargeable gain before taper relief	18,624

For taper relief purposes the shares have been owned for 6 years. The gain after taper relief is £14,899 (£18,624 × 80%)

ANSWERS (Task 2.2)

There is no taxable gain or allowable loss as a car is exempt from CGT.

ANSWERS (Task 2.3)

	£
Proceeds	71,000
Less: cost	
$£80,000 \times \dfrac{71,000}{71,000+95,000}$	(34,217)
	36,783
IA (£34,217 × 0.062)	(2,121)
Chargeable gain before Taper relief	34,662

For taper relief purposes the land has been owned for six years (including the additional year) so 80% of the gain is chargeable after taper relief – £27,730

ANSWERS (Task 2.4)

	£
Rent receivable (£4,800 – £500)	4,300
Loss b/fwd	(1,600)
Net Schedule A income	2,700

Tutorial note. Rental income is taxable on an accruals basis.

ANSWERS (Task 2.5)

INCOME	£
Schedule A (task 2.4)	2,700
Less PA (restricted)	(2,700)
Taxable income	–

	Total
	£
GAINS	
Gain on shares (task 2.1)	14,899
Gain on car (task 2.2)	0
Gain on land (task 2.3)	27,730
	42,629
Annual exemption	(7,900)
	34,729

Capital gains tax payable:	£
£1,960 × 10%	196.00
£28,540 × 20%	5,708.00
£4,229 × 40%	1,691.60
	7,595.60

MEMO

To: Jeanette Alsop

From: Accounting Technician

Date: 1 June 2004

Ref: Late declaration of income

It is always important, when you are dealing with the Inland Revenue, to be as honest as possible. I would therefore recommend that you make a late declaration of income, so that the Inland Revenue has the full picture of your income for 2002/03.

The Inland Revenue will view your mis-declaration as being a submission of an incorrect tax return. Normally, the penalty for this is a charge of up to 100% of the amount of tax underpaid as a result of the incorrect return.

Once the building society interest is taken into account, you will be a 40% taxpayer so you will have made an underpayment of tax. You will therefore need to pay both the underpayment and the penalty.

Lecturers' Resource Pack Activities

Note to Students

The answers to these activities and assessments are provided to your lecturers, who will distribute them in class.

If you are not on a classroom based course, a copy of the answers can be obtained from Customer Services on 020 8740 2211 or e-mail publishing @bpp.com.

Note to Lecturers

The answers to these activities and assessments are included in the Lecturers' Resource Pack, provided free to colleges.

If your college has not received the Lecturers' Resource Pack, please contact Customer Services on 020 8740 2211 or e-mail publishing @bpp.com.

Lecturers' Practice Activities

1 Mary

Mary, a single 24 year old, has earnings of £14,000. She also receives building society interest of £6,400 net, dividends of £1,800 (net), and pays a charge of £2,500 (gross) each year. How much cash will she have available to spend in 2003/04?

2 Tom Tulliver

Tom Tulliver has been appointed sales director of Pembridge plc, a large company in the building industry. In addition to a basic salary of £50,000 he has been offered a comprehensive benefits package. The proposed deal is as follows.

(a) The company will provide him with a new 1,400 cc motor car which together with accessories will cost £19,500. The car emits CO_2 of 255g/km. Petrol for private use will be provided but Mr Tulliver must make a contribution of £400 per year towards its cost.

(b) A loan of £5,200 interest free will be made to him on appointment and need only be repaid on his leaving the company. This will be used by Mr Tulliver to purchase a boat.

(c) He has a choice of meals in the company canteen, which is open to all staff free of charge or luncheon vouchers worth £5 per day, an amount equivalent to the normal cost of the meals. He has decided to accept the luncheon vouchers. The normal working year is 200 working days.

(d) His son, aged three, is presently attending a private nursery; this costs £2,000 per year. Pembridge has offered to give his son a free place in their own day nursery at their offices. Mr Tulliver would like to continue the existing arrangement and for Pembridge to continue paying the fees to the existing nursery.

Mr Tulliver's appointment will date from 1 April 2004 and he wishes to examine his tax position before the start of the fiscal year 2004/05.

Tasks

(a) Calculate the taxable benefits arising from Mr Tulliver's employment package as it stands.

(b) Advise him of any changes you consider that he should make to maximise the tax efficiency of the proposed package.

Notes

(a) The official rate of interest should be taken to be 5%.

(b) Use benefit rules for 2003/04 throughout.

3 Simon Harris

During the tax year 2003/04 Simon Harris had the following income:

	£
Salary	28,000
UK dividends (cash amount)	1,800
Building society interest (cash amount)	1,744
Rental income (amount due)	6,000
National savings bank ordinary account interest (cash amount)	100

He works for a large UK company and was provided with the following benefits:

- A petrol engined motor car with a list price of £10,667. The CO_2 emissions of the car was 170 g/km. The company paid for all petrol.

- An average outstanding loan of £8,000 to help purchase his main residence. The company charged him a flat rate of 2.75% interest. Simon had no other loans from any source.

- Medical insurance. The company paid £575. A similar scheme would have cost Simon £650 if he had obtained the cover himself.

Tasks

(a) Calculate the income tax payable by Simon for the year 2003/04.

(b) How will the company notify the Inland Revenue of the benefits provided to Simon, and by what date must this be done?

(c) How will the company notify the Inland Revenue of the total pay paid to and the total tax deducted from Simon for the year? By what date must this be done?

Assume the official rate of interest is 5%.

4 Albert

Albert owns a lock-up shop which he had let for some years to Jim at a rent of £2,400 a year payable on the first of each month in advance. The tenancy terminated on 30 June 2003 and the premises remained vacant until 1 October 2003.

On 1 October 2003 Albert let the shop to Jean a rent of £10,400 a year payable quarterly in advance.

Expenditure on repairs incurred by Albert (who was responsible for all repairs) during the year ended 5 April 2004 was as follows.

	£
Period to 30 June 2003	700
1 October 2003 to 5 April 2004	650

Task

Compute Albert's Schedule A income for 2003/04.

5 Joe Joseph

(i)   In the tax year 2003/04 Joe Joseph realised a net capital gain after taper relief (but before the annual exemption) of £12,000. His total taxable income for that year was £28,700.

Task

Calculate the capital gains tax payable.

(ii)   Jim made disposals of non-business assets during 2003/04 resulting in a gain before taper relief of £12,000 and a loss of £3,000. The asset sold at a gain had been purchased in 1988. He has unrelieved losses brought forward of £6,000.

Tasks

(a)   What is Jim's taxable gain after taper relief and the annual exemption?
(b)   What is his loss left unrelieved at the end of 2003/04?

6 Thomas More

In the year to 5 April 2004, Thomas More made the following disposals.

(a)   A flat in a house that he had purchased on 31 March 1982 for £40,000. The house had never been occupied as his main residence and had been consistently let during his period of ownership. The property had been converted into two flats in September 1985 at a cost of £18,000. The flat was sold for £71,000 on 1 December 2003 and out of this legal fees of £2,000 were paid. It was agreed that the value of the other flat was £65,000 in December 2003.

(b)   An investment property which cost £60,000 in December 1983 and which was sold for £160,000 in December 2003.

Tasks

(a)   Calculate the chargeable gain arising on the sale of the flat, after taper relief if applicable.

(b)   Calculate the chargeable gain arising on the sale of the investment property, after taper relief, if applicable.

Assume indexation factors

March 1982	79.4
December 1983	86.9
September 1985	90.1
April 1998	162.6

7 Cecelia

Cecelia acquired 2,500 shares in Black plc on 6 October 1989 for £4,000 and another 2,500 shares for £16,000 on 1 June 1999. She sold the shares on 26 June 2003 for £39,000. The shares are not a business asset for taper relief purposes.

Cecelia's sold no other assets during 2003/04.

Task

Calculate the chargeable gain, after taper relief if applicable, arising on the disposal of the shares.

Assume indexation factors

October 1989 = 109.5
April 1998 = 162.6

8 Cubist

Cubist bought and sold three paintings as follows.

Painting	Date bought	Purchase price	Date sold	Selling price
		£		£
A	31.3.82	2,500	4.6.03	7,200
B	16.5.98	7,000	6.8.03	4,800
C	25.6.99	4,000	1.2.04	6,300

All selling prices are shown net of 10% commission paid to the auctioneer. Cubist did not make any other disposals in 2003/04.

Task

Compute Cubist's net chargeable gain for 2003/04 after taper relief but before the annual exemption.

Assume indexation factor

March 1982 – April 1998   1.048

9 John Hood

John Hood made the following disposals of assets during the tax year 2003/04.

    (i)   16 July 2003, 2,000 shares in ABC plc were given to his son in reward for him passing his accounting examinations. These were the only shares held by John and had cost him £3,000 in September 1998. The stock exchange daily listing on 16 July 2003 showed closing prices of £4.50 and £4.90. Dealings during the day were made at £4.40, £4.50, £4.60, £4.90 and £5.00.

    (ii)   19 August 2003. A house was sold for £640,000. This had cost John £66,000 in August 1985. John had lived in the house from August 1985 to August 1995. Thereafter he had lived in a second house he had bought as his principal private residence. The house was let from August 1995 to August 2003.

John was a 40% taxpayer for income tax purposes. None of the assets were business assets for taper relief.

The Inland Revenue had issued a tax return to John on 6 June 2004.

Tasks

    (a)   Calculate John Hood's chargeable gains for 2003/04.

    (b)   Calculate the capital gains tax payable.

    (c)   State how these gains will be reported to the Inland Revenue and when payment of the tax is due.

    (d)   By what date(s) must John return his self assessment form for 2003/04 to the Inland Revenue?

    (e)   What penalties may be imposed by the Inland Revenue if John misses the deadline for submitting his tax return?

Assume indexation factors

August 1985 – April 1998   0.703

Lecturers' Practice Exam

LECTURERS' PRACTICE EXAM

TECHNICIAN STAGE – NVQ4

UNIT 19

Preparing Personal Taxation Computations

Time allowed – 3 hours plus 15 minutes' reading time.

DO NOT OPEN THIS PAPER UNTIL YOU ARE READY TO START UNDER TIMED CONDITIONS

INSTRUCTIONS

This examination paper is in TWO sections.

You have to show competence in BOTH sections.

You should therefore attempt and aim to complete EVERY task in EACH section.

You should spend about 120 minutes on Section 1 and 60 minutes on Section 2.

COVERAGE OF THE PERFORMANCE CRITERIA

The following performance criteria are covered in this practice exam.

Element	PC Coverage
19.1	**Calculate income from employment**
A	Prepare accurate computations of emoluments including benefits
B	List allowable expenses and deductions.
D	Make computations and submissions in accordance with current tax law and take account of current Inland Revenue practice
G	Maintain client confidentiality at all times
19.2	**Calculate property and investment income**
A	Prepare schedules of dividends and interest received on shares and securities
B	Prepare schedules of property income and determine profits and losses
D	Apply deductions and reliefs and claim loss set off
E	Record relevant details of property and investment income accurately and legibly in the tax return
F	Make computations and submissions are made in accordance with current tax law and take account of current Revenue practice
I	Maintain client confidentiality at all times
19.3	**Prepare income tax computations**
A	List general income, savings income and dividend income and check for completeness
B	Calculate and deduct charges and personal allowances
C	Calculate income tax payable
E	Make computations and submissions in accordance with current tax law and take account of current Revenue practice
H	Maintain client confidentiality at all times
19.4	**Prepare capital gains tax computations**
A	Identify and value disposed of chargeable personal assets
B	Identify shares disposed of by individuals
C	Calculate chargeable gains and allowable losses
D	Apply reliefs and exemptions correctly
E	Calculate capital gains tax payable
G	Make computations and submissions in accordance with current tax law and take account of current Revenue practice
I	Maintain client confidentiality at all times

SECTION 1

Data

You went to a meeting held on 19 September 2004 with Mrs Joan Davis, whose husband, Albert, died suddenly on 31 March 2004.

Mrs Davis has asked that we sort out both her and her late husband's tax position for 2003/04. She has supplied the following information regarding her own affairs.

Income for 2003/04

(i) Pension from old employers ICD plc £7,035 gross (tax deducted £1,945)

(ii) State retirement pension £3,926

(iii) **Statement of Rental Income and Expenditure**

Letting of furnished properties	14 West Crescent		Harbour Cottage	
	£	£	£	£
Rental income receivable		5,400		4,000
Less: Legal fees re tenancy agreement	800		–	
Insurance	300		300	
Decoration	240		460	
Repairs	2,800		1,900	
Council Tax	410	(4,550)	290	(2,950)
Surplus for year		850		1,050

Notes

(1) Both properties were fully let all year and are fully furnished.

(2) Repairs comprise:

14 West Crescent – installation of central heating £2,800
Harbour Cottage – repairs to roof damaged during storm £1,900

(3) Joan claims wear and tear allowance instead of the renewals basis.

(iv) **Statement of Savings Income**

	£
Interest on Halifax Building Society account	
Amount credited – on 31 December 2003	720
– on 31 December 2004 – estimated	800
Interest on HSBC bank deposit account	
Amount credited – on 30 June 2003	300
– on 31 December 2003	260
– on 30 June 2004	340
Interest on National Savings Bank ordinary account	
Amount credited – on 31 December 2003	200
– on 31 December 2004 – estimated	250

(v) **Statement of Dividend Income**

		£
Dividends on Interweb plc shares purchased in 2003		
Cheques received	– on 19 July 2003	280
	– on 3 December 2003	350
	– on 4 May 2004	400

(vi) Miscellaneous income – Since her retirement, Joan has sold flowers and bouquets on a part time basis. It has been agreed with the Inland Revenue to treat this income as assessable under Schedule D Case I. The amount assessable for 2003/2004 has been agreed as £2,800.

Payments for 2003/04

Cheque for £250 to NSPCC – a charity – under the gift aid scheme
Cheque for £300 to BUPA for private medical care

Task 1.1

Calculate the Schedule A rental income for 2003/04.

Task 1.2

Prepare schedules showing taxable interest and dividend income for 2003/04.

Task 1.3

Prepare an income tax computation for 2003/04.

Task 1.4

Complete the extract from Mrs Davis' tax return for the year ended 5 April 2004.

Task 1.5

State the dates by which Mrs Davis' tax return for 2003/04 should be submitted.

Mr Albert Davis – deceased – personal details

Income for 2003/04

Employment with Vanhire Ltd – salary – £14,250, PAYE tax deducted £2,085.
 – benefits – Petrol engined car with CO_2 emissions 207g/km. List price of car £16,800. Capital contributions towards the original cost of the car were £800. In 2003/04 £600 was paid towards the private use of the car. Vanhire Ltd paid for all petrol.

Vanhire Ltd paid other expenses of £460 which relate to a training course which Albert was required to attend by Vanhire Ltd.

Albert was also provided with a TV and video system for use at home. The original cost of this was £1,200.

Task 1.6

Calculate the taxable earnings of Mr Albert Davis for 2003/04.

SECTION 2

Data

In 2003/04 Mrs Davis sold a number of assets in anticipation of moving house in early 2005. She has supplied the following information on these sales.

		£
(i)	*Antique bookcase* – gross proceeds 15.5.2003	6,900
	Auctioneer's fee	510
	Cost on 31.3.2000	200
(ii)	*Antique clock* – proceeds 4.9.2003	7,200
	Cost on 31.3.1982	3,000
(iii)	*Harbour Cottage* – proceeds 29.3.2004	81,000
	Cost on 15.3.2002	40,000
(iv)	*8,000 shares on Speculate plc* – proceeds 15.12.2003	48,000

Joan had bought 3,000 shares in April 1988 for £6,000 and a further 7,000 shares on 3 June 2002 for £28,000. A bonus issue had been made of one for two in June 2003. These shares are a non-business asset for taper relief purposes.

Joan has unrelieved capital losses of £50,000 at 6 April 2003.

Task 2.1

Calculate the capital gains on the disposals in 2003/04.

Task 2.2

Calculate the capital gains tax payable.

Albert's nephew, Rodney Davis, understands that he is a beneficiary in Albert's will. He has left a message on our answerphone asking if we will send him a letter setting out Albert's average annual income and a list of his assets.

Task 2.3

Draft a letter replying to Rodney for me to review.

Income for the year ended 5 April 2004

Inland Revenue

LAND AND PROPERTY

Name

Tax reference

Fill in these boxes first

If you want help, look up the box numbers in the Notes.

Are you claiming Rent a Room relief for gross rents of £4,250 or less?
(Or £2,125 if the claim is shared?)
Read the Notes on page LN2 to find out
- whether you can claim Rent a Room relief; and
- how to claim relief for gross rents over £4,250

Yes [ ]

If 'Yes', tick box. If this is your only income from UK property, you have finished these Pages

Is your income from furnished holiday lettings?
If not applicable, please turn over and fill in Page L2 to give details of your property income

Yes [ ]

If 'Yes', tick box and fill in boxes 5.1 to 5.18 before completing Page L2

Furnished holiday lettings

- Income from furnished holiday lettings — **5.1** £

■ *Expenses* (furnished holiday lettings only)

- Rent, rates, insurance, ground rents etc. — **5.2** £
- Repairs, maintenance and renewals — **5.3** £
- Finance charges, including interest — **5.4** £
- Legal and professional costs — **5.5** £
- Costs of services provided, including wages — **5.6** £
- Other expenses — **5.7** £

total of boxes 5.2 to 5.7 — **5.8** £

Net profit (put figures in brackets if a loss) — box 5.1 *minus* box 5.8 — **5.9** £

■ *Tax adjustments*

- Private use — **5.10** £
- Balancing charges — **5.11** £

box 5.10 + box 5.11 — **5.12** £

- Capital allowances — **5.13** £
- Tick box 5.13A if box 5.13 includes enhanced capital allowances for environmentally friendly expenditure — **5.13A** [ ]

Profit for the year (copy to box 5.19). If loss, enter '0' in box 5.14 and put the loss in box 5.15

boxes 5.9 + 5.12 *minus* box 5.13 — **5.14** £

Loss for the year (if you have entered '0' in box 5.14)

boxes 5.9 + 5.12 *minus* box 5.13 — **5.15** £

■ *Losses*

- Loss offset against 2003-04 total income — **5.16** £
- Loss carried back — see Notes, page LN4 — **5.17** £
- Loss offset against other income from property (copy to box 5.38) — see Notes, page LN4 — **5.18** £

SA105

Other property income

■ Income

		copy from box 5.14		
•	Furnished holiday lettings profits	**5.19** £		
•	Rents and other income from land and property	**5.20** £	Tax deducted **5.21** £	
•	Chargeable premiums	**5.22** £		
•	Reverse premiums	**5.22A** £		boxes 5.19 + 5.20 + 5.22 + 5.22A **5.23** £

■ Expenses (do not include figures you have already put in boxes 5.2 to 5.7 on Page L1)

•	Rent, rates, insurance, ground rents etc.	**5.24** £	
•	Repairs, maintenance and renewals	**5.25** £	
•	Finance charges, including interest	**5.26** £	
•	Legal and professional costs	**5.27** £	
•	Costs of services provided, including wages	**5.28** £	
•	Other expenses	**5.29** £	total of boxes 5.24 to 5.29 **5.30** £

Net profit (put figures in brackets if a loss)
box 5.23 *minus* box 5.30
5.31 £

■ Tax adjustments

•	Private use	**5.32** £	
•	Balancing charges	**5.33** £	box 5.32 + box 5.33 **5.34** £
•	Rent a Room exempt amount	**5.35** £	
•	Capital allowances	**5.36** £	
•	Tick box 5.36A if box 5.36 includes a claim for 100% capital allowances for flats over shops	**5.36A**	
•	Tick box 5.36B if box 5.36 includes enhanced capital allowances for environmentally friendly expenditure	**5.36B**	
•	10% wear and tear	**5.37** £	
•	Furnished holiday lettings losses (from box 5.18)	**5.38** £	boxes 5.35 to box 5.38 **5.39** £

Adjusted profit (if loss enter '0' in box 5.40 and put the loss in box 5.41)
boxes 5.31 + 5.34 *minus* box 5.39
5.40 £

Adjusted loss (if you have entered '0' in box 5.40)
boxes 5.31 + 5.34 *minus* box 5.39
5.41 £

•	Loss brought forward from previous year	**5.42** £

Profit for the year
box 5.40 *minus* box 5.42
5.43 £

■ Losses etc

•	Loss offset against total income (read the note on page LN8)	**5.44** £
•	Loss to carry forward to following year	**5.45** £
•	Tick box 5.46 if these Pages include details of property let jointly	**5.46**
•	Tick box 5.47 if **all** property income ceased in the year to 5 April 2004 **and** you don't expect to receive such income again, in the year to 5 April 2005	**5.47**

Now fill in any other supplementary Pages that apply to you.
Otherwise, go back to page 2 of your Tax Return and finish filling it in.

BS 12/2002net   TAX RETURN ■ LAND AND PROPERTY: PAGE L2

TAXATION TABLES

Capital gains tax

Annual exemption £7,900

Indexation Allowance

Retail Price Index (RPI) for:

March 1982	79.4	September 2003	180.3
April 1988	105.8	December 2003	180.9
April 1998	162.6	March 2004	181.5
June 2002	176.2		

Income tax

Allowances	£
Personal allowance	4,615

Rates of income tax

Taxed @ 10%	First £1,960
Taxed @ 22%	Next £28,540
Taxed @ 40%	The balance

Car fuel benefit

Set figure £14,400

Official rate of interest   5%

See overleaf for information on other
BPP products and how to order

AAT Order

To BPP Professional Education, Aldine Place, London W12 8AW

Tel: 020 8740 2211. Fax: 020 8740 1184
E-mail: Publishing@bpp.com Web:www.bpp.com

Mr/Mrs/Ms (Full name) _____
Daytime delivery address _____

Postcode _____
Daytime Tel _____
E-mail _____

	5/03 Texts	5/03 Kits	Special offer	8/03 Passcards	Tapes
FOUNDATION (£14.95 except as indicated)				Foundation	
Units 1 & 2 Receipts and Payments	☐	☐	Foundation Sage Bookkeeping and Excel Spreadsheets CD-ROM free if ordering all Foundation Text and Kits, including Units 21 and 22/23 ☐	£6.95 ☐	£10.00 ☐
Unit 3 Ledger Balances and Initial Trial Balance	☐				
Unit 4 Supplying Information for Mgmt Control	☐				
Unit 21 Working with Computers (£9.95) (6/03)	☐				
Unit 22/23 Healthy Workplace/Personal Effectiveness (£9.95)	☐				
Sage and Excel for Foundation (CD-ROM £9.95)	☐				
INTERMEDIATE (£9.95 except as indicated)					
Unit 5 Financial Records and Accounts	☐	☐		£5.95 ☐	£10.00 ☐
Unit 6/7 Costs and Reports (Combined Text £14.95)	☐				
Unit 6 Costs and Revenues	☐	☐		£5.95 ☐	£10.00 ☐
Unit 7 Reports and Returns	☐	☐		£5.95 ☐	
TECHNICIAN (£9.95 except as indicated)					
Unit 8/9 Managing Performance and Controlling Resources	☐	☐		£5.95 ☐	£10.00 ☐
Spreadsheets for Technician (CD-ROM)	☐		Spreadsheets for Technicians CD-ROM free if take Unit 8/9 Text and Kit ☐		
Unit 10 Core Managing Systems and People (£14.95)	☐	☐		£5.95 ☐	£10.00 ☐
Unit 11 Option Financial Statements (A/c Practice)	☐	☐		£5.95 ☐	
Unit 12 Option Financial Statements (Central Govnmt)	☐	☐		£5.95 ☐	
Unit 15 Option Cash Management and Credit Control	☐	☐		£5.95 ☐	
Unit 17 Option Implementing Audit Procedures	☐	☐		£5.95 ☐	
Unit 18 Option Business Tax (FA03)(8/03 Text & Kit)	☐	☐		£5.95 ☐	
Unit 19 Option Personal Tax (FA 03)(8/03 Text & Kit)	☐	☐		£5.95 ☐	
TECHNICIAN 2002 (£9.95)					
Unit 18 Option Business Tax FA02 (8/02 Text & Kit)	☐	☐			
Unit 19 Option Personal Tax FA02 (8/02 Text & Kit)	☐	☐			
SUBTOTAL	£	£	£	£	£

TOTAL FOR PRODUCTS
£ _____

POSTAGE & PACKING

Texts/Kits

	First	Each extra	
UK	£3.00	£3.00	£
Europe*	£6.00	£4.00	£
Rest of world	£20.00	£10.00	£

Passcards

UK	£2.00	£1.00	£
Europe*	£3.00	£2.00	£
Rest of world	£8.00	£8.00	£

Tapes

UK	£2.00	£1.00	£
Europe*	£3.00	£2.00	£
Rest of world	£8.00	£8.00	£

TOTAL FOR POSTAGE & PACKING
£ _____
(Max £12 Texts/Kits/Passcards – deliveries in UK)

Grand Total (Cheques to *BPP Professional Education*)
£ _____

I enclose a cheque for (incl. Postage) ☐
Or charge to Access/Visa/Switch

Card Number ☐☐☐☐☐☐☐☐☐☐☐☐☐☐☐☐

Expiry date _____ Start Date _____

Issue Number (Switch Only) ☐☐☐

Signature _____

We aim to deliver to all UK addresses inside 5 working days; a signature will be required. Orders to all EU addresses should be delivered within 6 working days. All other orders to overseas addresses should be delivered within 8 working days. * Europe includes the Republic of Ireland and the Channel Islands.

AAT Order

To BPP Professional Education, Aldine Place, London W12 8AW

Tel: 020 8740 2211. Fax: 020 8740 1184

E-mail: Publishing@bpp.com Web:www.bpp.com

Mr/Mrs/Ms (Full name) _____

Daytime delivery address _____

Postcode _____

Daytime Tel _____

E-mail _____

OTHER MATERIAL FOR AAT STUDENTS	8/03 Texts	3/03 Text
FOUNDATION (£5.95)		
Basic Mathematics	☐	
INTERMEDIATE (£5.95)		
Basic Bookkeeping (for students exempt from Foundation)	☐	
FOR ALL STUDENTS (£5.95)		
Building Your Portfolio (old standards)	☐	
Building Your Portfolio (new standards)	☐	☐

£ ☐   £ ☐

TOTAL FOR PRODUCTS £ ☐

POSTAGE & PACKING

Texts/Kits	First	Each extra	
UK	£3.00	£3.00	£ ☐
Europe*	£6.00	£4.00	£ ☐
Rest of world	£20.00	£10.00	£ ☐
Passcards			
UK	£2.00	£1.00	£ ☐
Europe*	£3.00	£2.00	£ ☐
Rest of world	£8.00	£8.00	£ ☐
Tapes			
UK	£2.00	£1.00	£ ☐
Europe*	£3.00	£2.00	£ ☐
Rest of world	£8.00	£8.00	£ ☐

TOTAL FOR POSTAGE & PACKING £ ☐

(Max £12 Texts/Kits/Passcards - deliveries in UK)

Grand Total (Cheques to *BPP Professional Education*) £ ☐

I enclose a cheque for (incl. Postage)

Or charge to Access/Visa/Switch

Card Number ☐☐☐☐☐☐☐☐☐☐☐☐☐

Expiry date _____ Start Date _____

Issue Number (Switch Only) _____

Signature _____

We aim to deliver to all UK addresses inside 5 working days; a signature will be required. Orders to all EU addresses should be delivered within 6 working days. All other orders to overseas addresses should be delivered within 8 working days. * Europe includes the Republic of Ireland and the Channel Islands.

Review Form & Free Prize Draw – Unit 19 Preparing Personal Taxation Computations (FA 2003) (8/03)

All original review forms from the entire BPP range, completed with genuine comments, will be entered into one of two draws on 31 January 2004 and 31 July 2004. The names on the first four forms picked out on each occasion will be sent a cheque for £50.

Name: _____   Address: _____

_____

_____

How have you used this Assessment Kit?
(Tick one box only)

☐ Home study (book only)

☐ On a course: college _____

☐ With 'correspondence' package

☐ Other _____

Why did you decide to purchase this Assessment Kit? *(Tick one box only)*

☐ Have used BPP Texts in the past

☐ Recommendation by friend/colleague

☐ Recommendation by a lecturer at college

☐ Saw advertising

☐ Other _____

During the past six months do you recall seeing/receiving any of the following?
(Tick as many boxes as are relevant)

☐ Our advertisement in *Accounting Technician* magazine

☐ Our advertisement in *Pass*

☐ Our brochure with a letter through the post

Which (if any) aspects of our advertising do you find useful?
(Tick as many boxes as are relevant)

☐ Prices and publication dates of new editions

☐ Information on Assessment Kit content

☐ Facility to order books off-the-page

☐ None of the above

Have you used the companion Interactive Text for this subject?   ☐ Yes   ☐ No

Your ratings, comments and suggestions would be appreciated on the following areas

	Very useful	Useful	Not useful
Practice activities	☐	☐	☐
Practice exams	☐	☐	☐
Specimen exam	☐	☐	☐

	Excellent	Good	Adequate	Poor
Overall opinion of this Kit	☐	☐	☐	☐

Do you intend to continue using BPP Interactive Texts/Assessment Kits?   ☐ Yes   ☐ No

Please note any further comments and suggestions/errors on the reverse of this page.

The BPP author of this edition can be e-mailed at: suedexter@bpp.com

Review Form & Free Prize Draw (continued)

Please note any further comments and suggestions/errors below

Free Prize Draw Rules

1   Closing date for 31 January 2004 draw is 31 December 2003. Closing date for 31 July 2004 draw is 30 June 2004.

2   Restricted to entries with UK and Eire addresses only. BPP employees, their families and business associates are excluded.

3   No purchase necessary. Entry forms are available upon request from BPP Professional Education. No more than one entry per title, per person. Draw restricted to persons aged 16 and over.

4   Winners will be notified by post and receive their cheques not later than 6 weeks after the relevant draw date.

5   The decision of the promoter in all matters is final and binding. No correspondence will be entered into.